SO-AID-460

PrincetonReview.com

BUSINESS SCHOOL ESSAYS THAT MADE A DIFFERENCE

BY NEDDA GILBERT
AND THE STAFF OF THE PRINCETON REVIEW

Random House, Inc.
New York

Copyright © 2010 by The Princeton Review, Inc.
111 Speen St., Suite 550
Framingham, MA 01701

All rights reserved under International and Pan-American Copyright
Conventions. Published in the United States by Random House, Inc.,
New York, and simultaneously in Canada by Random House of Canada
Limited, Toronto.

ISBN 978-0-375-42784-8
ISSN 1948-9331

Senior VP—Publisher: Robert Franek
Editor: Laura Braswell
Print Production: Best Content Solutions, LLC
Production Editor: Kristen O'Toole

Printed in the United States of America on partially recycled paper.

9 8 7 6 5 4 3 2 1

ACKNOWLEDGMENTS

A book such as this is truly a collaborative effort. Many of the ideas and insights presented here belong not to me, but to the extraordinary business school admissions individuals who generously agreed to share their insights and essays with me.

I am particularly indebted to three schools for jumping into this project from the get-go. Their can-do attitude made the success of this project much more probable.

At Babson College, a sincere thanks goes to Kate Klepper, Director of MBA Admissions, Olin Graduate School of Business.

At the University of Chicago's Graduate School of Business, I am especially grateful to Don Martin, Director of Admissions, and to Allan Friedman, Director of Executive Communications.

At the Tuck School of Business, my deepest thanks go to Kiki Keating, Director of Public Relations, and to Kristine Laca, Director of Admissions.

Other business school folks who provided thoughtful inspiration and essay materials are:

Glenn Berman, Director of Admissions, Rutgers Business School at Rutgers, The State University of New Jersey

Pamela Black-Colton, Assistant Dean for MBA Admissions and Administration, William E. Simon Graduate School of Business Administration, University of Rochester

Evan Bouffides, Assistant Dean and Director, MBA Admissions and Financial Aid, Olin School of Business, Washington University in St. Louis

Erin Ernst, MBA Admissions Director, Michael G. Foster School of Business, University of Washington

Ute Frey, Haas School of Business, University of California—Berkeley

Rod Garcia, MBA Admissions Director, Sloan School of Management, MIT

JUN 08 2011

Daniel Garza, Director of Marketing, McCombs School of Business, University of Texas at Austin

Christine Gill, Director of Marketing and Admissions, Weatherhead School of Management, Case Western Reserve University

Rebekah Lewin, Director of Admissions, Simon School of Business, University of Rochester

Brian T. Lohr, Director of MBA Admissions, Mendoza College of Business, University of Notre Dame

John McLaughlin, Assistant MBA Admissions Director, Sloan School of Management, MIT

Linda Meehan, Assistant Dean of Admissions, Columbia Business School, Columbia University

Mark Miester, Editor, Office of University Publication, Tulane University

Erin L.C. Nickelsberg, Director, Admissions and Recruitment, Wisconsin School of Business, University of Wisconsin

Emile Pilafidis, MBA Program Director, Peter F. Drucker School of Management, Claremont Graduate University

Bill Sandefer, Director of Admissions and Financial Aid, A. B. Freeman School of Business, Tulane University

Barbara Schneider, Director of Admissions and Financial Aid, Crosby MBA Program, University of Missouri

Melanie Standridge, Assistant Director of Marketing and Recruiting, Peter F. Drucker Graduate School of Management, Claremont Graduate University

Mary Spreen, Director of Admissions, Henry B. Tippie School of Management, University of Iowa

Matt W. Turner, PhD, Director of Admissions, McCombs School of Business, University of Texas at Austin

Sherry Wallace, Director, MBA Admissions, Kenan-Flagler Business School, University of North Carolina at Chapel Hill

Jeanne Wilt, Assistant Dean of Admissions and Career Development, University of Michigan

Jenni Winslow and Lisa Guglielmi, first-year students at Haas School of Business, University of California—Berkeley

Heartfelt thanks goes to my editors who were instrumental in bringing this book to fruition. I'd also like to thank Rob Franek for the opportunity to write another book. He's so good. He is Hollywood.

A small circle of friends and family also needs to be acknowledged.

My children tried to endure my immersion in this project. My youngest, still at home, felt my best work would be done with her at my side. Despite an arsenal of distractions, she could not be deterred from rollerblading over my toes during phone interviews. I truly could claim that this book took blood, sweat, and tears.

That said, both of my daughters desire to be famous, so here goes: Kaela and Lexi, thank you for letting me do my work. You make the difference in my life.

Thanks also go to my dearest friends, Janine Molinaro and Susan Smotrich, for seeing me through several crises; my father, Dr. Irving Buchen, for providing thoughts on being a great writer; Livingston Johnson, who dropped everything to retrieve a document sent into computer oblivion; and Peter and Leslie Tilles for generously offering their home to my children so that I could write.

Final thanks go to my husband (and Harvard MBA), Paul Gilbert. I promised him I would not involve him in this book. I failed him miserably.

CONTENTS

Chapter 11

INTRODUCTION

It's never easy to write a book. This was especially the case with this one. Perhaps because I was already established as someone who writes about business schools (my first book was The Princeton Review's *Best Business Schools*), I thought that writing a companion book would be relatively uncomplicated.

Where my first book had several chapters on how to put together a winning application, this book would elaborate on that theme by focusing solely on the essay portion of the application process.

The essays can count for up to 75 percent of your application. So critical are they in the admissions process that neither the highest test scores and grades nor the most stellar work experience can salvage a candidate with problematic essays. I reasoned that this book was sorely needed. Not only would it provide detailed information on how to write a winning essay, it would feature loads of actual b-school essays, accompanied by critiques from the admissions officers themselves on what worked and what didn't.

But life is full of surprises. In my very first phone call to a school that in years past had provided me with generous access to its inside workings, I hit a wall. This school, one of the nation's most prestigious, did not believe that real winning essays should be made public. Their concerns were several: First, publishing these essays might encourage an act of plagiarism. Second, they did not want to provide an advantage in their applicant pool to purchasers of this book. Third, they did not want to sanction essay-writing assistance. Finally, they thought students would use these essays too literally and treat them as formulaic blueprints.

I considered this school's positions seriously. These are legitimate concerns. I had equally strong concerns for not doing this book, though, which I'll explain a bit later.

That said, I share some of the business school's concerns about this type of book. So before advising you any further on your essays, a cautionary note is necessary.

A Word of Warning

First, do not use these essays as specific templates for your own story-telling. This book shows you the depth and breadth of good essays, how mature self-awareness is expressed, and how goals and limitations are explored. They are meant to provide you with an example of how one person chose to answer a question. Use these essays to inspire you and get you on the right track.

Second, as you read through the essays, bear in mind that one lone essay did not win the applicant his or her admission. Many factors enter into an admissions decision. Each essay in this book was part of an application that included many criteria. It was the consistency throughout the application that won individuals with an essay in this book admission.

Finally, though it goes without saying, don't plagiarize the essays in this book. That's worth repeating: **Do not plagiarize the essays you read in this book.** We encourage you to note buzzwords, structures, and themes that you like, but draw the line at copying paragraphs, sentences, or even phrases.

Many schools have begun to hire outside consultants for the sole purpose of catching those who plagiarize, lie, and cheat in their applications. This includes catching those who hire someone to write their essays for them. The writing section of the GMAT is one of the factors used to verify that your essay writing is your own. Obviously, schools expect the essays you compose at home, which undergo many rewrites, to be superior to those undertaken on the GMAT. Still, admissions officers are skilled enough to identify troubling discrepancies. If you get busted, you won't get into b-school at all. Plus, plagiarism is simply wrong, so don't do it. Period.

Chapter 1

BUSINESS SCHOOL ADMISSIONS: A BRIEF OVERVIEW

Although admissions requirements vary among business schools, most rely on the following criteria: GMAT score, college GPA, work experience, your essays, letters of recommendation (academic and/or professional), an interview with an admissions representative, and your extracurriculars. The first four are generally the most heavily weighted. The more competitive the school, the less room there is for weakness in any area. Any component out of sync, such as a weak GMAT score, is potentially harmful.

Happily, the admissions process at business school is one where great emphasis is placed on getting to know you as a person. The essay component is the element that allows the schools to do just that. Your essays can refute weaknesses, fill in gaps, and in general, charmingly persuade an admissions board that you've got the right stuff. They are the single most important criteria in business school admissions.

But as we've just said, they're not the only criteria. All pieces of your application must come together to form a cohesive whole. It is the entire application that determines whether you win admission.

ANTICIPATE AND COORDINATE

The application process is very time-consuming, so anticipating what you need to accomplish within the admissions time frame is critical. To make the best use of our advice, you should first contact each of the programs on your personal list of schools. Their standards and criteria for admission may vary, and you'll need to follow their specific guidelines. Please note that the less competitive a school is, the more easily you may be able to breeze through (or completely omit) the rigorous requirements we identify as crucial in the application process for the top programs.

In addition, business school applicants are often overwhelmed by how much they have to do to complete not only one, but several applications. Proper management of the process is essential, since there are so many factors to coordinate in each application.

You'll have to prep for the GMAT, then actually take the test, round up some writers for your recommendations, follow up with those chosen to write recommendations, make sure the recommendations are submitted on time, have your college transcript sent, and finally, write the essays. Of course, some schools require an interview as well. What makes all of this particularly challenging is that many applicants have to fit this in among the demands of a full-time job.

We know that it takes a supreme force of will to complete even one application. As grad school applications go, a top business school's is pretty daunting. If you don't stay focused on the details and deadlines, you may drop the ball.

There are many common and incredibly embarrassing mistakes you can avoid with prudent early planning. They include allowing your recommendation writers to miss the deadline, submitting an application full of typos and grammatical errors, sending one school an essay intended for another, or forgetting to change the school name when using the same essay for several applications. Applicants who wind up cramming for the GMAT or squeezing their essay writing into several all-nighters seriously shortchange themselves.

APPLY EARLY

The best advice is this: Plan and apply early. The former diminishes the likelihood of an accidental omission or a missed deadline. The latter increases your chances of acceptance.

The filing period ranges anywhere from six to eight months. The earlier you apply, the better your chances. There are a number of reasons for this:

1. Early on, there's plenty of space available. As the application deadline draws near, fewer spaces are left. Pretty logical, right?

2. In the beginning, admissions officers aren't yet sure how selective they can be. An early application may be judged more on its own merit than on how it stacks up against the competition. This is in your favor if the applicant pool turns out to be especially competitive.

3. By getting your application in early, you're showing strong interest.

One caveat: You might not want to be the very first one in line. It's best to be close to the front, but not absolutely first.

ROUNDS VS. ROLLING ADMISSIONS

Applications are processed in one of two ways: rounds or rolling admissions. Schools that use rounds divide the filing period into approximately three timed cycles. Applications are batched into the round in which they are received and reviewed in competition with others in that round. A list of a b-school's round dates can be obtained by contacting their admissions office if they employ this method. Applications to schools with rolling admissions are reviewed on an ongoing basis as they are received.

GMAT and GPA

The GMAT and GPA are used in two ways. First, they're "success indicators" for the academic work you'll have to slog through if admitted—will you have the brainpower to succeed in the program? Second, they're used as benchmarks to compare each applicant to other applicants within the pool. At the more selective schools, you'll need a higher score and average to stay in the game.

The Educational Testing Service (ETS) administers the GMAT. You'll need to register to take the exam by calling 800-GMAT-NOW (800-462-8669) or by registering online at www.mba.com. Many applicants take the exam more than once to improve their scores. Test preparation is also an option for boosting your numbers—call 800-2Review (800-273-8439) for more information about The Princeton Review's GMAT courses.

Your college transcript is a major factor in the strength of your candidacy. Some schools focus more closely on the junior- and senior-year grades than the overall GPA, and most consider the reputation of your college and the difficulty of your course selections. A transcript loaded with offerings like "Tao of Hip-Hop" and "The Child in You" won't be valued as highly as one packed with calculus and history classes.

Letters of Recommendation

Letters of recommendation act as a reality check. Admissions committees expect them to support and reinforce what they're seeing in the rest of your application. When the information doesn't match up with the picture you've painted, it makes you look bad. Because you won't see the recommendation (it's sent in "blind"), you won't even know there's a problem. This can mean the end of your candidacy. That's why you need to take extreme care in selecting your references.

Scan each application for guidelines on choosing your references—business schools typically request an academic or professional reference. The academic reference should be someone who can evaluate your performance in an academic environment. It's better to ask an instructor, teacher's aide, or mentor who knew you well than a famous professor who barely knew your name.

The same holds true for your professional reference. Seek out individuals who can evaluate your performance on many levels. The reference will be far more credible. Finding the right person to write your professional reference, however, can be trickier. You may not wish to reveal to your boss early on that you plan on leaving, and if the dynamics of your relationship are not ideal (hey, it happens once in a while), he or she might not make an appropriate reference. If this is the case, seek out a boss at a former job or someone who was your supervisor at your current job but has since moved to another organization. Avoid friends, colleagues, and clients as references unless the school explicitly says it's okay.

Advise your writers on themes and qualities you highlighted in your application. Suggest that they include real-life examples of your performance to illustrate their points. In other words, script the recommendation as best you can. Your boss, even if he or she is your biggest fan, may not know what your recommendation should include.

A great recommendation is rarely enough to save a weak application from doom. But it might push a borderline case over to the "admit" pile. Mediocre recommendations can be damaging; an application that is strong in all other areas now has a weakness, an inconsistency.

A final warning on this topic: Procrastination is common here. Micromanage your references so that each recommendation arrives on time! If need be, provide packaging for an overnight letter, have your reference seal it up, and then ship it out yourself.

The Interview

Not all business schools attach equal value to the interview. For some, it's an essential screening tool. For others, it's used to make a final decision on those caught somewhere between "admit" and "reject." Some schools may encourage, but not require, the interview. Others make it informative, with little connection to the admissions decision.

Like the letters of recommendation, an interview may serve as a reality check to reinforce the total picture. It may also be used to fill in the blanks, particularly in borderline cases.

If an interview is offered, take it. In person, you may be an entirely more compelling candidate. You can further address weaknesses or bring dull essays to life. Most important, you can display the kinds of qualities—enthusiasm, sense of humor, maturity—that often fill in the blanks and positively sway an admissions decision.

Act quickly to schedule your interview. Admissions departments often lack the time and staff to interview every candidate who walks through their doors. You don't want your application decision delayed by several months (and placed in a more competitive round or pool) because your interview was scheduled late in the filing period.

A great interview can tip the scale in the "admit" direction. How do you know if it was great? You were calm and focused. You expressed yourself and your ideas clearly. Your interviewer invited you to go rock climbing with him next weekend. (Okay, let's just say you developed a solid personal rapport with the interviewer.)

A mediocre interview may not have much impact, unless your application is hanging on by a thread. In such a case, the person you're talking to (harsh as it may seem) is probably looking for a reason not to admit you, rather than a reason to let you in. If you feel your application may be in that hazy, marginal area, try to be extra-inspired in your interview.

Approach this meeting as you would a job interview. Dress and act the part of a professional. But at the same time, remember: You're being sized up as a person in all of your dimensions. Avoid acting stiff or like a stuffed shirt. Limit your use of business jargon. Be personable. Gear yourself up for an enjoyable conversation in which you may discuss your hobbies or recent cross-country trip. Talk about your passions or any areas in which you have achieved excellence—even something like gourmet cooking. Just avoid stunt-like gimmicks (we don't advise you to pull out a platter of peppercorn pâté sautéed in anchovy sauce). The idea is to get the interviewer thinking of you as someone who will contribute greatly to the quality of campus life. Try to be your witty, charming, natural self.

How to Blow the Interview

1. **Wear casual clothes.**
   This is an automatic ding. Wearing anything but professional attire suggests you don't know or don't want to play by the rules of the game.

2. **Bring your mom or dad. Or talk about them.**
   Business schools value maturity. If Mom or Dad takes you to the interview, or your answer to the question "Why an MBA?" begins with "Dad always told me . . . ," the interviewer is going to wonder how ready you are for the adult world of b-school.

3. **Talk about high school.**
   Again, they'll question your maturity. Stories about high school, and even college, suggest you haven't moved on to more mature, new experiences. Exceptions: Explaining a unique situation or a low GPA.

4. **Show up late.**
   This is another automatic ding at some schools. Short of a real catastrophe, you won't be excused.

5. **Say something off the wall or inappropriate.**
   No doubt, the conversation can get casual, and you may start to let your guard down. But certain things are still off-limits: profanity, ethnic jokes, allusions to sex, your romantic life, and anything else that might signal to the interviewer that the cheese fell off your cracker.

---

6. **Chew gum or munch on one of those designer mints.**
   Your teacher always said, "Don't chew gum in class." The same rule applies here.

7. **Forget to write a thank-you note to your interviewer.**
   Sending a thank-you note means you know how to operate in the business world, and it goes a long way toward convincing the interviewer you belong there.

Work Experience

Business schools are particularly interested in your work history. It provides tangible evidence of your performance in the business world thus far and hints at your potential. It's one thing to show academic wherewithal as demonstrated by your grades and GMAT score, but your work experiences best demonstrate your leadership, strategic abilities, and creativity in a business environment.

Your work experience will also be examined for the following: Have you progressed enough (or too far) to benefit from a business school education? Have you advanced within your organization/career? What industry perspective will you bring to the program? It's the job of the Admissions Office to create balanced, diverse classes, so applicants hailing from under-represented fields—health care and public service, for example—may be particularly appealing.

Now that we have an understanding of what the entire application process is about, we're ready to focus on the essays.

Chapter 2

THE IMPORTANCE OF
THE ESSAY

An essay is any school's Rorschach test when considering your candidacy. Whether you're applying to business school, law school, or medical school, what you write says more about you than your GPA or test score.

Unlike the law or med school admissions processes, b-school admissions are unique in their request for many essays and their heavy weighting of those essays. Although grades and standardized tests are considered key benchmarks for admission, they function more as a threshold. Your stories are what close the deal one way or the other.

THE REAL YOU,
REVEALED AND DISSECTED

In b-school admissions, the essays tie all the pieces of your application together. They weave a narrative of who you are and why you belong in a particular program. They provide a framework for your personal and professional activities, highlighting your choices and attitudes as well as your analytical and communication skills. They also reveal your character and integrity. That's because those onerous essay questions are designed to elicit thumbnail profiles of the real you, which is arguably the most heavily weighted criterion in the admissions process. For these reasons, the essays are invaluable screening tools.

At the top business schools, evaluating a candidate's character, genuine accomplishments, and potential has always been pivotal. That's because b-schools operate like micro-communities, and there is an expectation that you will work well and make connections within that community. Furthermore, the curriculum is designed so that you learn from your classmates. Therefore, each student's perspective, experience, and behavior is vital. B-school learning is also team-oriented, so a cooperative spirit (or lack thereof) says a lot about whether you're a strong fit for a particular program.

But perhaps most important, b-schools are a primary source of future business leaders. So attributes like honesty (yes, that includes what you put on your resume), leadership, and ethics matter. In the wake of Enron, WorldCom, Tyco, Lehman Brothers, and other corporate scandals, they matter more than ever. You can almost hear the collective b-school groan when the latest Wall Street violator turns out to be another MBA.

Figuring out whether you'll one day prove to be a source of pride or an embarrassment to your alma mater and the business community is the gray zone in admissions. So how does a b-school attempt to get at your true character and determine your potential as a business leader?

While it may be almost impossible to make such a prediction, the essays are good indicators of character strengths and flaws. So as you compose your stories, know that you're being looked at through many different lenses.

B-School Applicants Need an Advocate

... and that's exactly why we decided to produce this book.

The truth is, I've always been on the side of those pinning their dreams on getting into the most highly regarded program they can, wanting to make something of themselves by going to one of the "best" programs. In fact, I've always secretly identified with those applicants.

Perhaps it's because admissions decisions can seem arbitrary, or because admissions boards wield such a degree of power in young lives. Who wouldn't need a little guidance for such a daunting task?

I had other reasons for wanting to help candidates with their essays. As we mentioned earlier, b-schools are uniquely interested in nontest-score characteristics. High on their list is emotional maturity, self-awareness, leadership ability, creativity, teamwork potential, and morality. Even the venerable Harvard Business School has a stated mission to do no less than "educate leaders who make a difference in the world." To screen for all these qualities, the schools rely on the essays. And herein lies the problem.

An Essay Can Be an Imperfect Screener

It may be difficult for an engineer who will one day launch a new product that will transform an industry to craft a compelling self-narrative. How many great business leaders might be disqualified from getting their MBA at a top school because their writing or storytelling skills are poor, or because at this young age they don't know how to show self-awareness or articulate it in their essays?

In this way, the essays on b-school applications can be overreaching. But they're imperfect in other areas as well. When you consider the questions posed by the most selective programs, you realize that it's genuine frontline caretakers, like social and health care workers, who may best embody the value systems b-schools are looking for. It's by virtue of their chosen profession that caretakers demonstrate such value systems. On the other hand, also by virtue of their chosen profession, such redeeming qualities in would-be MBAs are often less evident.

CAUGHT BETWEEN A ROCK AND A HARD PLACE

Ironically, success and financial reward are part of the b-school hype. Indeed, many schools are judged each year on their career placement statistics (translation: the number of grads who secure high-paying positions, and how quickly they do so), so they work hard to ensure that their statistics are competitive. But an applicant who articulates too much interest in the very pot of gold the MBA dangles may be penalized for lacking the softer skills b-schools desire these days.

The truth is that the negative aspect of the MBA stereotype might at times be true; many pre-MBAs are ambitiously preoccupied with success and financial reward. But why should that be considered unattractive? As you can see, these essay questions don't necessarily play to a would-be MBA's strengths. The essay writers of today need an advocate.

So how does one navigate between posturing as a sincere do-gooder and an ambitious future financial officer?

It's a difficult challenge. The majority of b-school applicants are deeper than their stereotypes would suggest. As we said before, they are reflective, accountable, and morally sound. Finessing all that in a series of short stories with strict word limits is no easy task.

Chapter **3**

HOW TO CRAFT YOUR ESSAYS

Hidden Agendas

Now that you know that the essays are used to check applicants for a range of qualities, it makes sense that each question on the application has a reason for being there. Even seemingly straightforward essay questions such as those in the vein of, "Why do you want the MBA? Why do you want the degree at this juncture in your life? And why here?" have an agenda.

As essay questions go, this one is fairly clear-cut. Although you'd rather do anything (including clean the bathroom) than sit down to suss out an honest and intelligible response, it seems doable. So why do so many applicants fail to answer the question successfully? Because even a straightforward question needs to be thought through.

Here's the inside line: Schools consider this essay the ballast to your candidacy. They want to see well-crafted goals for your education and career outlined here. When I explain this to applicants, it surprises them. After all, they argue, b-school is a journey, and part of the journey is not knowing what lies ahead. Would-be MBAs treat this essay as an opportunity to share their excitement about the discovery. But if you're not sure where you're headed or why, it's nearly impossible to answer such questions convincingly.

It is critical that you present well-defined goals and expectations in your essays. At the best schools, admissions committees want you to lay down a compelling rationale for why you need the MBA and why their program specifically meets your needs. If you can't do that, why should they award you one of their coveted spots? They want students who will value the resources at their program, not those in need of a two-year pit stop.

Half the battle in writing a winning essay is in knowing what the essay question is attempting to draw out, and we aim to offer some guidance in that respect. We don't want you to spend hours working on one question and completely miss the mark. Later on we'll identify and translate commonly asked essay questions. But let there be no mistake about it, equally important to the content, or the "what" of the essay, is the "how."

The "How" of an Essay Is Important

Think of your essay-writing this way: All written communication lives or dies on the "how" in its message. The way you present yourself in your essays and frame your subject is crucial to the impression you create. Ever receive an apology letter that felt warm and real (as opposed to perfunctory)? Did it have a positive impact on how you felt about the person after you read it? If it did, you saw an example of a good use of "how."

Still not sure what the "how" is? It's

- The mood and tone in your writing

- Your writing style and skill and the clarity of your thinking

- Your ability to follow directions

- The judgment you use in selecting your subject matter

- The impact you leave on the reader

Tone and mood can communicate that you are candid, warm, friendly, and a true leader by example. It can also betray negativity, inappropriateness, or a lack of maturity.

There are many variables to the "how" of anyone's writing. There is no one formula we can hand off to you. What might work for one essay or person won't necessarily work for another. The trick is to be self-aware.

COMPOSING A SYMPHONY, ONE NOTE AT A TIME

It is said that Mozart's patron, the Emperor of Austria, once uttered to Mozart, "You have too many notes in this piece." Mozart, who knew that his piece was balanced and perfect, replied, "Your Highness, which note would you like me to take out?"

Think of each essay as one note in your carefully orchestrated song. That song should sing of your capabilities, strengths, and accomplishments. As we said, it should reflect self-awareness and concern for the welfare of others and the world at large. Some of the high notes to hit are dignity, humility, perspective, morality, and wisdom. But your song should also address weak points and anticipate what details in your record might be of concern to the admissions committee.

As you compose your essays, you must determine which notes to hit, which to amplify, and which to play softly. You must orchestrate well. Every note must have a critical reason for being, complementing those that come before and those that follow.

WHAT YOUR ESSAYS SHOULD SAY ABOUT YOU

Applicants tend to place great emphasis on their accomplishments and strengths. But as we said before, there is more to writing an essay than this. You'll need to carefully weave evidence of these favorable qualities into your essay so you can appear in the best possible light without boasting, lying, or being mushy or corny. In other words, the trick is to navigate between maintaining a modest position and showcasing your accomplishments.

As you compose your essays, remember to remain aware of what the details of your stories actually reveal about you.

Your essays should suggest that you are:

A leader

Humble

Mature

Goal-oriented

Creative

Dignified

Intelligent

Hard-working

Concerned for others

Team-oriented

Positive, with a can-do attitude

Introspective

Moral and ethical

Accountable

Able to recognize and learn from mistakes and failure

Wise

Self-aware

Unique

Of sound mind and perspective

Your essays should avoid communicating that you are:

Arrogant

Vain

Entitled

Egotistical

Competitive

A perfectionist

Blindly ambitious

Angry or quick to blame

Immature

Overly bookish

Mediocre

Prejudiced regarding race and/or gender

A poor or boring writer

One who exercises poor judgment
One who sets unrealistic goals

Now Add Two Shakes of Salt . . .

Take the favorable qualities from the first list that best describe you, and jot those down. It's time for you to find a vehicle through which to convey your finest features.

Consider what compelling stories you have to tell and sketch them out. Reflect on what each story says about you and what kind of picture each paints. Then when you sit down with your application, you'll start to draw connections between your stories and the questions that are asked of you.

Chapter **4**

CASE STUDIES

Many years ago I was hired by several Wall Street investment banks in New York City to assist their corporate analysts with their applications to b-school. During this time, I interacted with a wide variety of clients, each with his or her own unique set of strengths, weaknesses, and circumstances.

Below you will find eight tales of business school hopefuls, whose stories may serve both as inspiration and warning. As you read them, you may identify with the applicants' challenges in completing a winning application. Their stories may also help you figure out how to best describe your experiences to showcase your most desirable qualities.

1. A Tale of Two Brothers

I met two brothers, just a year apart in age, who were both applying to Harvard. Each had exceptional credentials, although one brother had near-perfect grades and test scores and had gone to Harvard as an undergrad; the other went to Bowdoin.

At that time, one of the essay questions inquired about a favorite extracurricular activity. As both were expert skiers, skiing was an obvious choice. The two brothers were born and raised in affluence on Fifth Avenue in New York City and, unsurprisingly, they had learned to ski in glamorous locations. The Swiss Alps was the most frequented and memorable locale.

One brother made the Midwest the scene of his essay and mentioned the location only once. His story focused on the bumps on a "skull and crossbones" run he did over and over for days until he got it right. He spoke of the importance of earning performance, about always working harder than the guy next to you. This was the bedrock of everything he did—challenging himself again and again until he had mastered the task at hand. Skiing, as a metaphor for all of his pursuits, was about being the best he could be and, through sheer force of will, attaining his goals.

He also spoke of the beauty of the mountainous terrain, of his awe of nature, and the freedom he felt when speeding down vertigo-inducing runs. He made creative use of his passion and talent for skiing, and he made a compelling analogy between his core ethos of hard work and the commitment he would bring to b-school. The unique twist to his material was refreshing, and it was on message. Even though the only skiing I've ever done is down my driveway on a cafeteria tray, I could relate to his story.

The other brother chose to write about skiing in Switzerland and chronicled other ski trips abroad. His story was basically about the exhilaration of skiing. Unfortunately, this essay was predictable, and the setting in the Alps was a turn-off. In the absence of gripping insights, the venue came to be front and center. He came off as just another pampered candidate. This was the brother who had the superior grades, Harvard undergrad degree, and better test scores.

Have you guessed the ending to this story? The brother who wrote about conquering the "skull and crossbones" run won admission to Harvard Business School. The brother with the presumed edge in his academics did not.

It's important to note, though, that it was not just this one essay that earned one brother an admission and the other a rejection. It was the consistency of their themes in the remaining essays. For the brother admitted, these themes painted an appealing picture of a hard worker with leadership and teamwork abilities.

In fact, knowing both brothers, I would say the essays ultimately did reflect their true personalities. One was indeed pompous. The other was thoughtful and self-aware.

As you can see, the "how" in your writing is powerful enough to elevate you or sink you.

2. Spousal Privilege, Denied

Here's another example. An applicant I worked with had to write about the person he admired most. This was a common essay question at the time, and it stumped a lot of applicants. Most applicants assumed the subject of the essay had to be famous or powerful, which made the task more daunting. Once they decided on an individual, they were often at a loss as to what to write about.

As we've said before, knowing the agenda in a question goes a long way. This question is really asking you about the character traits and strengths you value in others, as well as in yourself, which is revealed in your selection. Whom you select is not as important as what you say about him or her, so your choices can be humble.

This particular gentleman chose to write about his wife. The moment he picked her, I knew the essay was at risk of being compromised. Would you want to work alongside someone whose view of the world ends at his front door? This essay was too intimate for a b-school application, and it demonstrated that he was inward-focused and myopic.

How does this story end? This candidate was not aiming for schools like Harvard, but nonetheless, schools that were selective. He was accepted into one of them. In spite of this acceptance, though, it would be unwise to conclude that this essay didn't impact his application negatively. The essay certainly reflected questionable judgment.

There is also tremendous variability in admissions factors to take into account. During the year in which this candidate applied, applying to b-school was not as popular as in previous years, so he was in a less competitive pool. Furthermore, many business schools have favorite hunting grounds for recruiting applicants. He worked at one of them—a prestigious Wall Street firm. He had a solid and impressive work history.

In all likelihood, the admissions board found this essay problematic but was able to overlook it in light of other redeeming factors. Nonetheless, times have changed. The demand for admittance to b-school remains high, and schools are more sensitive to issues of character. If the same person applied with the same essay now, I think an admissions board would give far more weight to this one essay, and it would be more damaging.

3. Maid in Manhattan

Many years ago, community service was not the popular and accepted activity it is now. But we have become a society of do-gooders—so much so that a majority of our nation's high schools now integrate community service into their requirements. At b-schools, service through organizations like Habitat for Humanity is an equally acknowledged staple of student life. In this process, volunteerism is important because it reflects empathy and interest in others—both critical to effective leadership.

When I met this next applicant, schools were just getting jazzed about the concept of volunteerism. He was savvy enough to recognize that a volunteer activity would indeed communicate his positive attributes and put him ahead of the curve. Several of the b-school applications he was working on required an essay about the applicant's greatest accomplishments. He wanted one of those accomplishments to be his commitment to community service. The problem? He didn't have one.

Shortly thereafter he hit upon an idea. Late one night when he was burning the midnight oil, he was still at work when the cleaning crew came in. He noticed that the woman who cleaned his office spoke little English. He decided to help her learn English as a second language; he thought this might allow her to do something more than cleaning up after others. This became the subject of one of his essays on his greatest accomplishments.

If you've already learned a thing or two through these examples, you may know where I'm heading with this one.

This essay was a stretch. The concept of helping someone could have been moving, but this act of kindness seemed self-serving. Common sense says that someone who wants to go out and help others actually leaves his building to do so. Although helping this woman was noble, as a greatest accomplishment it came off like a bad Hollywood movie. The premise also seemed flimsy because of the timing; a genuine history of service to others dates back to some period of time before your application is due.

I can't tell you exactly what happened with this candidate because I lost contact with him. I do know he was struggling to come up with material for not only this essay, but also many others. He was hampered by the fact that he was relatively young, that he had only two years of work experience, and that those experiences were very typical of an investment banker. With all work and no play, and nothing truly dramatic in his life, it was a challenge to create a compelling essay.

Hey, no one said this was going to be easy.

4. THIRD-GENERATION DROPOUT

By contrast to the last tale, this next candidate had a genuinely unique background. He had worked in his family business since college, and he was a third-generation executive in a true mom-and-pop operation. As he was an only child, the legacy of this company would be in his hands.

This candidate seemed to have such rich material to work with. First, his family was in the business of wholesaling comic books, a nontraditional industry if ever there was one. (To build diversity, b-schools seek out candidates from diverse venues like this.) From the story of how his grandparents built their business from nothing to his future plans for the business, there was great opportunity for creativity in his essays. Surely there were many issues he could touch upon to describe what the MBA could offer him.

Naturally, I was surprised when I read his essay addressing why he wanted the MBA. Overall, the essay was passive. It lacked passion and focus. Nowhere was there anything about his vision for the comic book company, how the comic book industry was evolving, what the threats and opportunities in the marketplace were. He wrote nothing of the need for this company to integrate accounting principles, business strategy, or professional marketing into its practices.

Of all the candidates I had met at that point, he seemed to have the strongest, most genuine need for the MBA.

Or so it seemed. The truth was, like many family businesses, this one was embroiled in family power struggles. The "Mom" and "Pop" of this business, the applicant's grandparents, did not want to relinquish control, and his father was wrestling for dominance. This candidate might have been the next generation, but the business was in his father's hands for the time being.

As for his personal life, it was equally stalled. Friends from college had married or moved on with their professional lives. He felt out of sync and uninspired. His real reason for wanting to go to b-school was to figure out what he wanted to do with his life.

This unstated objective was unfortunately quite evident. As we said before, b-schools are not pit stops for figuring out what you want to do with yourself. If you're not clear on your professional objectives in the short and medium term, how can you select the most appropriate program to help you achieve those objectives?

It was hard for this candidate to map out a potential career plan, but he did it. He articulated it well in the rewrite of his essay, and the plan did not include a career in the field of comic books.

He applied to six schools, many of which were state programs, reasonable choices given his academics—a B average and decent test scores. He was admitted to all but one and chose to attend a school in Texas, far from his family.

5. DISABLED, BUT NOT DISADVANTAGED

This story is about an applicant who was injured in a farming accident when he was a child, which left him with a devastating physical handicap. Despite this handicap, he had done exceptionally well and was in a senior position at a blue-chip investment bank.

When I met him, his application was almost complete. Each essay I read was better than the last—well crafted, passionate, interesting, and reflective. I had almost no feedback for him. He had excellent test scores but only average grades, and he had done his undergrad at a little-known college in the Midwest. His target list of b-schools consisted of the most prestigious, top-tier programs.

Even today, almost every application has a personal statement essay, or what I call a bonus question. Although it's optional, I almost always encourage individuals to submit something here, as it is an invaluable opportunity to provide the admissions board with additional information. It can be used to communicate something remarkable, or it can be used to explain poor grades or test scores (this is where many applicants indeed do this, but we'll get to the "how" of that later).

Obviously, I thought this candidate could make use of the personal statement opportunity. But he was quite resolute that with what he'd communicated in his other essays, there was nothing more to say.

End of story? Almost.

You won't be surprised to learn that he was admitted to his first-choice schools. You may be surprised, however, to learn that not a single essay in any of his applications made mention of his childhood accident or of the resulting handicap. And yet an essay about this injury would go straight to the heart of character, as would a story about overcoming adversity. But this applicant did not want his essays to elicit sympathy. He had spent his whole life trying to make his handicap a nonissue, and he was admitted solely on the merits of his candidacy.

6. If at First You Don't Succeed—Grow Up

Analysts are generally hired straight out of college. They spend two years in an analyst training program, after which they are expected to matriculate at a business school or find other work. Post-MBA, they often return to the bank in a more senior capacity, but this is not a contractual agreement. These analysts are often a "safe" or "easy" admit; the banks are considered feeder programs to the schools because success in the job often correlates with success at b-school.

I worked with one applicant who was a second-year analyst at a prestigious Wall Street investment bank. She was the top-ranked analyst in her second-year program, an honor bestowed upon her for her outstanding work. She had good grades, but unfortunately just an average GMAT score. At less competitive schools, her score would not have been a problem, but she was fixated on getting into one of the nation's best programs. I couldn't blame her.

Her essays would have to promote her candidacy above the penalty of a low score. She began by addressing her GMAT score in the "personal statement" section. She explained that she had test anxiety and that despite taking the exam on two different occasions, she was unable to improve her score. Because she scored lower on the Math portion of the GMAT, she played up her success in calculating complex financial transactions for the bank. I thought she had proactively put her problematic scores into context.

Unfortunately, her other essays were predictable. They lacked introspection and passion. She was driven and ambitious—assets in her line of work, but hardly qualities that would make her an engaging dinner partner. Despite my feedback explaining that her essays were boring, her rewrites were no better. She wasn't able to tell a compelling story.

Younger applicants would generally need more years of experience to accrue the professional and emotional maturity that older applicants have. For an applicant from a feeder program like this, there is probably a discount factor. That is, schools may not expect the most inspiring essays. But in her case, the bad essays gave them no reason to admit her over the highly qualified competition.

This candidate applied to five schools and was rejected by all of them. Because I had worked with other candidates with similar backgrounds and scores, I was able to determine that her essays were the death blow. I encouraged her to reapply after she had left the bank and gained some maturity.

She spoke a little French, so she chose to attend a graduate-level, one-year foreign language immersion program involving overseas study. She became fluent in French and lived abroad. When she applied to b-school again, she composed essays that sang with excitement; they spoke of her passion for France and her experiences while there. She reapplied to three of her original b-school targets and won admission to her first-choice school, a bastion of finance. At graduation, she returned to a life of investment banking, her greatest passion.

The moral of this story is not that you have to go to Paris or change your life completely to write a great essay; it's that you have to write about something that inspires or excites you. For this woman, it took getting out of the box to find that inspiration.

A final note: Later on, it occurred to me that the b-school had truly lost out in not admitting this applicant the first time, proof again that essays are imperfect predictors. She quickly took on a leadership role at that school and became a genuine champion of the program. For the time she was there, she made a difference. Perhaps this school had underestimated how great a contribution she would have made the first time she applied.

7. A NEAR-MISSED OPPORTUNITY

Shortly thereafter, I worked with another second-year analyst at a different investment bank. She, too, was a bright star at her firm. Unfortunately, like the applicant above, her GMAT scores were mediocre.

Unsurprisingly, she had targeted top schools for admission. Her first choice was regarded as the "in" school and had just been chosen as number one by a widely read business magazine. It offered not only a great education, but also a dramatic departure from the cut-throat atmosphere of other programs, as its focus was on teamwork and other "soft skills." It was going to be extremely difficult to get into this already popular number-one program.

This applicant worried about her GMAT score, and for good reason. Like the analyst applicant we mentioned earlier, she was able to make a compelling argument for why she could manage the academic rigor of b-school and that she should not be judged by her score. She focused on portraying herself as the type of student who fit with the culture of this school. She slaved over her essays.

Unlike the other analyst, this applicant had a unique advantage: She had founded, almost single-handedly, a volunteer program aimed at getting Wall Street executives and analysts out of their offices and into community service projects. The program set new standards in this industry. It not only succeeded where others had failed (Wall Streeters are not exactly known for their altruism), but it also became "in" to volunteer with this program. Again, this was about fifteen years ago, before we were becoming a nation of do-gooders. At the time, this was highly novel.

You've already jumped to the punch line with this applicant. Yes, she was accepted into that number-one school. But it wasn't necassarily a slam dunk.

When the applicant first sat down to write her essays, she initially got hung up on a lot of details about her work (too much detail and techno-babble is always a mistake). In the essay that asked for a discussion of her accomplishments, she failed to articulate her volunteer program as a major achievement. I know that seems unbelievable, but this is exactly the kind of opportunity that gets missed without careful introspection and self-awareness.

Perhaps because of the intensely competitive culture in which she worked, she was overly focused on professional accomplishments. She didn't recognize what would be most valued by a b-school. Her best story nearly got buried.

After I had several discussions with her, her community service program came to be front and center in her essays. Still, she was never fully confident that this one achievement would override her GMAT score or that it would have more significance than her work history. Fortunately, her essays did articulate her accomplishment, and she stood out among a sea of applicants. Her essays also made it clear that she was a genuine fit with this school. Her GMAT score became a nonissue.

The epilogue to this story is that she had what it takes. She just wasn't going to showcase her best advantage until someone showed her the way.

8. The Job-Hopper

Another individual I worked with was an ex-analyst at one of the investment banks for which I was a consultant. He had attended one of my information sessions when he was a first-year analyst. Shortly after we met, he left the bank's training program because he found it rigid and limiting. He had kept my business card, and years later he phoned me.

After leaving the program, he had found a position at a smaller firm. He then went to work in finance at a service-oriented company. After that job, he was a project manager in a technology firm. By the time we spoke almost four years later, it seemed as though he had changed jobs every six months. Not only that, but the companies he had worked at were no-name firms.

Before we go on, I will give you some personal background: This applicant was born and raised in India. He had attended a selective college in America, had good grades and a solid, though not exceptional, GMAT score. He was feeling tremendous pressure from his parents, who were still in India. They did not consider business a worthy profession, so getting into a world-famous b-school was critical to earning their approval. It was equally critical to his life plan.

When he phoned me, I had been retired from my consulting work for several years, and I had just had a baby. He talked me into working with him and was very persistent, calling almost every day. To say the least, he was difficult to work with.

He was also convinced that b-schools had a bias against Indians and that it would therefore be more difficult for him to win admission. I didn't think this was true. What is in fact true is that all applicants are vulnerable to the diversity b-schools are aiming to create. But they also benefit from it.

He decided that only one school would do. I cautioned him that his chances were better if he applied to a mix of schools, but he was fixated on just one. With all that was riding on his acceptance, I worried that he was setting himself up for a letdown. His patchwork of jobs was problematic. His essay on this subject would have to compensate for a lot.

He used many essays to write movingly about his family and life in India. A socio-economic analysis he made of the Indian caste system was fascinating. He related it to behavioral expectations placed on him as a member of the elite. His mother and father, both medical doctors, were considered professional aristocrats. But because the tax rate in India at that time was around 95 percent, they were not rich. The rigidity of the caste system kept them at the upper rung of society, but ironically, they could not offer him financial support in college or thereafter. In the context of the American standard of living, he was poor. He spoke eloquently of the impact of those inconsistencies.

Now he had to answer the essay question on his professional experiences. Not all of the job switching was his doing, which gave me hope. At one organization, an entire department was eliminated; at another, the company was sold. As I've said in other sections of this book, the trick with a background like this is to focus on how you overcame adversity and what you learned about yourself.

He did speak of a personal ethos of determination and about how much he had learned, but some of this was a stretch. At many of his jobs he was overqualified—he was simply biding his time until he could figure out the next step. His work history came off less as a case of bad luck and more as a case of a young man unable to stay on a chosen path.

He was rejected from his choice school. Ever persistent, he insisted on speaking to an admissions officer to find out why he was a no-admit. The feedback was hardly surprising; the admissions board found his work background of serious concern. They found the remainder of his application and essays compelling, however, and they encouraged him to reapply.

My advice to him was to find a job he was passionate about and stay put for a year.

He did. Right on cue, many months later, he came knocking at my door. This time, his "problem" essay spoke of more stability and genuine passion. He reapplied early in his choice school's first round and got in.

There are several points to this story. First, an essay can blow your emotional cover. Genuine passion or sincerity is hard to manufacture. In this case, the insights he took away from having worked so many jobs lacked fire. Second, even an application full of great essays, such as this applicant's essays about his family, may not overcome an inherent problem.

As we've said before, there are many variables in the admissions process. At another school, perhaps one that was less selective, he would have been admitted in the first round. At this particular school, his application full of moving, well-crafted stories made an impression on the board, which probably had something to do with his being encouraged to reapply. When he did, they remembered him. Fondly.

chapter 5

COMMON ESSAY QUESTIONS
(AND WHAT THEY'RE REALLY ASKING)

CREATING PERFECTION TAKES TIME

"Essays are the love letter of why a student wants to attend business school."
—Julia Min,
Director of MBA Admissions at Stern School of Business,
New York University

No one ever said it was going to be easy. Depending on where you're applying and how prolific a writer you are, a b-school application will take anywhere from fifty to one hundred hours to complete. Sound excessive? Go ahead and try it. You'll probably scrap and rewrite an essay many times over. It takes time for thoughts to gestate. Indeed, it might feel like a fine wine ages faster than you write an essay.

You'll need to look at every essay question on each of your applications to determine how to optimally allocate your stories and anecdotes. One story might work well for either a leadership essay or an essay about failure. But you might have several good stories for leadership, and none for failure. Mapping out how you're going to allocate your anecdotes and stories is critical to your overall strategy.

Take a look at a recent year's essay questions from Harvard and Wharton below to get an idea of what you're up against. Keep in mind that not all schools will require you to write such exhaustive essays. The more selective a school is, the more rigid and demanding their standard for admission will be. That said, we're going to focus on the most brutal applications. They are the gold standard for essays, and their questions demand the greatest efforts.

Harvard Business School

1. Discuss an experience that has had an impact on your development as a leader. (400-word limit)

2. What are your three most substantial accomplishments, and why do you view them as such? (600-word limit)

3. Recognizing that successful leaders are able to learn from failure, discuss a situation in which you failed and what you learned. (400-word limit)

4. Discuss an ethical dilemma that you experienced firsthand. How did you manage and resolve the situation? (400-word limit)

5. Provide a candid assessment of your strengths and weaknesses. (400-word limit)

6. What are your career aspirations, and how can Harvard Business School help you to reach them? (400-word limit)

7. (Optional) Is there any other information that you believe would be helpful to the Board in understanding you better and in considering your application? Please be concise.

The Wharton School, University of Pennsylvania

1. Describe how your experiences, both professional and personal, have led to your decision to pursue an MBA at the Wharton School this year. How does this decision relate to your career goals for the future? (1,000 words)

2. Describe a situation where leadership and teamwork were critical to the outcome of a project in which you were directly involved. What did you learn from the experience and how have you applied what you learned to other situations? (1,000 words)

3. Describe a personal achievement that has had a significant impact on your life. Give specific details. What did you learn from this experience? How did it help shape your understanding of yourself and the world around you? (500 words)

4. Please tell us something else about yourself that you feel will help the Admissions Committee know you better. (500 words)

READING BETWEEN THE LINES

Being a great storyteller and gifted writer can be a major advantage to the prospective b-school student. But be forewarned: A wonderful answer to a question not asked will not help you here. We can't stress enough that you must answer the question.

Each school has its own set of questions. Although posed differently, all search for the same insights. Here's a list of commonly asked questions and what's behind them.

THEME 1: CAREER GOALS AND THE MBA

Describe your specific career aspirations. How will your goals be furthered by an MBA degree and by our MBA program in particular?

How do you feel the "X" school MBA degree can help you attain your specific career and personal goals for the five years after you graduate?

Discuss your career progression to date. What factors have influenced your decision to seek a general management education? Based on what you know about yourself at this time, how do you envision your career progressing after receiving the MBA degree? Please state your professional goals, and describe your plan to achieve them.

Translation:

What do I want to be when I grow up, and how will the MBA get me there?

This may be the most important essay question. It lays out the reasons why you should be given one of the cherished spots in the program. Even if your post-MBA future is tough to envision, this question must be answered.

A good way to frame this essay is to discuss how the MBA makes sense in light of your background, skills, and achievements to date. Why do you need this degree? Why now? One common reason is being stymied in your work by a lack of skills that can be gained in their program. Or you may want to use the MBA as a bridge to the next step. For example, an actress who wants an MBA to prepare for a career in theater management. The more specific, the better.

It may be easier to provide specifics by breaking your plans into short-term and long-term objectives.

Don't be afraid to present modest goals. If you're in accounting and want to stay there, say so. Deepening your expertise and broadening your perspective are solid reasons for pursuing this degree. On the other hand, feel free to indicate that you'll use the MBA to change careers; 70 percent of all students at b-school are there to do just that.

If you aspire to lofty goals, like becoming a CEO or starting your own company, be especially careful that you detail a sensible, pragmatic plan. You need to show you're realistic. No one zooms to the top. Break your progress into steps.

Finally, this essay question asks how a particular program supports your goals. Admissions committees want to know why you've selected their school. That means you not only have to know, but also show, what's special about their program and how that relates specifically to your career aspirations. Hint: Many admissions officers say they can tell how much someone wants to go to their school by how well their essays are tailored to the offerings in their program.

Theme 2: Extracurriculars and Social Interaction— Our Nonwork Side

What do you do for fun?

What are your principal interests outside of your job or school?

What leisure and/or community activities do you particularly enjoy? Please describe their importance in your life.

Translation:

Would we like to have you over for dinner? Do you know how to make friends? What are your special talents—the b-school Follies needs help. Are you well-balanced, or are you going to freak out when you get here?

B-school is not just about business, case studies, and careers. The best programs buzz with the energy of a student body that is talented and creative and that has personality. You won't be spending all your time in the library.

Are you interesting? Would you contribute to the school's vitality? Are you the kind of person other MBAs would be happy to meet? Describe activities you're involved in that might add something to the b-school community.

Are you sociable? B-school is a very social experience. Much of the work is done in groups. Weekends are full of social gatherings. Will you participate? Initiate? Get along with others? Communicate that people, not just your job, are an important part of your life.

Can you perform at a high level without being a nerd?

B-school can be tough. It's important to know when to walk away and find some fun. Do you know how to play as hard as you work?

How well-rounded are you? Business leaders have wide-angle perspectives; they take in the whole picture. How deep or broad are your interests? A warning: Don't just list what you've done. Explain how what you've done has made you unique.

Theme 3: Whom You Most Admire

If you were able to choose one person from the business world, past or present, to be your personal professor throughout the MBA program, who would this person be and why?

Describe the characteristics of an exceptional manager, using an example of someone whom you have observed or with whom you have worked. Illustrate how his or her management style has influenced you.

Translation:

What are your values? What character traits do you admire?

This is the curveball question. The committee isn't looking to evaluate your judgment in selecting some famous, powerful person in your firm or in the world. What they're really after, which you reveal in your selection of the person, are the qualities, attributes, and strengths you value in others, as well as in yourself. Some important qualities to address: drive, discipline, vision, ethics, and leadership. As always, provide specific examples. And avoid choosing anyone too obvious.

Since the person you select is not as important as what you say about him or her, your choices can be more humble. You might write about a current boss, business associate, or friend. Bad choices are your mother or father.

If you like, it's perfectly fine to go for a famous figure. Indeed, there may be someone whose career and style you're passionate about. Make sure your essay explains why you find this person so compelling.

On page 21, read about an applicant who chose a very intimate subject for this question—his wife.

THEME 4: TEAMWORK—HOW DO YOU WORK WITH OTHERS IN A GROUP SETTING?

At X School, a team, which consists of approximately five first-year students, is often assigned group projects and class presentations. Imagine that, one year from now, your team has a marketing class assignment due at 9:00 a.m. on Monday morning. It is now 10:00 P.M. on Sunday night; time is short, tension builds, and your team has reached an impasse. What role would you take in such a situation? How would you enable the team to meet your deadline? [Note: The specific nature of the assignment is not as important here as the team dynamic.] Feel free to draw on previous experiences, if applicable, in order to illustrate your approach.

Translation:

We need cooperative, one-for-all-and-all-for-one students here. Are you cut out to be one, or are you a take-over type who has all the answers? Are you likely to help everyone get along and arrive at solutions? (We like those kinds of students.) Can you lead others to order and synergy? (We especially like leaders.) Or do you retreat or become a follower?

This, too, is a curveball question. But you can't afford to get it wrong. After the career goals question, it probably ranks as the most critical essay you write. Here the committee isn't looking to see how you save the team (so put yourself on ego alert as you sit down to write this one); they want to see how you can create an environment in which everyone contributes so that the sum is greater than its parts. Bottom line—the admissions committee is looking to see whether you have "emotional intelligence." Understand that schools today believe that emotional intelligence, the ability to navigate emotion-laden situations, is as important as strategic and analytical skills. This question is intended to illustrate this particular type of ability.

Expect to shift gears with this essay. Almost the entire application process thus far has asked you to showcase "me-me-me." Now the focus of your story needs to be on the "we" and how you made the "we" happen.

As you write your essay, consider that when you get to school, some team members will be from different countries where cultural attitudes play into team dynamics. Your sensitivity to these cultural differences, as well as to personality types, will go a long way toward demonstrating your emotional intelligence. For example, a team member hailing from a certain culture may withhold an opinion in an attempt to foster consensus. How can you help this person make a contribution? Likewise, consider differences among team members in terms of their academic and professional strengths. If the assignment is heavy on numbers, finance students may dominate teammates from softer sciences. How can you ensure that everyone feels valued? Teams are inspired to success when everyone is motivated and taking ownership within a context of respect.

Remember, the team in this particular essay is at an impasse, as most teams are at some point in time. Write about how you "unjammed" the jam. Ideas: A change of scene, food, twenty push-ups, a quick round-the-room confessional about why you came to b-school. Introducing some process is also useful; ground rules such as voting, speaking times, a division of labor, and a time line all create a method from the madness. Perhaps you encourage members to adopt roles—business or otherwise. Hint: The leader or CEO in this case might be your most soft-spoken team member. Whatever you do in this essay, be careful not to present yourself as the one who single-handedly gets the team dynamic going.

THEME 5: DIVERSITY AND WHAT MAKES YOU UNIQUE

Our business school is a diverse environment. How will your experiences contribute to this?

During your years of study in the X program, you will be part of a diverse multicultural, multiethnic community within both the Business School and the larger university. What rewards and challenges do you anticipate in this environment, and how do you expect this experience to prepare you for a culturally diverse business world?

Translation:

What about you is different in terms of your background, your experience, or your cultural or geographic heritage? Can we count on your unique voice and perspective in our wide-ranging classroom discussions? How will you support the diverse cultural climate we are fostering here?

This essay gets at two concerns for the admissions committee: How will you enrich the student body at this school? And what is your attitude toward others' diverse backgrounds? Today's business leaders must be able to make decisions in situations that cut across geographic and cultural boundaries. If your essay reveals that you have dinosaur-era, only-white-males-rule thinking, you're going to close the door on your candidacy.

So what if you are a white male? Or you have no immediate point of distinction? Maybe a grandparent or relative is an immigrant to this country and you can discuss the impact of his or her values on your life. Perhaps you are the first individual in your family to attend college or to attend graduate school. What does that mean to you? Perhaps you are involved in a meaningful or unusual extracurricular activity. How has this changed your perspective? Perhaps you did a business deal with a foreign country. What did you observe about that culture, and how did it affect your decisions?

Whatever you write about need not be dramatic—maybe you take art classes, coach a little league team, or race a motorcycle. Sound goofy? It's all in the framing. Racing a motorcycle might be about the physical and mental stamina, the ability to take risks, the commitment to learning something new.

This question can be relatively easy to answer if, of course, you have diversity or some unique element in your background. If you don't have something obvious, then you're going to have to dig a bit and find something you can amplify to suggest you bring a unique voice to the school.

THEME 6: YOUR GREATEST PERSONAL ACHIEVEMENT/ACCOMPLISHMENT

Describe a personal achievement that has had a significant impact on your life. In addition to recounting this achievement, please analyze how the event has changed your understanding of yourself and how you perceive the world around you.

In reviewing the last five years, describe one or two accomplishments in which **you** demonstrated leadership.

Translation:

Do you know what an achievement is? Have you done anything remarkable? What made it remarkable to you? Bonus points if you showed leadership or inspired others in some way.

This is one of those maddening essay questions because on the one hand, b-schools seek out applicants whose average age is twenty-seven (a relatively young age to have achieved much of anything). On the other hand, the schools want to know what miracles you've performed. Don't pull your hair out yet. There is a way out. Like all the others, this essay is just one more prove-to-us-you-have-some-character hoop you'll have to jump through. It's less about the achievement and more about who you are and how you see yourself.

Again, this question can be easy to answer if you have some clear accomplishment or event in your background. But if you're like the rest of us—you guessed it—you'll have to rely on framing.

Let's cover bad essay topics for achievements. Getting straight A's in college is not an achievement because everyone else at b-school has probably done the same. Surviving a divorce or breakup is a bad accomplishment topic. Personal stories are acceptable, but one taboo area is romance and marriage. If this is all you can come up with, you're going to look like you're as deep as a doughnut.

The accomplishment you choose might show some of the following qualities: character, sacrifice, humility, dedication, high personal stakes, perseverance over obstacles, insight, and learning. You need not have published a business article or won an award to answer this question. This essay is not about excellence of outcome, but what it took for you to reach some personal worthy objective. Maybe you didn't lead a sports team to a victory. The victory may be just that you made it onto the team.

Modesty Matters

Kate Klepper, Director of Admissions at Babson, on how to avoid being arrogant or boastful in the achievement essay:

"Many applicants over-amplify their accomplishments and strengths. This is a common pitfall in this and other essays. But this is one of those frustrating application conundrums. First, the schools exhort you to engage in self-praise, and then you're penalized if you take it too far. But it's hard for an applicant to know where the line is between demonstrating performance and boasting.

"One way to avoid boasting is to frame the accomplishment in terms of why it was meaningful to you. There are many levels to this; one might be the opportunity you had to grow, another the privilege to be lauded by your peers. Still another level might be the chance to gain new skills, and the last might be what you felt at a deeply personal level.

"Of course, one man's accomplishment may be another person's failure. Someone might use this essay to talk about being the slugger who hits the most home runs in baseball. Someone else might use this essay to share that the mere act of making the team, even though they spent the season in the dugout, was their greatest accomplishment.

One's greatest accomplishments in life may not be the big blockbuster ones like a promotion, or acquisition of a company. The most inspiring stories here can run counter to what you think might be impressive."

THEME 7: FAILURE/WHAT MISTAKES HAVE YOU MADE?

Discuss a nonacademic personal failure. In what way were you disappointed in yourself? What did you learn from the experience?

Translation:

Can you admit to a genuine failure? Do you have enough self-awareness to know what kind of failure is real? Can you learn from your mistakes? Do they lead to greater maturity and self-awareness? Do you take responsibility when the fault is yours?

Many applicants make the mistake of answering this question with a failure that is really a positive, such as "I'm a perfectionist and so therefore I was too demanding on a friend when she was in a crisis." Or they never really answer the question, fearful that any admission of failure will throw their whole candidacy into jeopardy. The truth is, if you don't answer this question with a genuine failure or mistake, one that the committee will recognize as authentic, you may have jinxed your application.

In this essay you want to write about a failure that had some high stakes for you. Demonstrate what you learned from your mistake and how it helped you mature. What's the relevance to b-school here? Your ability to be honest, show accountability, and face your failures head-on reflects what kinds of decisions and judgments you will make as a business professional.

Can't think of a time you failed? Discuss the essay question with a friend or family member. An outsider's perspective may jog your memory. Remember, if your whole application has been about work, work, work, this is a great place to convince the committee you're a real person.

THEME 8: ETHICS

Describe an ethical issue you have faced in your professional life and how you dealt with it. What was the outcome?

Translation:

Do you even know what an ethical dilemma looks like? Are you tomorrow's corporate miscreant? What kinds of decisions and judgments might you make in your future practices as a business leader?

The last few years have brought attention to the ethical issues of the business world and the failure of corporate self-governance. In the aftermath of many high-profile scandals, b-schools don't want to turn out graduates who are fast into their suspenders, fast into a deal, and fast to swindle their clients and shareholders.

The above question tests your judgment, integrity, and perspective. It's most important to present a legitimate ethical dilemma here, one that has consequences. Applicants often write about the dilemma of not obeying a supervisor's orders because they wanted to do things their way, a known better way. But this is not an ethics problem (unless the order was improper or illegal); it's a management problem. Likewise, handing in a report to your boss that you know is full of errors is also not an ethical problem; it's a trivial, single-impact, easy-to-fix problem.

If you were thinking of telling a story like one of those mentioned above, it may be because you wanted to play it safe. This is one of those uncomfortable, hot-seat essays after all. But playing it safe here would only make you appear clueless or morally bereft.

This essay requires you to roll up your ethical shirtsleeves and get down in the dirt. True ethical issues are neither clean nor pretty. Don't shrink away from a discussion of failure here or present an overly optimistic, no-loose-ends solution.

It's key that you write about an ethical dilemma in which there was no easy course—one that entailed costs either way. For example, let's say you sold a product to a client and later discovered the product was faulty; your employer wanted you to keep mum. You'd built your sales relationships on trust and personal attention, so you wanted to be forthcoming. What did you do?

This essay must show that you can work through a complex ethical impasse, and it must highlight your sense of honor and conduct. This essay screams relevance. Make sure you shout back that you know right from wrong.

Chapter **6**

THE (OPTIONAL) PERSONAL STATEMENT: HOW, IF, AND WHEN TO USE IT

We mentioned earlier that most applications have an optional essay question, also known as the personal statement. It can be used to fill in the blanks—to address any topic that you were unable to weave into the required essays. We'll show you how this question might best be used to your advantage, depending on what shortcomings (if any) are present in your application.

Theme: The Personal Statement

Does this application provide the opportunity to present the real you?

The admissions committee would welcome any additional comments you may wish to provide in support of your application.

What question should we have asked you?

Translation:

What did we miss? Appeal to us in any way you want; this is your last chance. Be real.

I call this the "bonus" question. If you have an experience or personal cause that says something interesting about you, and it hasn't found a place in any other essay, this is the time to stick it in. Keep in mind that you are hoping to present yourself as unique—so show some passion!

The Tuck School of Business gives you further direction on how to complete their personal statement: "Complete this section only if you feel your credentials and application do not fully represent your candidacy." This last part of the question is saying, "Okay applicant, what did we miss?" But it's also saying, "Tread carefully with your content here; don't waste our time."

How and When to Craft an Essay that Explains a Weakness (or Rebuts a Weakness with a Strength)

How does an applicant go about writing an essay that addresses his or her weaknesses? Well, it's a complex art, and the potential communication pitfalls are many. For example, how much should you tell the admissions officers? Do you apologize for the problem, or just defend its circumstances? When have you made your point without over-explaining? How do you evoke empathy, but not pity? Is there a valid excuse for bad scores?

The efficacy of your explanation is critical here. You want to make sure that the message you intend to send out is exactly what is received. When you're offering explanations, there is no room for miscommunication with style, tone, or content. Rambling or whining in this essay will kill not only the message, but also your candidacy.

Keep in mind that you are composing essays for people who have seen real hardships and real causes for performance or employment gaps. Perched at a sort of crossroads to life, the admissions board has heard it all—anything and everything that has ever happened to anyone. Chances are, they've lived through some of these things too. They don't expect you to sail through life unscathed. They do, however, expect you to own up to your shortcomings and move on with confidence.

What Is Legit?

Before you can craft an explanation, you have to first identify what is a legitimate problem and what is a legitimate excuse. This calls into play your self-awareness, and it can be tricky. What you think is legitimate, someone else might see as lame. For example, if your explanation for bad grades in college is simply that you partied too much, well, you've just dug yourself an even bigger hole. You highlight your true personality through the topics you choose to write about, so think before you choose a foolish topic.

A general rule of thumb is this: Unless the problem has negatively impacted you in some way relevant to the application process, it may not need to be brought up at all. Ask yourself: Why am I telling the admissions officers this story? What's my point? You don't have to bring to the attention of the admissions board every misfortune or mishap you've experienced, even if its effect on you was quite dramatic.

Paid His Own Way

Here's an example of a situation that doesn't warrant an explanation or even a mention in the application. A friend of mine put himself through school and held down two part-time jobs while attending college full-time. While this could have conceivably made it more difficult for him to dedicate time to his studies, his grades did not suffer as a result of these jobs. There is consequently no weakness to address and no excuse to be given. He could have mentioned this in the personal statement as evidence of his focus and determination, but it might have sounded lame.

Loss of a Parent

Another friend of mine suffered through her mother's battle with cancer while attending an Ivy League college. Her mother passed away when my friend was a sophomore. Years later, when she applied to graduate school, she didn't focus on this. Why? She got straight A's, graduated with the highest of honors, and received good scores. She had moved on. She did not have excuses, although she did have adversity. There is a difference.

"Hold on," you say. That has the making of a great essay! And you would be right. While you could use this topic for a personal statement, as an added value it would be better-positioned front and center as a main essay. This story is so rich that she could have used it in response to a question about unique qualities or achievements, or even a question about a person you admire or three people with whom you would most like to have dinner.

Now, if this friend had received bad grades, it'd be a different story. In that scenario, I would advise that she write about the loss of her mother as a main essay with a theme of triumph over adversity and in a straightforward and confident tone, use the personal statement to explain why her grades were bad and why her academic performance would be different at business school. Each of these essays would support and reinforce the other.

Circumstances and Weaknesses Commonly Addressed in Business School Personal Statements:

Acts of God (flood, fire, accidents)

Bad grades

Low GMAT score (overall, Math, or Verbal)

Test anxiety

Learning disability

Handicap

Multiple college transcripts/on-and-off attendance

Birth of a child

Illness (physical or mental)

Death or loss

Divorce or marriage

Family problems

Financial hardship

Job loss

Lack of career progress/promotions

Addressing Some Common Problems

Now we'll go one step further and advise you in more detail on how to craft your personal statement to address the most common concerns.

Pink Slips

In this brutal economy, b-schools know that seamless resumes are a relic of the past. Many applicants may have lost not one, but two or more jobs, particularly those who have transitioned through the dot-com era; some never even secured that first job out of school. Don't worry, though; you won't automatically be penalized for a spotty resume, as long as you fill in the gaps. You won't be blamed for layoffs, and you won't be blamed for the fact that the company failed.

In order to properly address this issue in the personal statement, you'll want to share the circumstances of your departure, but avoid providing too much detail. Play up what you learned and focus on any other positive details of your experience at the company. Were you able to stay in a single industry and build upon your prior work experiences? Perhaps you were with an Internet startup that went bust. In this case, describe how you stayed at the helm to the bitter end, and focus on the leadership you demonstrated in so doing.

If you had to grab a paycheck, be honest. Don't communicate self-blame or embarrassment. Again, put it in the context of what you learned. Talk about how you used each job to acquire specific skills or contacts.

If you were fired due to work performance, that's okay; we've all been there, too. Use the suggestions above to write self-assuredly of your experience.

Bad Grades

If you were working two full-time jobs to pay for college, or were lettering in three sports, it's fairly obvious why your grades were a casualty. This is an understandable scenario. But perhaps you perceived college as just one long party, or you're a street-smart person who doesn't shine academically. Maybe you were just lazy, and getting by was good enough for you.

Whatever the case may have been then, you are marketing yourself now, so place yourself in the best possible light. Tell them you've left behind your partying and desultory ways. Demonstrate how in your current profession you have evolved into a highly motivated, capable, and hard-working professional. Focus on who you are today. Speak to your maturity and renewed commitment to academics.

You may also wish to provide concrete examples of academic excellence in other areas. If you scored high on the GMAT, mention it as evidence of your brainpower, but be subtle; your straight-C average and 90th percentile scores may really convince the committee you're a goof-off. Don't forget to stay in tight control of your message. Emphasize the fact that the great GMAT score means you can handle the academic rigors ahead. You're not goofing off anymore. Additional examples of academic success are courses or training programs you've taken in which you've excelled.

BAD SCORES AND TEXT ANXIETY

It's okay to admit that you don't do well on standardized tests. You won't be the first one to do so. You may even want to note that you took it twice to improve your score.

Whatever you do, don't whine on this one. Own up to the weakness and give the admissions officers plenty of reasons (with supporting evidence) to admit you anyway. Convince them you have the intellectual wherewithal to perform successfully in their program. Provide them with other professional and academic examples of your brainpower.

If your Math score is weak, showcase your quantitative skills at your job and elsewhere; if your Verbal score is poor, well then, you'd better submit essays that shine and provide other evidence of your outstanding verbal skills.

LEARNING DISABILITY

This is a slippery slope. If a learning disability is the reason for poor academic performance, this is quite legitimate. But you may be portraying it as a weakness that is an inherent part of your makeup. You can't frame this as something you can move on from, so this may be one of those instances where you can make things worse. The admissions committee's main concern, after all, is that you can keep pace with your b-school peers and the volume of work.

It's hard to advise whether someone in this situation should admit to it on the application, even though it's the most legitimate of explanations. If you do, put the learning disability in the context of tenacity and hard work. Highlight any areas of academic excellence.

IN SUMMARY

We'd like to offer some general recommendations for utilizing the personal statement to explain a weakness or a problem.

- Discuss problems in a forthright, straightforward manner.

- Don't make whiny, shopworn excuses. Have a legitimate point to make.

- Write confidently about your mistakes and weaknesses; don't hide behind shame. Rebut a weakness with a strength.

- Illustrate what you've learned and how you've moved on and recovered.

- Don't focus on yesterday. Talk about who you are today.

- Be positive. Emphasize that you are a can-do person.

- Don't get too intimate with the details. What works on *Oprah* is too personal for a b-school essay.

- Avoid sounding defensive, self-pitying, or self-absorbed. Showcase how you overcame adversity.

Chapter **7**

IN CASE YOU SLEPT
THROUGH ENGLISH CLASS

Like any good writing, your business school essays should be clear, concise, candid, structurally sound, and 100 percent grammatically accurate. Go ahead and get the story out, but then make sure to edit with a fine-tooth comb. Here's how.

THE ESSENTIALS

Clarity and conciseness are usually the products of a lot of reading, re-reading, and rewriting. Without question, repeated critical revision by yourself and by others is the surest way to trim, tune, and improve your prose.

Candor is the product of proper motivation. Honesty, sincerity, and authenticity cannot be superimposed after the fact; your writing must be candid from the outset. Also, let's be frank: You're probably pretty smart and pretty sophisticated. You could probably fake candor if absolutely necessary, but you shouldn't. For one thing, it's a hell of a lot more work. Moreover, no matter how good your insincere essay may be, we're brazenly confident that an honest and authentic essay will be even better.

Structural soundness is the product of a well-crafted outline. It really pays to sketch out the general themes of your essay first; worry about filling in the particulars later. Pay particularly close attention to the structure of your essay and to the fundamental message it communicates. Make sure you have a well-conceived narrative. Your essay should flow from beginning to end. Use paragraphs properly, and make sure the paragraphs are in a logical order. The sentences within each paragraph should also be complete and in logical order.

It is critical that you avoid all grammatical errors. We just can't stress this enough.

You aren't allowed to misspell anything. You aren't allowed to use awkwardly constructed or run-on sentences. You aren't allowed to use verbs in the wrong tenses. You aren't allowed to misplace modifiers. You aren't allowed to make a single error in punctuation. A thoughtful essay that offers true insight will stand out, but if it is riddled with poor grammar and misspelled words, it will not receive serious consideration. In fact, making sure your essays are 100% grammatically accurate is so important that we've prepared a little primer for you. Even if you're already a brilliant writer, it can't hurt to have a little review,

Don't neglect your spelling and grammar check

We imagine you'll probably write your essay on a computer. It's a very good idea. Use a computer with a spell-checker. Turn on the spelling- and grammar-checking options. Your computer is only as smart as you are, so carefully consider the advice your computer offers. Your computer is not going to know the difference between "there" versus "their," but you should.

MOST COMMON GRAMMAR MISTAKES

Chances are you know the difference between a subject and a verb. So we won't spend time here reviewing the basic components of English sentence construction (however, if you feel like you could use a refresher, check out our book, *Grammar Smart*.) Instead we will focus on problems of usage.

Below is a brief overview of the seven most common usage errors among English speakers. These are errors we all make (some more than others) and knowing what they are will help you snuff them out in your own writing.

Mistake #1: Misplaced Modifier

A modifier is a descriptive word or phrase inserted into a sentence to add dimension to the thing it modifies. For example:

Because he could talk, Mr. Ed was a unique horse.

Because he could talk is the modifying phrase in the sentence. It describes a characteristic of Mr. Ed. Generally speaking, a modifying phrase should be right next to the thing it modifies. If it's not, the meaning of the sentence may change. For example:

Every time he goes to the bathroom outside, John praises his new puppy for being so good.

Who's going to the bathroom outside? In this sentence, it's John! There are laws against that! The descriptive phrase *every time he goes to the bathroom outside* needs to be near *puppy* for the sentence to say what it means.

When you are writing sentences that begin with a descriptive phrase followed by a comma, make sure that the thing that comes after the comma is the person or thing being modified.

Mistake #2: Pronoun Agreement

As you know, a pronoun is a little word that is inserted to represent a noun (*he, she, it, they,* etc). Pronouns must agree with their nouns: The pronoun that replaces a singular noun must also be singular, and the pronoun that replaces a plural noun must be plural.

During your proofreading, be sure your pronouns agree with the nouns they represent. The most common mistake is to follow a singular noun with a plural pronoun (or vice versa), as in the following:

If a writer misuses words, they will not do well on the state exam.

The problem with this sentence is that the noun ("writer") is singular, but the pronoun ("they") is plural. The sentence would be correctly written as follows:

If a writer misuses words, he or she will not do well on the state exam.

Or

If writers misuse words, they will not do well on the state exam.

This may seem obvious but it is also the most commonly violated rule in ordinary speech. How often have you heard people say, *The class must hand in their assignment before leaving. Class* is singular. But *their* is plural. *Class* isn't the only tricky noun that sounds singular but is actually plural. Following is a list of "tricky" nouns—technically called collective nouns. They are nouns that typically describe a group of people but are considered singular and therefore need a singular pronoun:

Family

Jury

Group

Team

Audience

Congregation

United States

If different pronouns are used to refer to the same subject or one pronoun is used to replace another, the pronouns must also agree. The following pronouns are singular:

Either

Neither

None

Each

Anyone

No one

Everyone

If you are using a pronoun later in a sentence, double-check to make sure it agrees with the noun/pronoun it is replacing.

Mistake #3: Subject-Verb Agreement

The rule regarding subject-verb agreement is simple: singular with singular, plural with plural. If you are given a singular subject (*he, she, it*), then your verb must also be singular (*is, has, was*).

Sometimes you may not know if a subject is plural or singular, making it tough to determine whether its verb should be plural or singular. (Just go back to our list of collective nouns that sound plural but are really singular).

Subjects joined by *and* are plural:

Bill and Pat *were* going to the show.

However, nouns joined by or can be singular or plural—if the last noun given is singular, then it takes a singular verb; if the last noun given is plural, it takes a plural verb.

Bill or Pat *was* going to get tickets to the show.

When in doubt about whether your subjects and verbs agree, trim the fat! Cross out all the prepositions, commas, adverbs, and adjectives separating your subject from its verb. Stripping the sentence down to its component parts will allow you to quickly see whether your subjects and verbs are in order.

Mistake #4: Verb Tense

As you know, verbs come in different tenses—for example, *is* is present tense, while was is past tense. The other tense you need to know about is "past perfect."

Past perfect refers to some action that happened in the past and was completed (perfected) before another event in the past. For example:

I had already begun to volunteer at the hospital when I discovered my passion for medicine.

You'll use the past perfect a lot when you describe your accomplishments to admissions officers. For the most part, verb tense should not change within a sentence (e.g., switching from past to present).

Mistake #5: Parallel Construction

Remember this from your SATs? Just as parallel lines line up with one another, parallelism means that the different parts of a sentence line up in the same way. For example:

Jose told the career counselor his plan: he will be taking the GMAT, attend business school, and become a CEO.

In this sentence, Jose is going to *be taking*, *attend*, and, *become*. The first verb, *be taking* is not written I the same form as the other verbs in the series. In other words, it is not parallel. To make this sentence parallel, it should read:

Jose told the career counselor his plan: he will take the GMAT, attend business school, and become a CEO.

It is common to make errors of parallelism when writing sentences that list actions or items. Be careful.

Mistake #6: Comparisons

When comparing two things, make sure that you are comparing what can be compared. Sound like double-talk? Look at the following sentence:

Larry goes shopping at Foodtown because the prices are better than Shoprite.

Sound okay? Well, sorry—it's wrong. As written, this sentence says that the prices at Foodtown are better than Shoprite—the entire store. What Larry means is that the prices at Foodtown are better than the *prices* at Shoprite. You can only compare like things (prices to prices, not prices to stores).

The English language uses different comparison words when comparing two things than when comparing more than two things. Check out these examples:

more (for two things) vs. **most** (for more than two)

Ex.: Given Alex and David as possible dates, Alex is the *more* appealing of the two. In fact, of all the guys I know, Alex is the *most* attractive.

less (for two things) vs. **least** (for more than two)

Ex.: I am *less* likely to be chosen than you are.

I am the *least* likely person to be chosen from the department.

better (for two things) vs. **best** (for more than two)

Ex.: Taking a cab is *better* than hitchhiking.

My organic chemistry professor is the *best* professor I have ever had.

between (for two things) vs. **among** (for more than two)

Ex.: Just *between* you and me, I never liked her anyway.

Among all the people here, no one likes her.

Keep track of what's being compared in a sentence so you don't fall into this grammatical black hole.

Mistake #7: Diction

Diction means choice of words. There are tons of frequently confused words in the English language. They can be broken down into words that sound the same but mean different things (*there, they're, their*), words and phrases that are made up (*irregardless*) and words that are incorrectly used as synonyms (*fewer, less*).

Words that sound the same but mean different things are homonyms. Some examples are:

there, they're, their: *There* is used to indicate a location in time or space. *They're* is a contraction of "they are." *Their* is a possessive pronoun.

effect/affect: *Effect* is the result of something. *Affect* is to influence or change something.

conscience/conscious: *Conscience* is Freudian, and is a sense of right or wrong. *Conscious* is to be awake.

principle/principal: *Principle* is a value. *Principal* is the person in charge at a school.

eminent/imminent: *Eminent* describes a person who is highly regarded. *Imminent* means impending.

Imaginary words that don't exist but tend to be used in writing include:

Alot: Despite widespread use, *alot* is not a word. *A lot* is the correct form.

Irregardless: *Irregardless* is not in anybody's dictionary—it's not a real word. *Regardless* is the word that you want.

Sometimes people don't know when to use a word. How often have you seen this sign?

Express checkout: Ten items or less.

Unfortunately, supermarkets across America are making a blatant grammatical error when they post this sign. When items can be counted, you must use the word *fewer*. When something cannot be counted, you would use the word *less*. For example:

If you eat fewer French fries, you can use less ketchup.

Here are some other words people make te mistake of using interchangeably:

number/amount: Use *number* when referring to something that can be counted. Use *amount* when it cannot.

aggravate/irritate: *Aggravate* and *irritate* are not synonymous. To *aggravate* is to make worse. To *irritate* is to annoy.

disinterested/uninterested: *Disinterest* means impartiality; absence of strong feelings about something, good or bad. To be *uninterested*, on the other hand, indicates boredom.

Diction errors require someone to cast a keen, fresh eye on your essay because they trick your ear and require focused attention to catch.

Here's a handy chart to help you remember the most common grammar usage errors:

GRAMMAR CHART

Grammatical Category	What's the Rule?	Bad Grammar	Good Grammar
Misplaced Modifier	A modifier is word or phrase that describes something and should go right next to the thing it modifies.	1. Eaten in Mediterranean countries for centuries, the tomato was viewed the tomato with suspicion. 2. A **former greens keeper** now about to become the Masters champion, **tears** welled up in my eyes as I hit my last miraculous shot.	1. Eaten in Mediterranean countries for centuries, the tomato was viewed with suspicion by Northern Europeans. 2. I **was a former greens keeper** who was now about to become the Masters champion; **tears** welled up in my eyes as I hit my last miraculous shot.
Pronoun Agreement	A pronoun must refer unambiguously to a noun and it must agree in number with that noun.	1. Although **brokers** are not permitted to know executive access **codes**, **they** are widely known. 2. The **golden retriever** is one of the smartest breeds of dogs, but **they** often **have** trouble writing **personal statements** for law school admission. 3. Unfortunately, both **candidates** for whom I worked sabotaged their own **campaigns** by accepting a **contribution** from illegal **sources**.	1. Although **brokers** are not permitted to know executive access **codes, the codes** are widely known. 2. The **golden retriever** is one of the smartest breeds of dogs, but often **it has** trouble writing **a personal statement** for law school admission. 3. Unfortunately, both **candidates** for whom I worked sabotaged their own **campaigns** by accepting **contributions** from illegal **sources**.
Subject-Verb Agreement	The subject must always agree in number with the verb. Make sure you don't forget what the subject of a sentence is, and don't use the object of a preposition as a subject.	1. **Each** of the men involved in the extensive renovations **were** engineers. 2. Federally imposed **restrictions** on the ability to use certain information **has** made life difficult for Martha Stewart.	1. **Each** of the men involved in the extensive renovations **was** engineers. 2. Federally imposed **restrictions** on the ability to use certain information **have** made life difficult for Martha Stewart.

Grammatical Category	What's the Rule?	Bad Grammar	Good Grammar
Verb Tense	Always make sure your sentences' tenses match the time frame being discussed.	1. After he finished working on his law school essays he **would go** to the party.	1. After he finished working on his law school essays he **went** to the party.
Paralell Construction	Two or more ideas in a single sentence that are parallel need to be similar in grammatical form.	1. The two main goals of the Eisenhower presidency were a **reduction** of taxes and **to increase** military strength. 2. **To provide a child** with the skills necessary for survival in modern life is **like guaranteeing their** success.	1. The two main goals of the Eisenhower presidency were **to reduce** taxes and **to increase** military strength. 2. **Providing children** with the skills necessary for survival in modern life is **like guaranteeing their** success.
Cmparisons	You can only compare things that are exactly the same.	1. The **rules** of written English are **more stringent** than spoken **English.** 2. The **considerations** that led many colleges to impose admissions quotas in the last few decades **are similar to the quotas** imposed in the recent past by large businesses.	1. The rules of written English are **more stringent than those of** spoken **English.** 2. The **considerations** that led many colleges to impose admissions quotas in the last few decades **are similar to those** that led large businesses to impose quotas in the recent past.
Diction	There are many words that sound the same but mean different things.	1. Studying had a very positive **affect** on my score. 2. My high SAT score has positively **effected** the outcome of my college applications.	1. Studying had a very positive **effect** on my score. 2. My high SAT score has positively **affected** the outcome of my college applications.

PUNCTUATION

Now that we've got that covered, it's time to talk about punctuation. As a member of the LOL generation you might be great at turning punctuation into nonverbal clues, but colons and parentheses have other uses besides standing in as smiley faces at the end of your texts.

A formal essay is not like the notes you take in econometrics. "W/" is not an acceptable substitute for *with*, and neither is "b/c" for *because*. Symbols are also not acceptable substitutes for words (@ for *at*, & for *and*, etc.). (In fact, try to avoid the use of "etc."; it is not entirely acceptable in formal writing. Use "and so forth" or "among others" instead.) And please don't indulge in any "cute" spelling ("nite" for *night*, "tho" for *though*). This kind of writing conveys a message that you don't care about your essay. Show the admissions officers how serious you are by eliminating these shortcuts.

The overall effectiveness of your business school application essay is greatly dependent on your ability to use punctuation wisely. Here's what you need to know:

Commas (,)

Very few people understand every rule for proper comma use in the English language.

This lack of understanding leads to two disturbing phenomena: essays without commas and essays with commas everywhere. Here is a quick summary of proper comma use:

Use Commas to Set Off Introductory Elements.

- Breezing through my application essay, I wondered if everyone were as well prepared as I.

- Incidentally, I got a 750 on the GMAT.

- Before you jump to any conclusions, I was only taking a mote out of her eye.

Use Commas to Separate Items in a Series.

- She made hot chocolate, cinnamon toast, scrambled eggs with cheese, and coffee cake.

[Note: There's always great debate as to whether the final serial comma (before the *and*) is necessary. In this case, the comma must be added; otherwise, there will be a question about the contents of the scrambled eggs. In cases where no such ambiguity exists, the extra comma seems superfluous. Use your best judgment. When in doubt, separate all the items in a series with commas.]

Use Commas Around a Phrase or Clause that Could Be Removed Logically from the Sentence.

- The Analytical Writing section, the first section of the GMAT, always makes my palms sweat.

- Xavier, the student whose test was interrupted by marching band practice, would have liked to have had ear plugs.

Use a Comma to Separate Coordinate (Equally Important) Adjectives. *Do Not* Use a Comma to Separate Noncoordinate Adjectives.

- It was a dark, stormy night.

- It was messy triple bypass.

***Do Not* Use a Comma to Separate a Subject and a Verb.**

- Incorrect: My new GMAT study group, meets at the local café.

- Correct: My new GMAT study group meets at the local café.

Do Not Use a Comma to Separate Compound Subjects or Predicates.

(A compound subject means two "do-ers"; a compound predicate means two actions done.)

- Incorrect: My best friend Xavier, and his brother Lou always tell me the truth about my practice essays.

- Correct: My best friend Xavier and his brother Lou always tell me the truth about my practice essays.

- Incorrect: Because of the strange tickling in the back of my throat, I stayed in bed, and gave myself a break from studying.

- Correct: Because of the strange tickling in the back of my throat, I stayed in bed and gave myself a break from studying.

Colons (:)

Use a colon to introduce an explanation or a list.

- "I think you judge Truman too charitably when you call him a child: He is more like a sweetly vicious old lady." *Tennessee Williams*

- "When I am dead, I hope it may be said: 'His sins were scarlet, but his books were read.'" *Hilaire Belloc*

- "Everything goes by the board to get the book written: honor, pride, decency…" *William Faulkner*

Semicolons (;)

Use a semicolon to join related independent clauses in a single sentence (a clause is independent if it can logically stand alone).

- "An artist is born kneeling; he fights to stand." *Hortense Calisher*

- "Why had I become a writer in the first place? Because I wasn't fit for society; I didn't fit into the system." *Brian Aldiss*

Dashes (—)

Use a dash for an abrupt shift. Use a pair of dashes (one on either side) to frame a parenthetical statement that interrupts the sentence. Dashes are more informal than colons.

- "Like a lot of what happens in novels, inspiration is a sort of spontaneous combustion—the oily rags of the head and heart." *Stanley Elkin*

- "Writers should be read—but neither seen nor heard." *Daphne du Maurier*

- "Of all the cants which are canted in this canting world—though the cant of hypocrites may be the worst—the cant of criticism is the most tormenting." *Laurence Sterne*

Exclamation Points (!)

Use exclamation points sparingly. Try to express excitement, surprise, or rage in the words you choose. A good rule of thumb is *one* exclamation point per essay, at the most.

- "You don't know what it is to stay a whole day with your head in your hands trying to squeeze your unfortunate brain so as to find a word…. Ah! I certainly know the agonies of style." *Gustave Flaubert*

Question Marks (?)

Use a question mark after a direct question. Don't forget to use a question mark after rhetorical questions (ones that you make in the course of argument that you answer yourself).

- "Why shouldn't we quarrel about a word? What is the good of words if they aren't important enough to quarrel over? Why do we choose one word over another if there isn't any difference between them?" *G. K. Chesterton*

Quotation Marks (" ")

Use quotation marks to indicate a writer's exact words. Use quotation marks for titles of songs, chapters, essays, articles, or stories—a piece that is part of a larger whole. Periods and commas always go inside the quotation mark. Exclamation points and question marks go inside the quotation mark when they belong to the quotation and not to the larger sentence. Colons, semicolons, and dashes go outside the quotation mark.

- "That's not writing, that's typing." *Truman Capote* on Jack Kerouac

STYLE

Now that you've gotten a refresher in the building blocks of good writing, it's time to talk about the other half of the equation: style. If grammar and punctuation represent the mechanics of your writing, style represents the choices you make in sentence structure, diction, and figures of thought that reveal your personality to admissions officers. We can't recommend highly enough that you read *The Elements of Style*, by William Strunk Jr., E. B. White, and Roger Angell. This little book is a great investment. Even if you've successfully completed a course or two in composition without it, it will prove invaluable and become your new best friend—and hopefully also your muse.

ELIMINATING WORDINESS

Remember: Good writing is writing that's easily understood. You want to get your point across, not bury it in words. Make your prose clear and direct. **If an admissions officer has to struggle to figure out what you're trying to say, there's a good chance he or she might not bother reading further.** Abide by word limits and avoid the pitfall of overwriting. Here are some suggestions that will help clarify your writing by eliminating wordiness:

Address One Idea at a Time

Don't try to put too much information into one sentence. If you're ever uncertain whether a sentence needs three commas and two semicolons or two colons and a dash, just make it into two separate sentences. Two simple sentences are better than one long convoluted one. Which of the following examples seems clearer to you?

Example #1:

Many people, politicians for instance, act like they are thinking of the people they represent by the comments made in their speeches, while at the same time they are filling their pockets at the expense of the taxpayers.

Example #2:

Many people appear to be thinking of others, but are actually thinking of themselves. For example, many politicians claim to be thinking of their constituents, but are in fact filling their pockets at the taxpayers' expense.

Use Fewer Words to Express an Idea

In a 500-word essay, you don't have time to mess around. In an attempt to sound important, many of us "pad" our writing. Always consider whether there's a shorter way to express your thoughts. We are all guilty of some of the following types of clutter:

Cluttered	Clear
due to the fact that	because
with the possible exception of	except
until such time as	until
for the purpose of	for
referred to as	called
at the present time	now
at all times	always

Test Yourself: Eliminating Wordiness Exercise

Another way in which unnecessary words may sneak into your writing is through the use of redundant phrases. Pare each phrase listed below down to a single word:

cooperate together_____

resulting effect_____

large in size_____

absolutely unprecedented_____

disappear from sight_____

new innovation_____

repeat again_____

totally unique_____

necessary essentials_____

Use Fewer Qualifiers

A qualifier is a little phrase we use to cover ourselves. Instead of plainly stating that "Former President Reagan sold arms in exchange for hostages," we feel more comfortable stating "*It's quite possible* that former President Reagan *practically* sold arms in *a kind* of exchange for people who were *basically* hostages." Over-qualifying weakens your writing. Prune out these words and expressions wherever possible:

kind of	basically
a bit	practically
sort of	essentially
pretty much	in a way
rather	quite

Another type of qualifier is the *personal qualifier*, where instead of stating the truth, I state the truth "in my opinion." Face it: Everything you state (except perhaps for scientific or historical facts) is your opinion. Personal qualifiers like the following can often be pruned:

to me

in my opinion

in my experience

I think

it is my belief

it is my contention

the way I see it

Use Fewer Adverbs

If you choose the right verb or adjective to begin with, an adverb is often unnecessary.

Use an adverb only if it does useful work in the sentence. It's fine to say "the politician's campaign ran smoothly up to the primaries," because the adverb "smoothly" tells us something important about the running of the campaign. The adverb could be eliminated, however, if the verb were more specific: "The politician's campaign sailed up to the primaries." The combination of the strong verb *and* the adverb, as in "the politician's campaign sailed smoothly up to the primaries," is unnecessary because the adverb does no work. Here are other examples of unnecessary adverbs:

very unique

instantly startled

dejectedly slumped

effortlessly easy

absolutely perfect

totally flabbergasted

completely undeniable

Test Yourself: Eliminating Wordiness Exercise (part 2)

Rewrite these sentences to make them less wordy.

1. It can be no doubt argued that the availability of dangerous and lethal guns and firearms are in part, to some extent, responsible for the undeniable explosion of violence in our society today.

_____

_____

_____

_____

2. Why is it always imperative and necessary for the teaching educational establishment to subdue and suppress the natural spirits and energies of adolescents in scholarly settings?

_____

_____

_____

_____

3. It seems to me that I believe one must not ignore the fact that Hamlet was a heroic character as well as a tragic and doomed character fated to suffer.

_____

_____

_____

_____

4. No one would deny the strong and truthful fact that young teenage pregnancy is on the rise and is increasing at unbelievable rates each and every single day of the year.

_____

_____

_____

_____

Test Yourself: Eliminating the Passive Voice Exercise

Put each of the following sentences into the active voice:

1. The Constitution was created by the Founders to protect individual rights against the abuse of federal power.

_____

_____

_____

_____

2. Information about the Vietnam War was withheld by the government.

_____

_____

_____

_____

3. The right to privacy was called upon by the Supreme Court to form the foundation of the *Roe v. Wade* decision.

_____

_____

_____

_____

4. Teachers in many school districts are now often required by administrators to "teach to the test."

_____

_____

_____

_____

5. Residents of planned communities are mandated by Block Associations to limit the number of cars parked in their driveways.

_____

_____

_____

_____

6. Mistakes were made by the President.

_____

_____

_____

_____

7. The gaze of the tiny porcupine was captured by the headlights of the oncoming Range Rover.

_____

_____

_____

_____

Using Nonsexist Language

Pronoun agreement problems often arise because the writer is trying to avoid a sexist use of language. Because there is no gender-neutral singular pronoun in English, many people use *they*, as in the incorrect sentence above. But there are other, more grammatically correct ways of getting around this problem.

One common, albeit quite awkward, solution is to use *he/she* or *his/her* in place of *they* or *their*. For example, instead of writing, "If someone doesn't pay income tax, then they will go to jail," you can write, "If someone doesn't pay income tax, then he or she will go to jail." A more graceful (and shorter) alternative to *he/she* is to use the plural form of both noun and pronoun: "If people don't pay income tax, they will go to jail." Using nonsexist language also means finding alternatives for the word *man* when you are referring to humans in general. Instead of *mankind* you can write *humankind* or *humanity*, instead of *mailman*, you can use *mail carrier*, rather than stating that something is *man-made* you can call it *manufactured* or *artificial*.

There are a number of good reasons for you to use nonsexist language. For one thing, it is coming to be the accepted usage; that is, it is the language educated people use to communicate their ideas. Many publications now make it their editorial policy to use only non-gendered language. In addition, nonsexist language is often more accurate. Some of the people who deliver mail, for example, are female, so you are not describing the real state of affairs by referring to all of the people who deliver your mail as *men* (since it is no longer universally accepted that *man* refers to all humans). Finally, there is a good chance that at least one of your readers will be female, and that she—or, indeed, many male readers—will consider your use of the generic "he" to be a sign that you either are not aware of current academic conventions or do not think that they matter. It is best not to give your readers that impression.

Use of non-sexist language can feel awkward at first. Practice until it comes to seem natural; you may soon find that it is the old way of doing things that seems strange.

Style Chart

Style Category	What's the Rule?	Bad Style	Good Style
Wordiness	Sentences should not contain any unnecessary words.	1. The medical school is accepting applications **at this point in time.** 2. She carries a book bag that is made out of **leather and textured.**	1. The medical school is accepting applications **now.** 2. She carries a **textured, leather** book bag.
Fragments	Sentence should contain a subject and a verb and express a complete idea.	1. **And** I went to the library.	1. I went to class and I went to the library.
Run-ons	Sentences that consist of two independent clauses should be joined by the proper conjunction.	1. The test has a lot of difficult information **in it, you should** start studying right away.	1. The test has a lot of difficult information **in it, and you should** start studying right away.
Passive/Active Voice	Choose the active voice, in which the subject performs the action.	1. **The ball was hit by the bat.** 2. **My time and money were wasted** trying to keep www.justdillpickles.com afloat single-handedly.	1. **The bat hit the bat.** 2. **I wasted time and money** trying to keep www.justdillpickles.com afloat single-handedly.
Nonsexist Language	Sentences should not contain any gender bias.	1. A professor should correct **his** students' papers according to the preset guidelines. 2. From the beginning of time, **mankind** used language in one way or another. 3. Are there any **upperclassmen who** would like to help students in their Lit classes?	1. Professors should correct **their** students' papers according to the preset guidelines. 2. From the beginning of time, **humans** used language in one way or another. 3. Are there any **seniors** who would like to help students in their Lit classes?

What Not to Do: Sixteen Sure-Fire Ways to Torpedo Your Application

Besides grammatical concerns, business school applicants should keep in mind the following points while writing their admissions essays:

1. Write about the high school glory days.

Unless you're right out of college, or you've got a great story to tell, resist using your high school experiences for the essays. What does it say about your maturity if all you can talk about is being editor of the yearbook or captain of the varsity team?

2. Submit essays that don't answer the questions.

An essay that does no more than restate your resume frustrates the admissions committees. After reading 5,000 applications, they get irritated to see another long-winded evasive one. Don't lose focus. Make sure your stories answer the question.

3. Fill essays with industry jargon and detail.

Many essays are burdened by business-speak and unnecessary detail. This clutters your story. Construct your essays with only enough detail about your job to frame your story and make your point. After that, put the emphasis on yourself—what you've accomplished and why you were successful.

4. Write about a failure that's too personal or inconsequential.

Refrain from using breakups, divorces, and other romantic calamities as examples of failures. What may work on a confessional talk show is too personal for a b-school essay. Also, don't relate a "failure" like getting one C in college (out of an otherwise straight-A average). It calls your perspective into question. Talk about a failure that matured your judgment or changed your outlook.

5. Reveal half-baked reasons for wanting the MBA.

Admissions officers favor applicants who have well-defined goals. Because the school's reputation is tied to the performance of its graduates, those who know what they want are a safer investment. If b-school is just a pit stop on the great journey of life, admissions committees would prefer you make it elsewhere. However unsure you are about your future, it's critical that you demonstrate that you have a plan.

6. Exceed the recommended word limits.

Poundage is not the measure of value here. Exceeding the recommended word limit suggests you don't know how to follow directions, operate within constraints, organize your thoughts, or all of the above. Get to the crux of your story and make your points. You'll find the word limits adequate.

7. Submit an application full of typos and grammatical errors.

How you present yourself on the application is as important as what you present. Although typos don't necessarily knock you out of the running, they suggest a sloppy attitude. Poor grammar is also a problem. It distracts from the clean lines of your story and advertises poor writing skills. Present your application professionally—neatly typed and proofed for typos and grammar. And forget gimmicks like video. This isn't America's Funniest Home Videos.

8. Send one school an essay intended for another—or forget to change the school name when using the same essay for several applications.

Double check before you send anything out. Admissions committees are (understandably) insulted when they see another school's name or forms.

9. Make whiny excuses for everything.

Admissions committees have heard it all—illness, marital difficulties, learning disabilities, test anxiety, bad grades, pink slips, putting oneself through school—anything and everything that has ever happened to anybody. Admissions officers have lived through these things, too. No one expects you to sail through life unscathed. What they do expect is that you own up to your shortcomings.

Avoid trite, predictable explanations. If your undergraduate experience was one long party, be honest. Discuss who you were then, and who you've become today. Write confidently about your weaknesses and mistakes. Whatever the problem, it's important you show you can recover and move on.

10. Make the wrong choice of recommenders.

A top-notch application can be doomed by second-rate recommendations.

This can happen because you misjudged the recommendors' estimation of you or you failed to give them direction and focus. As we've said, recommendations from political figures, your uncle's CEO golfing buddy, and others with lifestyles of the rich and famous don't impress (and sometimes annoy) admissions folk—unless such recommenders really know you or built the school's library.

11. Let the recommender miss the deadline.

Make sure you give the person writing your recommendation plenty of lead time to write and send in their recommendation. Even with advance notice, a well-meaning but forgetful person can drop the ball. It's your job to remind them of the deadlines. Do what you have to do to make sure your recommendations get there on time.

12. Be impersonal in the personal statement.

Each school has its own version of the "Use this space to tell us anything else about yourself" personal statement question. Yet many applicants avoid the word "personal" like the plague. Instead of talking about how putting themselves through school lowered their GPA, they talk about the rising cost of tuition in America. The personal statement is your chance to make yourself different from the other applicants, further show a personal side, or explain a problem. Take a chance and be genuine; admissions officers prefer sincerity to a song and dance.

13. Make too many generalizations.

Many applicants approach the essays as though they were writing a newspaper editorial. They make policy statements and deliver platitudes about life without giving any supporting examples from their own experiences. Granted, these may be the kind of hot-air essays that the application appears to ask for, and probably deserves. But admissions officers dislike essays that don't say anything. An essay full of generalizations is a giveaway that you don't have anything to say, don't know what to say, or just don't know how to say whatever it is you want to say.

14. Neglect to communicate that you've researched the program and that you belong there.

B-schools take enormous pride in their programs. The rankings make them even more conscious of their academic turf and differences. While all promise an MBA, they don't all deliver it the same way. The schools have unique offerings and specialties. Applicants need to convince the committee that the school's programs meet their needs. It's not good enough to declare prestige as the primary reason for selecting a school (even though this is the basis for many applicants' choice).

15. Fail to be courteous to employees in the admissions office.

No doubt, many admissions offices operate with the efficiency of sludge.

But no matter what the problem, you need to keep your frustration in check. If you become a pest or complainer, this may become part of your applicant profile. An offended office worker may share his or her ill feelings about you with the boss—that admissions officer you've been trying so hard to impress.

16. No gimmicks, no gambles.

Avoid tricky stuff. You want to differentiate yourself but not because you are some kind of daredevil. Don't rhyme. Don't write a satire or mocked-up front-page newspaper article. Gimmicky essays mostly appear contrived and, as a result, they fall flat, taking you down with them.

PROOFREADING

Have three or four people read your essay and critique it. Proofread your essay from beginning to end, then proofread it again, then proofread it some more. Read it aloud. Keep in mind, though, that the more time you spend with a piece of your own writing, the less likely you are to spot any errors. You get tunnel vision. Ask friends, boyfriends, girlfriends, professors, brothers, sisters—somebody—to read your essay and comment on it. Have friends read it. Have an English teacher read it. Have an English major read it. Have the most grammatically anal person you know read it. Hire an editor if you feel it is necessary. We don't care. Just do whatever it takes to make sure your essay is clear, concise, candid, structurally sound, and 100 percent grammatically correct.

Always consider your audience. A big part of your overall strategy ought to be to keep in mind what it would be like to be the reader. Ultimately, you are giving a portrait of yourself in words to someone who doesn't know you and who may never meet you, but who has the power to make a very important decision about the course of your life. It's a real person who will read your personal statement, though—someone with real human traits who puts on her pants one leg at a time, just like you. Keep this person interested. Make this person curious. Make this person smile. Engage this person intellectually.

JUMP-START YOUR WRITING

Depending on where you're applying and on how prolific a writer you are, you can expect to spend anywhere from twenty-five to one hundred hours composing your stories. The process is time-consuming and maddening. Indeed, many applicants find the writing aspect of the application so unpleasant that they reach a plateau and give up. The results are mediocre, half-baked essays.

We want you to stay the full course and make every essay stand out. If you start to run out of fuel, or can't even get started, try the following for a little octane in your writing tank: Get some free feedback. There are limits and perils to self-analysis. Call a friend or colleague for a feedback session. Ask them to recount your strengths and weaknesses. Have them list your personal and professional accomplishments. They may remind you of concrete examples and provide you with fresh insights. Chat with your references, teachers, bosses—basically anyone who knows you well.

Some specific questions you may want to ask are:

- What are my strengths and weaknesses? Do you remember specific examples of this?

- What do you admire most about me? Least?

- Overall, how would you describe me? What adjectives come to mind?

- Can you think of an example of where I showed leadership, even in a small way?

Look for inspiration. Read the essays in this book, but go and seek out articles in other places. Good examples of what a well-written personal essay looks like can be found in a number of national magazines and newspapers. In *The New York Times Magazine*, testimonial-like essays can be found in the vibrant "Lives" column. No one expects you to write like a *New York Times* columnist, but study these and you may find inspiration.

You don't need to consult a publication as highbrow as *The New York Times*, though; even *Reader's Digest* is full of real-life testimonials. You'll notice how people write passionately about their experiences and what matters to them. There must be something in your life that matters to you. Make a list and return to your essays.

Let the story out. If you build it, it will come. You may have some idea of what you want to write about, but your writing skills are not up to the task. Let the content lead the way.

However unformed your thoughts are, just get it all down on paper. Afterward, you can prioritize and organize your points, complete half-thoughts, and delete what's extraneous. Find the central theme and keep building upon it. If none of the above work, try clustering.

Clustering (Or Oranizing Your Chaos)

It works like this: Grab a plain piece of paper. Take a main thought or idea, and write it in the middle of the page. Then float all of your ideas around that middle concept. Write them around the perimeter of the page and make lists.

Once you've got a page full of your chaotic thoughts, begin to prioritize your ideas by numbering them in order of importance. Delete what is extraneous, and add whatever important information you have left out.

Now start to cluster your thoughts in terms of chronology. What should go first, then next, and so on and so forth? At the end of this exercise you should have found enough ideas and sentence fragments to compose a rough draft.

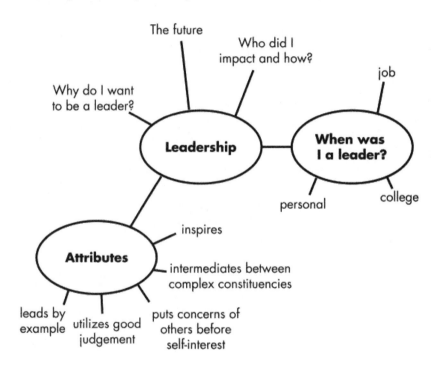

FOR THE ESSAYS

- Communicate that you're a proactive, can-do sort of person.
- Leaders take initiative and aren't thwarted by roadblocks.
- Put yourself on ego alert; stress what makes you unique, not what makes you great. You want admissions officers to respect and like you.
- Position yourself as a stand-out from the crowd; emphasize your distinctiveness.
- Make sure your leadership qualities really come through. Admissions officers want to hear about skills that enabled you to rally folks around your solution.
- Communicate specific reasons why you're a "fit" for a school, (but avoid vague, fluffy statements such as "I am the ideal or perfect candidate for you program"). Do your research. Relate your specific interests to the school's academics, specific professors,
- culture, quality of life, and location. If you use an essay for more than one school, make sure each is tailored to be school specific.
- Bring passion to your writing—admissions officers want to know what you're really excited about.
- Break out of your perceived mold. Use the essays to challenge any preconceived notions about who you are. Are you a numbers person or an engineer type? Challenge perceptions with unexpected portrayals that say, "There's more to me than you think." It could be that you're passionate about cooking, or that you organize a game of hoops every Saturday.
- Play up an unorthodox path to b-school. Admissions officers appreciate risk-takers. But be convincing about your ability to handle the program, especially quantitative skills that schools can take for granted in applicants in finance.
- Use your gender, ethnicity, minority, or foreign background—but only if it has affected your outlook or experiences.
- Avoid too many sentences that begin with "I." Use examples and anecdotes instead.
- Be subtle. If you call too much attention to a problem it becomes a bigger problem.
- Fill your essays with plenty of real-life examples to support your thesis and bring your story to life.
- Show a sense of humor or your vulnerability. These qualities make you likeable. They make your stories more personal.
- Don't write in a vacuum. Make sure that each of your essays reinforces and builds on the others. Think of each essay as one note in a song

Ready, Set, Write!

Hopefully what you've read here will help guide you through the process of writing a great personal essay and stand-out secondaries. Though there's no magic recipe, we're confident that if you follow our advice about what to put in and what to leave out, you'll end up with a memorable personal statement that will differentiate you from the larger applicant pool and make you a more competitive candidate. Take our word for it and give it your best shot.

Chapter **8**

STRAIGHT FROM THE MOUTHS OF EXPERTS: INTERVIEWS WITH STUDENTS

Won't take our word on b-school essays and admissions? We asked MBA students and business school admissions officers to share their thoughts on these matters. You might say we have the issue covered from every angle.

Lisa Guglielmi
Student, Haas School of Business,
University of California—Berkeley

Q: Lisa, how many schools did you apply to?

A: Six. Stanford, Harvard, Berkeley, UCLA, Kellogg, and Michigan. All in the first round.

Q: So all told, how many essays did you have to write?

A: Well they all have one common essay question. It's a version of "Why do you want the MBA, why now, and why at this school?" so this was one essay with slightly different versions. Several of the schools had the "What are your three greatest accomplishments?" question. The rest of the questions were very different. I easily wrote at least ten-plus essays.

Q: Which essay did you work on first?

A: The leadership essay.

Q: Why did you choose that one first?

A: It was the easiest one for me. I had a very good example of clear leadership.

Q: How did you go about writing your stories?

A: First, I put everything down on paper. Then I reread it to see if it communicated exactly what I wanted it to. That was the hardest part, making sure that what I wanted to say actually came forth. Because sometimes you'll write and write and write, but the point you're actually trying to get across doesn't come through.

In these kinds of essays, it's easy to write too much and provide too much detail. But what you want to focus on is who you are, and not the details that capture the *exact* experience.

Q: Did you take a test-prep course?

A: Yes.

Q: When?

A: I was working as an investment banker, and my firm paid for the course. I was very busy at work, so I didn't actually take the test until almost a year after the course. When I did take the test, however, it was six months before I worked on the essays and the rest of the application. I wanted to get the GMAT out of the way and focus on the application.

Q: What made you decide to apply in the first round?

A: I did a lot of research. Everyone seemed to say your odds were better in the first round. I also think that applying early in the filing period shows admissions that you're very serious, that this is something you've thought out very thoroughly.

Q: What was the hardest part of the application for you to work on?

A: The essays, definitely. It's so difficult in just four or five essays to accurately portray yourself and capture all your unique experiences.

Q: Which was the hardest essay for you to answer? Why?

A: I would say it was one of the Berkeley essays. Berkeley has two longer essays, then mainly short questions; this was very different from the other schools I was applying to.

   The essay that I really struggled with was "Whom would you like to have over for dinner?" I found this question to be a little more creative, whereas the others had been straightforward. You don't know what the admissions committee is looking for in this question, so I found it harder.

   But if you try to write what you think the admission person wants here, you just dig yourself a hole. It's always better to come from who you really are. I've gone back and read friends' essays who are here at Berkeley and at other schools. The ones that really stand out are those that are genuine. If you pose as someone you're really not in these essays, it's very easy for the admissions committee to see through it.

   But back to the "dinner" question. I guess the best way I can tell you how I answered this question is to tell you how I went about the entire essay-writing process.

   I got some great advice from a friend: Before working on any [of] the essays, sit down and make a list of the five or six qualities about yourself that you absolutely want to get across to the admissions committee. Then, go through each essay and make sure that you address one of these five or six big ideas in each one so that you create a complete picture of yourself. The application should really be seen as a total package.

This particular tool really helped me, because at first I was just so overwhelmed by it all. When you have to pick five or six qualities about yourself, it requires a lot of introspection. In this way, instead of looking at each specific question in a vacuum, I focused on getting these qualities across. As I said before, I would write and write, then reread and realize I had left out that one very important characteristic or aspect that I had made a goal to highlight.

So by the time I got to the dinner question, I had covered what I wanted to in the other essays. I could have a little more fun with this one, show a different side of me.

Q: What about your recommendations? How did you handle that?

A: My schools requested only professional recommendations. I had already selected two bosses for this—one current and one past. I chose the boss from my previous position, rather than someone else supervising me in my current job, because he knew me very well, he was an excellent writer, he was honest, and I knew he would support what I was saying about myself in the essays. The person who knows you the best is the one who should write your recommendations.

Q: What advice would you give an applicant about to embark on this journey?

A: Don't get overwhelmed. Look over the entire application and, as hard as it is, get everything down on paper. Step by step, list or outline what characteristics you want to highlight.

Have someone you don't know very well read your essays and give you their take on each one. They should be able to immediately pick out the characteristic you are trying to portray. The fact that your reader doesn't know you helps because they are not as inclined to just give their perception of you as a person.

It is also good to have people who know you well read your essays. These readers would say, wait a minute, you're not giving yourself enough credit for something, or you left out some of the specifics in this story that are meaningful to the point. It's not easy to brag about yourself and your accomplishments, and people who know you well can help you draw the line between bragging enough, but not too much. So both sets of readers were especially helpful.

I probably had five different sets of eyes look at my essays to see if they got what I intended. If the feedback was that they didn't, then I knew I was off my mark. I would scrap the entire essay, no matter how hard I had worked on it, and rewrite it completely, sometimes with entirely new topics.

JENNI WINSLOW
STUDENT, HAAS SCHOOL OF BUSINESS,
UNIVERSITY OF CALIFORNIA—BERKELEY

Q: Jenni, how many schools did you apply to?

A: Just four. Stanford, Berkeley, UCLA, and Kellogg.

Q: Where did you get in?

A: I got in to all four.

Q: What was the most daunting part of the application process?

A: The essays.

Q: Why?

A: The sheer quantity of the essays I needed to write was overwhelming. To deal with it, I first organized all of the applications together by creating a grid in Microsoft Excel. Then I wrote an essay question in each cell and looked for where there might be overlap.

Q: So your first strategy in the application process was to organize and examine all the essay questions for similarity?

A: Well, first I took a test-prep course. I took the class the spring before. The course ran from approximately January through March. Then I took the GMAT test in May with the knowledge that if I didn't do well as well as I wanted to, I could take it again and still have time to apply early for next year.

Q: Did you do well enough?

A: Yes, I did.

Q: How did your time line evolve from that point?

A: Well, I got to breathe a sigh of relief for the summer, which was nice. But by late August, as soon as all the applications were out, I had them in my hands—I had put my name on all the schools' lists so they would be sent to me immediately.

I also used the time in late August to contact all the admissions offices at each of the schools to schedule campus visits. I wanted to visit each of the campuses so I could figure out for myself what was different at each of these schools.

The gist of the visits was that I wanted to attend class, meet the people, meet the professors, and see the campus, so that I could write to that in my essays. Part of this process is figuring out which schools are right for you. I had figured out all were great options, but I needed to differentiate them for myself and in the essays. I also wanted to articulate what unique contributions I could make at a particular school. To do that, you need to do more than just read a brochure.

Q: So before you even put pen to paper, you had already done a tremendous amount of legwork and preparation?

A: Absolutely.

Q: Going back to the essays, how many essay questions did you have to answer?

A: Stanford [had] two. One of their questions was, "What is most important to you, and why?" and the second was, "Why do you want the MBA, and why here?" I think this last one is used at "X" school everywhere. So I got to recycle that last essay question, but I articulated unique differences at each school.

The Berkeley application was probably the most difficult in that there were six to eight short questions. Somehow that was harder than having to answer one long question. The question I found the most interesting to write—it was on Berkeley's application—was "Who would you most want to have dinner with and why?" That was fun.

Q: Whom did you pick?

A: Oprah Winfrey. She has been amazing in terms of how influential she has been. And while she is not known for this, she is an incredibly savvy businessperson.

After I got in at Berkeley, I learned that Madonna and Oprah are among the most common answers. Madonna is awesome because she, too, has built an empire. She has her public persona, as does Oprah, but these women are highly astute. They have built extraordinary businesses.

A number of people pick out a compelling figure from history as well.

Again, after I got in, I heard that with the Stanford essay, the most common answer to "What's most important to you and why?" is "balance in life."

Q: How often did you do a rewrite?

A: I probably did at least three or four rewrites of each question. Often what I would do is work on a question for a day. Then I would shelve it, leave it alone for a few days. Then I'd get perspective and go back and read it and work some more.

Another thing I did was to purchase three different books—one was a guidebook on the MBA, one was how to get into the top MBA programs, and the last one was a book with sample b-school essays, which proved very useful in getting ideas on how other people had done this.

Q: What would be your final piece of advice to someone about to start this process?

A: I applied in round one at three of my schools and round two at Kellogg. My advice is to start *early*. Figure out where you want to apply, and then map out your priorities. What needs to happen first at what school? When you say you want to apply to five schools in the first round, you might not be able to do that. I credit that I got into all four of my schools by applying early.

Chapter **9**

STRAIGHT FROM THE MOUTHS OF EXPERTS: INTERVIEWS WITH ADMISSIONS OFFICERS

Robert Wagner
Acting Director of MBA Admissions, Olin Graduate School of Business, Babson College

Q: What are some of the worst mistakes applicants make with their essays?

A: First and foremost, not answering the question. After completing the essays applicants should have someone read their responses without providing the questions. See if they can decipher from your essay responses what the original question was. Some applicants write generic responses that could fit any school or program. Copying and pasting the same essay responses for each school you are applying to is not effective. We also find the wrong school name in essays all the time, a very common mistake.

Q: What about types of essays, for example, where they're asked about their greatest achievement or something?

A: Well, that's a pretty consistent industry standard essay. Given our entrepreneurial focus at Babson, we take a different approach and ask applicants to describe their own entrepreneurial experiences to get a sense of their appreciation for the entrepreneurial mindset.

Q: So if you have a feeling of, "So what?" after reading an essay, that's the death knell?

A: Well, if the applicant has written a 4–5 sentence response, or it appears little effort was put into the essays, that's not a good sign. We're reading thousands of essays each year and comparing them to the other applicants in the pool. Applicants should really do some self reflection prior to writing the essay responses and be very clear [about] why they have chosen to apply to your program.

Q: How else do applicants try to impress but wind up having the opposite effect?

A: Essays that are 4–5 pages long will not impress us. Applicants should clearly and concisely respond to each question. 1–2 pages should be sufficient for each question. When an international applicant writes a perfect essay and the writing style is better than most U.S. candidates, we question whether the candidate wrote the essay [him or herself]. We do compare the writing style to the Analytical Writing Assessment on the GMAT.

Q: If you can sum it up quickly, what makes for a successful essay?

A: Genuine and sincere responses. We want to know who you are, what are your interests, background, experiences, and goals? How will you add value to our community and on teams? We are assessing if you be successful in our program and post-MBA.

Q: The economy has been brutal. How has this had an impact on the type of applicant you're seeing?

A: On the full time MBA application side, we are seeing an increase in applicants that are only 2–3 years post undergraduate. Candidates are seeking out the MBA earlier in their professional careers and many are career changers. At the same time career opportunities are changing so a growing trend is more interest in renewable energy and social responsibility careers.

Linda Meehan
MBA Admissions Director, Columbia Business School

Q: How heavily are the essays weighted in admissions at Columbia?

A: The essays are part and parcel of the entire application; they are not weighted higher or lower. They are utilized as a means of getting information that we want to know. We use them to see how people think and how they pull together all of the pieces to come to a solution. In other words, it's as much about how they arrive at the answer as the answer itself. For example, I'm thinking about the essay question that asks about an applicant's career goals and why they want the MBA and why at a particular school. This is without a doubt one of the most important essays they will write. Someone may say, "My short-term goal is to become an investment banker." What we want to know is how they plan on accomplishing this. This essay is meant to provide applicants with a vehicle to go through their entire thought process and bring us with them. Unfortunately, a lot of people miss that.

Q: What competencies are revealed in the questions you ask?

A: Their analytical abilities, written communication skills, organizational skills, and knowledge of themselves as well as their career paths are brought out in their essays. Assessing these competencies in their essays has become very difficult, given the amount of coaching available today.

Q: You bring up an interesting point. Is a "coached" essay easily visible to you?

A: What becomes evident are the irregularities you see among test scores and writing abilities. Those discrepancies make you more aware that they may have had help.

The analytical writing question on the GMAT helps provide a context for the skill level of the applicants' writing, though the GMAT no longer sends us the physical sample—we may request it. But generally speaking, if you have a low score, a 2 or 3 on the writing assessment, or your verbal GMAT score is very low, and we're reading an essay that is wonderful, there is a disconnect and it does raise flags.

Remember, there are so many checks and balances built into admissions. There are recommendations, which may speak of someone's communication skills; there is the GMAT we mentioned; work record; and in many cases, an interview. All of these elements help us make a decision.

Q: But what do you do when you see the irregularity?

A: Again, this is a holistic review process, and these irregularities are taken into account.

Q: Does your application ask if they have had any essay assistance?

A: No. Our application asks them to sign an honor statement that the work they present is their own. We have not asked specifically about essay help.

Q: How do you read through so many essays? What will be a "standout" to you?

A: First of all, I personally do not read each and every essay. My staff reads the essays and the entire application. They will then provide a summary of the application, which I then review. When there is something amazing or distinctive noted, I will refer back to that portion of the application.

Q: So yours are...another pair of highly important eyes?

A: Yes.

Q: The economy has been brutal. How would you suggest an applicant address a weak employment record? Is there less of a penalty these days?

A: I don't know that there was ever a penalty for unemployment. What's important is why you're unemployed. When you see someone not employed in good times, that's a trigger for something that may be amiss, but not always. For example, someone in the media world who is involved in production might hold four different jobs in four years. This would be normal for someone in this profession but not for someone working in marketing. Today you see people getting laid off due to a downturn in the economy.

You obviously would not hold that against them, as it is not their fault. But then we want to know, what are they are currently doing? How are they spending their time? This becomes what's important.

Q: What are some examples of good things they've been doing?

A: Pro bono work, giving their time and expertise to their communities. People have been working in unpaid internships at companies they hope to work for. There are those who have gone out on the creative side and done something they've always wanted to do. Some choose to travel, which may or may not serve their application well.

Q: What is your ideal use of the optional personal statement? What is a turn-off here?

A: The ideal is when the applicant tells us something that we need to know but they didn't have the opportunity to express earlier. Remember, this is an optional essay. If you feel you've done a great job in presenting yourself in your application, then you don't need to use the optional essay. But if there is something we failed to ask you that you wanted us to know, this is your opportunity. It is an open-ended essay not reserved for just the GMAT or GPA explanation.

Q: What's the biggest risk you saw an applicant take with an essay that worked?

A: Let me answer with this first: Sometimes people think they're being funny or cute in an essay. They don't realize that what may be funny or cute to them may be seen as inappropriate to an admissions committee. If you write very well and have the ability to use humor, then go ahead and do so. But if it's something you're trying to create but that doesn't come naturally to you, you can come off as flippant or too casual. This essay may crash and burn. There is an example of the best essay I ever read, where the premise could have backfired, but didn't. It needs a little setup. The author of this essay was a Latin American male who was applying to Columbia a few years ago. He wrote an essay about being very macho. According to this applicant, Latinos are, by nature, a macho culture. This meant that being the male in his marriage, he was the most important member of the couple. At the time, he was working as a banker. His wife was a psychologist. There was an important dinner for the principals at his firm, and obviously he felt it important to take his wife along. The day of the dinner, his wife received a phone call from a client in crisis. The wife worked with this client all through the day and gave thought to not going to the dinner because of the seriousness of the situation. The husband, Mr. Macho, thought this was horrible. How could his wife do something that might damage his career? The wife went to the dinner.

I know what happened here. The client killed himself. It didn't take the applicant long to rethink his priorities and recognize that he was indeed not the center of the universe. The part of this essay that could have gone awry was not just the macho part, but in handling the true drama of this story. What stuck with us, and still does years later, was his self-awareness. This was a very dramatic way for him to share with us his perspective. It certainly assisted him in gaining admission to Columbia Business School and several other top programs.

This is an example of an essay that had a major impact on someone's life. Many years ago, I worked in undergraduate admissions. I was speaking to an applicant's parents about their child, a young man whom they thought was the greatest. According to them, their son had everything: leadership, great grades and scores, wonderful extracurricular activities, and genuine commitment to these endeavors. So why, they wanted to know, did he get rejected from the school? Because, I had to answer, he looked like everyone else.

The point is, all of these candidates are great. At least 85 percent of the people who apply to the top ten business schools are all amazing, all are great. You just can't accept them all. That's a reality. So if applicants can distinguish themselves and let us get to know them, it may be the key to their admission.

Remember, we are trying to bring in to Columbia the most diverse and interesting class so that all may learn from one another.

BILL SANDEFER
DIRECTOR OF ADMISSIONS AND FINANCIAL AID, FREEMAN SCHOOL OF BUSINESS, TULANE UNIVERSITY

Q: How have things changed since you've been in MBA admissions?

A: The rankings are much more important. I started here ten years ago, and at that point you saw a lot of people referring to the rankings, but not many applications came directly from the rankings. In the last six years, business schools have seen a reduction in the number of applications but a much more focused set of applications. I think that's a function of people having a different information source. Instead of going to a professor and saying, "I'm interested in studying finance at graduate school, where do I go?" and then having the professor recommend schools they think would be good for you, prospective MBAs go to Business Week or U.S. News & World Report and say, "What's the best school in finance?" or "What's the best school in marketing?" And they'll start looking at those schools and benchmarking programs from that perspective.

Q: How has the Internet affected MBA admissions?

A: The Internet has been huge in the way people go about looking at schools. When we started offering online applications, the first year it was maybe 10 percent of our total applications. The next year, it was to the tune of 35 to 40 percent, so we're getting double-digit increases annually in online applications. That implies that the Net is also where they're gaining a lot of the information about the schools where they're applying. I think the Web has taken on a much bigger role, but not in the way that a lot of people think. People don't go online to learn about business schools in an advertising way. They tend to be much more selective when they go to the Web. They want immediate gratification related to their interests. If they're interested in financial aid or whether a school has a marketing program specifically for brand management, they want it right now in two clicks. If it's not there, they'll go to another website.

Q: Has the Internet bred a more savvy MBA shopper?

A: I was talking with a former admissions director at a top-tier school the other day. When we started, a big part of your day was spent telling people about the school or talking about very general issues—how do you apply, what materials you need, who needs to write your recommendations. Those days are gone. Very few applicants come in and say, "Who should I get to write my recommendations?" Because that information is there. Very quickly that comes across. People are increasingly self-selecting. The quality of our applicant pool is by far better than ever, and that seems to be a trend in the top-tier schools. I think that may be a real difference between schools that are nationally and internationally ranked and schools that have to inform applicants of every detail of the program.

Q: With so much information available online, what kinds of questions are applicants asking when they meet you in person?

A: Because people are much more savvy about their expectations in a school, they're asking a lot about what will be delivered in the program, about the team emphasis, about the breadth of requirements and the kind of knowledge you're going to get coming out of the program. People are much more specific: Why should I go to Tulane? What kind of experience am I going to have? What will the people I'm working with be like? How will it impact my future? Their questions are much, much more pointed. The idea of going to business school and knowing exactly what you want is a myth. While you might look at a business school and say, "This school has a very strong finance program and so I'm going to go there," you still haven't had the experience, the contact with people from all around the world, the opportunities you get from being immersed in such a program.

It's the sponge effect. When you encounter people, intellectual qualities, and academic qualities that you had no experience with before, it gives you an opportunity to see that things may be done differently in China or that things may be done the same way in Japan. So it either validates your current way of making decisions or it challenges you. And that may push you into looking at things differently. It should.

Q: How do you reconcile recruiting applicants with well-defined career goals with admitting applicants who are open to new experiences and ways of thinking?

A: If I could have any skill I don't possess, it would be clairvoyance. What you look for in applicants is a track record. Most have success written all over them, academic and professional. But what you're really looking for in an MBA applicant is not just a successful person but somebody who can recognize opportunities for change and incorporate them into his or her life. Some of our most recent essay questions seem to be very abstract and off-the-wall, and part of that is because we can already see what you're going to do with your career. Sitting where you are today, it's pretty obvious what your resume and your academic background will support. The things you can't see in an MBA application are how you go about making decisions, how you're influenced by other people, and how that influence manifests itself. In a community like the MBA program you're trying to get the exposure to diverse ways of thinking and new ideas, but it's only good if somebody is going to learn from it and walk away better because of it. Finding those applicants is the challenge.

Q: What are your essay questions?

A: We're running two right now. One is to identify the person that most influenced you in your life. That's pretty insightful not because of who it is—I would say 75 percent of the time it's Mom or Dad—but because it shows what influences people and how they react to it. That's something that has to be conveyed in the material you're presenting to the admissions committee. It's fine to say, "My mom made me honest," but was it through weekly beatings, was it through her exemplary behavior, or was it through the way she communicated with you?

Q: How long should an essay be?

A: I'm into brevity. One of the biggest challenges is to keep your essay within 200 words, which is like trying to summarize your life in a paragraph. Communicating effectively in a small space is a challenge. Not coincidentally, it's something you have to do in business school. Twenty-two-page essays are not a productive thing around here when you're trying to get through management communications.

Q: So one question is, "Who influenced you and why?"

A: Because we have a large international applicant pool, another essay question we've asked for a couple of years is to assemble a group and take them on a tour of your country. Tell us who will be in that group and what you will see. Part of what we're trying to gather there is the individual's perspective on the world. It's a twist on the old "If you could have dinner with anyone, who would it be and why?" But it's insightful for us because it gives insights into different nationalities and what those individuals would highlight about their backgrounds, history, countries, or needs in a way that is not so common to why would we admit you.

Q: Can you think of an essay response that impressed you with its unconventionality?

A: The tour essay that impressed me the most with its originality jumped across time to pull different people from history who had encountered the country and what readings about that person had influenced the applicant to think about or want to show about their country. I thought that was a really interesting way to approach the standard question.

Q: Is creativity important?

A: Creativity for its own sake is not a good thing. Most creative essays are not successful because in the essay I'm looking for some core values that are part of the person and how they're illustrating that. This is not the Faulkner Prize. We're trying to understand how you make decisions rather than how well you write. The GMAT includes two essays, so we already have a writing sample. The application essay is something you have a little more time to think about, and you should be able to produce something that is the best that's going to come out of the individual.

Q: How are the essays weighted?

A: If the applicant pool has self-selected itself to the point where they're close to qualifying academically and they're close to qualifying by their career interests, you're looking at a group of people who are fairly qualified on the objective measures. What you end up looking for are subtle skills that then get played out in the MBA program—how people interact with one another and function in an environment. So the essay and the interview tend to be more validating of how we expect people are going to function in the program and benefit from their experience.

Q: Can you think of an example where an essay made the difference, either for better or for worse?

A: We see both cases. An inconsistent application is the surest kiss of death. You want to open up an application and see that someone's resume, their recommendations, their essays, and their interview all support a set of goals that are compatible with what's going to happen to them over the next two years. Inconsistencies there raise red flags and, in a competitive pool, the red flag is what gets you taken off the table. So if somebody has a fabulous GMAT score, great verbal abilities, and an undergraduate degree in English and then his or her essay is riddled with errors, you look at that and say, "How attentive to detail is this person? How much effort was applied to writing that essay?" Something's wrong, and that will get you taken away. On the other hand, you might look at people who were very active as undergraduates or who did something that had [a negative] impact on their GPA, but then in talking to them and looking at their recent behavior, you might be a little bit more forgiving. So an interview and an essay that are very positive can have a heavier weight with some candidates.

Q: How have candidates changed in recent years?

A: A decade ago, people's bosses and parents encouraged them to go directly into graduate school. Remember [that] an MBA is a management program. These are people who are targeted for mid-level jobs when they get out of the program. Employers are looking for people who can be groomed quickly into supervisory roles, so with no prior experience—no track record of success—you really are at a disadvantage. I think that message has really been communicated over the last six or seven years, that you need experience.

Q: Has the economy had an impact on applicants?

A: I have a counter-cyclical theory. The students in top MBA programs tend to be much more focused on managing their careers. So while the economy has a role, it's only one factor in a long-term process. We see people who have been planning on an MBA since high school. They're on a twelve-year track. They've thought about this for years. They've kept tabs on the rankings for five or six years. They have a very refined idea of what they want to accomplish. With these applicants, I don't think the economy has an effect. Last year we witnessed some dramatic economic events, but only about 10 percent of the class could be traced to having a direct correlation to the economy. The remaining 90 percent of the class was basically on target for what they had planned on doing for a long period of time.

Q: What areas are applicants most interested in?

A: Eight years ago the emphasis was on general management with a broad range of skills and then whatever other experience you got thrown in was fine. Certainly in the case of all the major MBA programs, the first year was spent on a breadth of skills. That has largely changed. When you walk through the door, you need to be focused on the industries that you're interested in and the kinds of things they want, because those opportunities are going to appear much earlier in the MBA life cycle. You're going to be taking electives in that first semester, you're going to be exposed to speakers and opportunities in that first semester that have long-term career impacts.

Q: Is industry looking for specialization rather than a generalist?

A: I think that's definitely true. A company will come in and look for someone who has the training as an MBA, who understands marketing and finance and human resources, who has some knowledge of the international marketplace, but fundamentally you're being hired to run a finance department. Or you're being hired to run a brand in the case of the brand management area. So you have to understand all of those things but you also have to have deep knowledge in your subject, and you can get that through prior experience and specialization in your program.

BARBARA SCHNEIDER
DIRECTOR OF ADMISSIONS AND FINANCIAL AID,
CROSBY MBA PROGRAM
UNIVERSITY OF MISSOURI

FROM THE SCHOOL:

The University of Missouri Crosby MBA Program will help you discover and unleash your true potential—not just professionally, but personally. To that end, we've created an empowering community where you can thrive. You'll play an active role in taking on real challenges in new and exciting ways through experiential consulting courses and professional development initiatives. You'll gain real-world experience and perspective by working alongside executives and faculty who are genuinely focused on helping you attain your full potential. Your Crosby MBA colleagues will be a diverse group of individuals from all backgrounds, including science, engineering, liberal arts, journalism, agriculture and business and from many universities around the world. You can choose from specializations in finance, marketing, advertising, corporate or non-profit management, accounting, entrepreneurship, or your own unique career interest. You can also pursue a dual degree in law, health administration or industrial engineering.

As we review applications, we look for individuals who will both benefit from and contribute to our community. Essays provide you the opportunity to tell us your story and help us understand your goals and aspirations. Your written thoughts can convey your self-awareness, show how your experiences have informed your goals, and demonstrate your drive and passion. Use your essay to differentiate yourself in the application process and to tell us why you believe a University of Missouri Crosby MBA is right for you.

As you consider where to earn your MBA degree, it is important for you to find a program that best fits you—your interests, your goals, your hopes for the future. We invite you to visit campus to meet our students, faculty and staff and experience our community for yourself. At the University of Missouri Crosby MBA you can explore, you can collaborate and you can thrive!

Q: How heavily are the essays weighted in admissions at Crosby?

A: It is one of the important factors that we consider when we are evaluating an application. We are going to look at other factors as well, especially GMAT score and undergraduate academic performance. Essays are valued quite heavily in addition to those numbers as a way to differentiate.

What we're really looking for is to get to know that person, to see how well they know themselves and if they can connect their strengths (and/or weaknesses) with experiences they've had that leads them to want to be in our MBA program.

We're truly looking for an individual's personal story. We want to know about what they've been doing, something that shows they have drive, compassion, and interest in and where they want to go with it and why our program will help them get there.

Q: Are you able to easily recognize a "coached" essay?

A: Often we can. That's because it sounds a little canned. It's almost too perfect in terms of language and word selection, and it's also often not personalized.

Q: How do you read through so many essays? What will be a "standout" to you?

A: We have more than one person look at most applications. At the beginning of the process we talk about what we're looking for in applications, come up with guidelines for how to evaluate applications, and then we have specific people read different applications. Ultimately people who are admitted, or people we want to interview or look at further—there's more than one person reading that application.

Q: In recent years, so you find that applicants are using the essay to address a weak employment record? Is the essay the right place to address this?

A: I have not seen too much of that. In fact, people should probably address it more than they do. I think it would be a good idea to address it. At this point there's not necessarily a shame attached to having lost a job. I think it's probably good to address it and talk about how that may have affected them and how that may have contributed to their decision to go back and own a MBA.

Q: What are some of the worst mistakes applicants make with their essays?

A: The most obvious ones are grammatical errors. Also people who are obviously doing cutting and pasting and you see another school name in the essay…that's not good. If they're talking about something we don't have in our program and we know they've used the essay for someone else, or if they're not answering the question. Sometimes people will write the generic essay and send it of without really addressing what we've asked for and that's a big turn off for us.

Q: What's the biggest risk you saw an applicant take with an essay that worked?

A: A risk that can pay off is someone who will talk about a failure that they've had, in either a personal situation or a business setting, and address what they've learned from it and how it has changed things. It can be risky because you're talking about something that you did wrong, but if handled well and if it talks about lessons learned that we can believe are true lessons learned, that can be good.

Things that sometimes don't work out well is that people try to get too verbally dramatic about something. Lot's of times people will use quotes that they say have inspired them. It can work, but sometimes it sounds too affected. As if they're trying too hard to write what they think we want to hear rather than what is truly motivating them to apply to the program.

BRIAN T. LOHR
DIRECTOR OF MBA ADMISSIONS,
MENDOZA COLLEGE OF BUSINESS,
UNIVERSITY OF NOTRE DAME

FROM THE SCHOOL:

The Notre Dame MBA program asks more of business, by asking its students to lead with integrity, foster effective organizations and consider the greater good. With more than 90 elective courses, six concentration tracks and two formats, the Notre Dame MBA program provides students with a challenging and flexible educational experience.

Our MBA students learn leadership skills so that they can solve some of the toughest problems in business, and do so with a consciousness of how their actions impact the larger community. The curriculum provides a balanced mastery of all functional areas of business—finance, accounting, marketing and management. Signature courses in Problem-Solving and Innovation give students the tools to diagnose problems, understand the critical issues and frame innovative solutions.

Further, students are exposed to the complexities of global business through a series of engagements with leaders worldwide. Immersions in Asia and Latin America provide opportunities to experience other cultures first-hand. Signature lecture series, such as Ten Years Hence, bring in internationally renowned experts to discuss some of the most vital trends and issues facing the current age. Students also have the opportunity to broaden their problem-solving and entrepreneurial skills by participating in service projects in locations ranging from Jamaica, South Africa and Mexico, to here in the Midwest.

Q: How heavily are the essays weighted in admissions at Mendoza?

A: They are weighted equally with other facets of the application such as GMAT, work experience, GPA.

Q: What are the essay questions you guys ask? Is there more than one essay that is required?

A: We have one that is required, and that is "What are your career plans immediately after graduation? Explain how your past experiences prepare you for your desired position."

The second essay can be chosen from a group of 6, one relates to our MBA values statement, the second one relates to a personal failure and what they learned from it, the third involves trust or lack of trust and how that's impacted your professional experience; the fourth is describing a time when you were given a project in an area that was not well-defined and how you handles it; the fifth one is what brand would you most like to manage and how and why; and then sixth is a essay as it relates to the book *Risk and Other Four-Letter Words* which talks about the financial crisis of 2008–2009 and asks whether the book takes on the appropriate level of risk.

We also have a PowerPoint requirement in the application. We limit it to four slides. It's static, so we don't look for video, or music, or hyperlinks. It gives us a neat insight into the candidate. The business world relies on that type of communication so it's applicable to their future careers.

Q: What competencies are revealed in the questions you ask?

A: We're looking for creativity, insight into who they are as people outside of what we would learn through the application process. We get a lot of data—but this allows us to really look into that person and see what's important to them and how creative they can be.

Q: How do you read through so many essays?

A: Every application goes through at least two reads, then if there is a conclusion within the first two reads then we just move forward with that conclusion. If there is a divide it goes to third read which is part of the committee review and who we send it to depends on the issue.

Q: So you basically spend a lot of time with the essays?

A: We owe that to the applicants. They've put in a great deal of time and effort so we want to give everybody the fair valuation no matter what their background or GMAT score. It's just the right thing to do.

Q: What makes an essay a "standout"?

A: I can give you an example of one that stood out for me. A candidate [who] was from Jackson, Mississippi, who now works in New York for NBC in their finance area. He is an African-American man and his essay started off with essentially a description of his grandfather and his life prior to education. I can remember the sentence almost perfectly. He said, "My grandfather was tired of looking at the south end of a mule going north."

He made the determination that education was the way for his family to move along in life and get better. So essentially he was setting the foundation that education was the key to success. Then he just went on from there to talk about why he wanted to earn an MBA and what he planned to do with it.

I had another candidate who wanted to get into brand management and her essay started off with "Snap, Crackle, Pop…Snap, Crackle, Pop." Those things really stand out in my mind, but you need to be an excellent writer to do that. If you're not a good writer than you need to shift your methodology to more of a newspaper-type mode. For example, "I plan to go into investment banking in New York on Wall Street." Then build from there.

Q: What are some of the worst mistakes applicants make with their essays?

A: When they write what they think we want to hear. I don't think that is the way to go.

You need to write from the heart. If you believe in what you're writing and that's important to you, it's going to come through. The candidates that write what they think we want to hear—you can tell. When you read as many essays and Power Points that we do the ones that aren't from the heart really stick out. The applicants that do the "group/replace" mode in their essays—that really sticks out too. Spelling and punctuation and grammar have to be perfect.

Rebekah Lewin
Director of Admissions
Simon School of Business
University of Rochester

Q: How heavily are the essays weighted in admissions at the Simon School?

A: The essay is an important component that helps to differentiate candidates from one another beyond the basic metrics of work experience and GMAT score. It gives us a sense of what the candidate has to say about themselves and it is a way for us to assess their level of judgment in terms of what things they choose to share with us and fit with our program in terms of the background they bring and whether they have the potential to bring an interesting perspective to the MBA classroom.

Q: How important is fit?

A: Fit is quite important. I would say that the majority of the students who apply to our program are academically qualified. For the most part, these are students who can handle the rigor of a top MBA program and they've done their homework on places where they think they'd make the cut academically, so the essay is very important for getting to know the candidate and hearing about examples of prior work experience or volunteerism or leadership or team skills. Oftentimes that helps to determine which candidate we end up inviting for interviews.

Q: What competencies are revealed in the questions you ask?

A: Rochester has two required essays. One of the required essays asks the student to talk about their reasons for choosing to apply to business school at this particular juncture and specifically why they're interested in the Rochester MBA program and where they think the MBA will take them. It's very important to get a sense of their rationale and reason for pursuing school and the thought they've put into their post-MBA career search.

The other required essay asks students to discuss two leadership examples. That's important in terms of what students choose to write about and how that might translate into leadership inside or outside the classroom and after they graduate.

Q: How do you read through so many essays?

A: We have an admissions committee of full-time admissions officers whose goal is interacting with candidates during the recruiting season. We go out there and travel and met with candidates who come on campus for information sessions and interviews. We're heavily invested in the entire recruitment process and have a good sense of how to select candidates who are the right fit for the program.

We have our busy season, very similar in timeline to when accountants have their busy season, but ultimately we feel it's very important to invest the additional hours to read through the essays as part of the process of getting to know candidates and differentiating among them.

We're a very small program relative to some of the programs that are out there and so we want to be really careful and make sure that each of the students we are selecting is going to be part of the right mix. We really can't afford to make a mistake. So we spend a great deal of time trying to assess fit and background and all those sorts of things so that we're bringing together a class that's going to be the right mix for the type of environment we offer at Rochester.

Q: What is your ideal use of the optional personal statement?

A: Our optional essay is truly optional, and that's a big misconception among candidates. It is an opportunity for a candidate to talk about a weakness in the application that they feel needs an explanation, for example, a gap in their resume or a significantly below average academic record in college.

Q: What are some of the biggest mistakes students make?

A: Well, there are some fairly obvious things that some students may not fully consider in their desire to promote themselves to us. One really obvious thing is to pay attention to the nuances of the essay question. We realize that the candidate may be applying to multiple schools, but the topics tend to be slightly different depending on the school. The boilerplate essay template oftentimes doesn't fully reflect answering the question or even staying with the word limit. Those are some of the obvious ones along with spell checking your essay and grammar checking and that sort of thing.

In terms of the content, the most important thing is authenticity and also relevancy. Authenticity: being yourself, telling your story, and really helping us to get to know you but relevancy in terms of hearing the information that's most relevant to your b-school application. So there may things that are very authentic about you that have very little relevance to the b-school application process. Striking the right mix between authenticity in the way a candidate presents themselves while being concise and relevant and sharing the things that are really most important to answering the questions asked.

Q: What's the biggest risk you saw an applicant take with an essay that worked?

A: There have been instances when a candidate chose to be authentic in a relevant way but in a sense may have revealed a potential weakness but were able to do so in a way that was genuine and appropriate. This isn't something that's appropriate for every candidate—it just really depends on what the area of development is and whether it's relevant to the business school application. It is risky to be that transparent, but ultimately it come s down to us assessing the candidate's judgment in terms of what they choose to share with us about their background and the way that they choose to share it.

Erin Ernst
MBA Admissions Director
Michael G. Foster School of Business
University of Washington

From the School:

The Foster MBA Program, located in Seattle, offers a highly customizable MBA experience, top notch faculty, a collaborative learning environment and access to a diverse array of companies and industries. The Foster MBA is unique, and so is every candidate who applies. Think of the essays that you submit with your application as your voice to the admissions committee. The essays present you with an opportunity to tell the admissions committee exactly how this program is going to help you accomplish your goals. The Foster MBA application requires three essays – the first asks you discuss your career goals and how the Foster MBA fits into your plans, the second asks you to outline your plans for involvement in the program (beyond the classroom), and the third is a choice between two essay topics – your greatest professional accomplishment, or a time when you faced a great challenge. The first essay is by far the most important essay. Although most schools ask a similar question, it's crucial that you very specifically explain how the opportunities available at Foster will help you move closer to your short-term and long-term career goals. The other two essays take this a step further and help the admissions committee assess how you will contribute to the program in terms of your desire to get involved, your drive and leadership potential, and your ability to handle challenging situations. Finally, the Foster MBA application offers you the opportunity to write an optional essay. The optional essay is a great place to tell us something unique about yourself or to explain a potential area of concern in your application (such as a gap in your resume or a low GPA). In summary, the application essays are an excellent tool for helping the admissions committee understand not just what makes you a great candidate, but what makes you a great candidate for the Foster MBA Program.

Q: How heavily are the essays weighted in admissions at Foster?

A: Like other pieces of the application, it's just one part. In our application, there's no one piece that's weighted more than another. But don't underestimate the importance of the essay. There's a tendency to focus on things like the GMAT, and the essay can be the last thing that candidates think about, but I like to recommend starting on them really early because they are a great tool for helping the candidate think through why they want to be in school and why they are interested in a particular program. It helps them put together a better application and can help them interview better.

Q: What competencies are revealed in the questions you ask?

A: For our program, what we call the "goals essay" is important. It's basically telling us why you want to be here. We have three essays, but the goals essay is our first and longest. But for all that we ask the candidate to cover in the essays it's really not that long. One of the biggest challenges is addressing the whole question in a relatively short space. You really want to make sure that you specifically read the question. Our goals essay has several questions within a question and it is important to address all of them.

Q: Is a "coached" essay easily visible to you?

A: Getting feedback is not an issue, but you don't want your essay to be something that could be submitted to any school. You want to make sure that it's really specific to each school to which you're applying. I can tell when someone hasn't researched our school. You also want to make sure you're speaking from the heart. Rather than using clichéd phrases, I'd rather hear specifically what your plans are. For us, its more important that a candidate answers the questions and speaks very honesty than having a really eloquently written essay.

Q: How do you read through so many essays? What will be a "standout" to you?

A: We really do read every single essay. There's no applicant who applies to our program whose essays aren't read at least twice. But the strongest essays are the ones that very specifically answer the question and are honest and straight from the heart and you can tell that they genuinely want to be a part of the program. A real standout would be one that does all of these things and brings something unique in either their writing style or in a specific experience that they share.

Q: The economy has been brutal. How would you suggest an applicant address a weak employment record? Is there less of a penalty these days?

A: If someone is laid off from their job, particularly these days, it's not the being laid off that we're concerned about as much as what you do afterwards. Even if it's just really actively networking and researching your career goals, just spending all your time applying to business school isn't necessarily going to standout. If someone has been laid off, we are interested in hearing what they have been doing to keep their foot in the door.

The challenge with the goals essay is that you want to make sure that you are not too focused on our experience of the past. In the goals essay we're really curious about how did you get to where you are now and then where are you trying to go and how are you going to get there. Part of that might be telling us, "I was recently laid off and here's what I've done so far to get closer to accomplishing my career goals," and not just applying to MBA programs. That could mean asking for feedback on long-term goals or making preparations to be an engaged student.

Q: What are some of the worst mistakes applicants make with their essays?

A: It is important to abide by the minimum or maximum word count. A lot of people feel, "Well, you know. I have a lot of interesting things to say" but everyone has really interesting things to say. Part of the challenge is to say it succinctly and straightforwardly. The first priority for the essays is just to make sure you're answering the questions, and that might seem very obvious but people have such a tendency to want to really stand out and be unique but may tend to get caught up in piece of writing that is really nice to read but is not getting at the question. So the first priority is to make sure that you are very specifically answering the questions. If it's nice to read, that's sort of a bonus for the admissions committee.

Q: What's the biggest risk you saw an applicant take with an essay that worked?

A: Humor is one of those things that can be risky, and I don't necessarily recommend it to people. It's a talent to be able to add some humor into an essay and still be able to seriously state your reasons for wanting to go to business school. But some people do have a talent for maybe not making the whole essay funny to read, but throwing in little examples that are really just another way of speaking from the heart. I can think of a time when a candidate talked about getting up to give a presentation and he was really nervous and felt unprepared and how it was sort of the instigator that propelled him to want to go to business schools and learn to polish up these things. It was just an opener—he whole essay wasn't necessarily humorous after that, but it was a nice, personal example. If you're not sure, or you're worried that you're being too casual, you might want to veer away from that. I would also assess the culture of the school to which you are applying before you attempt to do that.

ERIN L.C. NICKELSBERG
DIRECTOR, ADMISSIONS AND RECRUITMENT, WISCONSIN SCHOOL OF BUSINESS, UNIVERSITY OF WISCONSIN

FROM THE SCHOOL:

The Wisconsin MBA is highly specialized. With ten different areas of specialization, our application requires that students not only complete the two general essays but also complete the two specialization-specific essays. Those essays range from covering good brand versus bad brand and brand and product management to why you want to be a part of a supply chain. Make sure you do your research and understand the program to which you are applying and make sure you have a passion for that specialization. Really capitalize on those essays to speak to that passion and explain why you would be a good fit.

Q: How heavily are the essays weighted in admissions at Wisconsin?

A: While we don't ascribe them a specific weight we do put a lot of emphasis on the essay. The essays are what allow us to get to know the individual on a personal level and usually precede an interview we would do with them. So we read the essays to get an idea of who they are and then we use the essay as a guide throughout the interview process to reconcile the two. Quite often you will get applicants who are heavily coached on their essays or choose to write their essays about an experience that is maybe only based 10 percent in fact. When we interview them we can very clearly see that there is a disconnect between the person in the essay and the person we are meeting face-to-face, and that's a huge red flag.

Q: Has there ever been an applicant who you normally wouldn't invite for an interview but who you decided to meet because the essay was so strong?

A: Absolutely. Here at Wisconsin we're a little different than most MBA programs because we offer a specialized program. We have ten different areas of specialization, and because of that, we are really looking for students with passion. If a student can clearly communicate and articulate their passion to us, we will very often invite them for an interview even though their metrics may not have qualified them for one.

Q: How can you tell if an essay has been "coached"?

A: A lot of big words…a lot of buzz words. It's very much the "thesaurus read." Coached essays also typically don't answer the questions. They're very political. They go all around the question but they never actually answer the question. I think there's a fine line between "coaching" and being smart enough to have people proof your essay. You certainly want as many eyes as possible to look at your essay and you want to choose people who know of your aspirations in business school as well as people who don't know and have them read it and tell you what they think your aspirations are, because that is what the admissions committee's take would be on it. So you want someone who can proofread it—if your mom is a high school English teacher all the better, because certainly those grammatical errors can be the kiss of death—and you want someone to proofread for content who may not know your aspirations and passions so they can assess whether your essay does a good job of communicating that.

Q: How do you read through so many essays?

A: We do read all of the essays that come to us. Again, here at Wisconsin, we're a little different. Our MBA program has ten specializations, and so within each specialization there is a team of people reading admissions essays and then there's also the admissions team that's reading them as a whole.

Q: The economy has been brutal. How would you suggest an applicant address a weak employment record? Is there less of a penalty these days?

A: You need to use your essay to address a lack of employment and talk specifically about the efforts you've made in the context of your employment difficulty. And it's not an excuse as much as an explanation. We want to see people who are talking about what they've done in the meantime since they haven't been able to find full time employment such as becoming involved in their community, volunteering, etc. We're not looking for people who have been sitting on their couch playing Wii all day long. We want people who are going to be out, and about, and involved. A few may have even taken a risk and taken an unpaid internship or started their own consulting firm—all of those types of things are things you ma want to include in an essay.

Q: What is your ideal use of the optional personal statement?

A: We look for people who can write about overcoming obstacles. Let's say a student has a low undergraduate GPA and they use the optional essay to address that and they talk about how they worked full time during school to support their family…those are obviously the things that we look at and take into consideration.

Q: What are some of the worst mistakes applicants make with their essays?

A: Besides grammatical errors, the one that we see most often is when people do a search and replace in their essay for the name of the school they are applying to and they don't catch them all. We get that all the time, and literally, we'll just cross you off the list immediately. It doesn't mater if you have a perfect GMAT or a perfect GPA and three years of perfect work experience—that's just enough for most schools to cross you off the list. The big mistake is not having another set of eyes look at it, because if you are the one reviewing the essay that you wrote you are not going to see all the mistakes that you may have made.

Q: What's the biggest risk you saw an applicant take with an essay that worked?

A: There's a fine line between sharing personal information and sharing personal information. That's always a risk people take and it also goes to their comfort level. Some of our programs are geared more towards people who have a personality where they might be more comfortable sharing personal information so that an essay that's more personal might actually give them a leg up. It just depends on the specific program to which they are applying. One of the biggest things students can do to prepare themselves is get to know the school. So do a lot of research, reach out to alumni, and really get to know the school that you are applying to and get to know the kinds of essays they are looking for. The people that are truly passionate about what they're writing, and the one ones that are succinct and detailed, grab your attention. I love the essays that I don't want to put down.

EVAN BOUFFIDES
ASSISTANT DEAN AND DIRECTOR,
MBA ADMISSIONS AND FINANCIAL AID
OLIN SCHOOL OF BUSINESS
WASHINGTON UNIVERSITY IN ST. LOUIS

Q: How heavily are the essays weighted in admissions at Olin?

A: Probably no more or less significant than any of the other components of the application we consider. Usually there's a few things that we look at and the essay bears as much weight as the other elements of the equation (test scores, academic record, work experience, interviews). The interesting thing about the essay is that it allows the applicant to tell us about his or her candidacy beyond just the objective data. The essay allows an applicant to more fully describe their candidacy to an admissions committee. So while it's not necessarily weighted any more or less than any of the other components, the essay is a very different type of data that we look at.

Q: What questions do you ask?

A: Our essay question currently is fairly broad. Historically we've asked all sorts of essay questions, but in this version of the application we ask for a statement of purpose. In the instruction we guide the person about some of the things we'd like them to touch upon and those things are typically related to their reasons for attempting to go into an MBA program, but frankly they can write whatever they want about themselves.

Q: I imagine this is a real source of creativity for some students and a fairly scary prospect for others.

A: That's right. If you look at something like academic record and standardized test scores it's pretty clear what's a good score and what's a bad score, a good GPA and a bad GPA; it's never completely clear what a good essay and what a bad essay is. Now, there are certain things that we look at, including a person's ability to express themselves in writing in a professional way, and perhaps even in a creative way. The rest of it is somewhat objective.

Q: What competencies are revealed in the questions you ask?

A: I can tell you that one of the important things that we look for in the essay is that the candidate can articulate their reasons for wanting to pursue an

MBA, wanting to pursue it at this point in time, and also wanting to pursue it at my specific institution. MBA programs have similarities, but they have dissimilarities as well and we want to make sure the applicant gives us evidence that they've done enough research to be able to comment intelligently about a particular institution and why the school is a good fit for them. Beyond that, we want to make sure the essay talks about the MBA as it relates to the landscape of their future, that they can articulate their professional goals. Most candidates (and rightly so) will talk about they expect to be doing from a professional perspective as they graduate the institution and about what will happen in at least the mid- to long-term future, not only right after graduation but 5 years from now, 10 years from now. That gives us a sense of each candidate's focus from a professional perspective and an idea of what they're trying to do with the MBA.

Q: How do you read through so many essays? What will be a "standout" to you?

A: There are essentially four people who do all of the file reading and most of the interviewing as well. We divide them up in the beginning in a very preliminary way to screen applicants to see who will be invited for an interview. In our process we interview everyone who is admitted to the program, but we can't possibly interview every applicant, so for us the first step is to do a preliminary screening and see who we would like to interview. During the file reading each person does an assessment of the application he or she has read and then we get together as an admissions committee we talk about each candidate and at that point a determination might be read or it may be that another reading has to be done by another person. I will do a reading of every applicant who comes across my desk, and particularly those we intend to admit.

Q: The economy has been brutal. How would you suggest an applicant address a weak employment record? Is there less of a penalty these days?

A: I think there are two places a person can address this: one is the essay and they other is the interview. Transparency is definitely important. I think that most schools, including our own, give applicants the change to complete an Optional Essay where they can talk about other points of their application that might not be clearly described in other parts of their application. So I think a person can address this in the standard question we ask or they can do it in the optional essay as well. We see that a lot these days. We see a number of people explaining various things that they might see as deficiencies in their applications and one of them can certainly be gaps in employment history.

Q: What are some of the worst mistakes applicants make with their essays?

A: One is obviously to cut and paste from one business school essay to another and leave the other school's name in it. That happens with more regularity than you might imagine. The problem is not so much the cutting and pasting but more that the person has not thoroughly proofread their essay. That we can extend to other issues of whether the applicant has attention to detail and is truly committed to the process.

Another example is an applicant's response to a specific question like "talk about your long and short-term goals." If a person avoids the question or answers a different question, that can be a very common problem. Making sure that an applicant reads the question carefully and makes sure they understand what the parameters of the question are is very important.

A lot of applicants are, for lack of a better term, "wishy washy" about what they're trying to do with an MBA and that might have something to do with their not having carefully thought out why they're pursuing the MBA. That can sometimes comes across in the essay when applicants talk about multiple things that they're interested in pursuing in terms of career goals, and multiple things that are completely divergent. I think it's fair to say that most admissions committees want people who have given careful thought to the notion of getting an MBA at their school and part of that answer has to be a fairly straightforward and relatively focused statement about what they're going to be doing in their professional life.

Q: What's the biggest risk you saw an applicant take with an essay that worked?

A: I think the risks sometimes have to do with the applicant wanting to express themselves in a creative way. This is one of the few areas of the application where an applicant's personality can come out. This is a chance for a great writer to shine. It's also a chance for a poor writer to make mistakes and take risks that maybe he or she should not have taken. When people do take risks and open up to the admissions committee and allow us to understand something about their personality--it can come through creativity, it can come through humor, it can through a lot of different ways—they really stand out as being successful beyond just answering the question.

OFFICIAL DISCLAIMER!

Our editors aren't asleep on the job.

The essays in this book appear exactly as they did for business school admissions officers. We only changed the layout, and in some cases, protected the anonymity of individuals, institutions, and organizations. Because we have not edited the essays, you may find errors in spelling, punctuation, and grammar. We assure you that we found these errors as well, but we thought it would be most helpful for you to see what the business school admissions officers saw—not what they could (or should) have seen. We still recommend that you carefully proofread your own personal statement, but should you miss an error, take comfort in the fact that others (accepted applicants, even!) sometimes did too.

Chapter 10

THE ESSAYS

CASE EXAMPLES: ADMISSIONS OFFICERS CRITIQUE WINNING ESSAYS

To show you how some applicants have answered the essay questions, we asked the b-schools for samples of "winning" essays. To show you what worked about them, we also asked the admissions officers to provide a Critique.

As you read through the essays, keep in mind that each was but one of several submitted by an applicant for admission. Moreover, they were part of a package that included other important components. One essay alone did not "win" admission.

One other reminder: The purpose of including essays in this book is to give you a nudge in the right direction, not to provide you with a script or template for your own work. It would be a mistake to use them this way.

Obviously, this collection is by no means all-encompassing. There are thousands of winning essays out there; we just couldn't include them all.

Editor's Note: Personal details, such as names, companies, and institutions, have been removed from these essays to protect the identities of the applicants. The essays have not been otherwise edited since they were submitted by the applicants.

BABSON COLLEGE
OLIN GRADUATE
SCHOOL OF BUSINESS

Essay #1

Question: a) What are your specific career goals immediately following graduation? b) What skills, competencies, and experiences do you have right now that will help you attain those goals?

Following graduation, I plan to become involved in projects that link business principals and models with innovative social programs, particularly those that support positive youth development. Most of my work life has focused on adolescents. I have worked for various youth service organizations, provided clinical services to youth and their families, and managed a program for young teens. Ultimately, I want to start a new organization that focuses on youth entrepreneurship, meaning that youth are supported in their efforts to innovate, organize and implement their plans. Learning about well-developed concepts in for-profit industries is essential for achieving my goals. The challenge will be to create ways to apply those principles in the non-profit sector.

As a social worker, the difficulties my clients face frustrate me less than the funding system within which services operate. Inefficient bureaucracy, weakly established means for linking research with service development, and turnover in funding limit my ability to expand and/or improve services. For example, the money that presently supports the program I manage was awarded to foster the development of "models" that prevent youth involvement in substance abuse and other risk behaviors. After two years of delivering services and refining the program, we have created a workable model. However, now that we have established ourselves and are capable of expansion, our contract is set to expire. In the search for new funds, there are two options: apply for one large grant or several small ones. Either option is likely to require that some parts of the current model be dropped or altered to meet the requirements of the new funders. This turnover in funding has a domino effect—management and front-line staff leave, which in turn disrupts operations. The social service organizations that house various programs are similarly effected, as staff positions come and go. The resultant organizational instability makes it nearly impossible to seek or develop alternative sources of capital, and the cycle repeats itself.

A related problem is the difficulty applying performance measures to non-profit entities. In nonprofits, results cannot be linked solely to revenue and expenses. Current tools for evaluating social service programs focus on concepts developed by social scientists. While those tools are essential for assessing clients' needs and developing programs, they are not adequate for measuring the performance of an organization over time. By combining new knowledge about various business concepts with my background in social science, I will be able to develop alternative ways to address this problem.

My MSW degree provided excellent clinical training and allowed me to gain skills in program development, evaluation, grant-writing and staff supervision. Over the last three years, I have tested those skills as a program manager. I have felt prepared to handle most youth and family concerns, staff issues and general oversight of daily activities, but I need further training in operations, marketing, application of technology, and strategy. I am obtaining an MBA to fill gaps in my current skill set, learn about venture start-up and expand my worldview. Babson's focus on entrepreneurship throughout the curriculum, and the opportunity for specialized training, will help me attain my goals.

Critique

This essay explained the clear direction that the student intends to take upon graduation. The student did a good job of connecting her prior work experience and education to future career goals. This is especially important when candidates are making a career change or are seeking employment in an environment or industry that is outside the norm for MBA recruiting. The student identified areas where MBA knowledge and skills would be an asset, recognized her lack of knowledge in certain areas, and succeeded in demonstrating to the admissions committee why the MBA—specifically the Babson MBA—was the appropriate next step in her career progression.

ESSAY #2

> Question: a) What are your specific career goals immediately following graduation? b) What skills, competencies, and experiences do you have right now that will help you attain those goals?

For the last decade, I have helped guide the career of [Band A] from a college band into a professionally touring and recording entity with a national impact. This evolution has endured many growing pains, but the band has persevered because of my vision, passion, and work ethic. My vision of growth for the organization and for myself helped us discover and create opportunities that put us in a position to succeed. In addition, my vision of survival helped us withstand an avalanche of challenges that would have ended the careers of most other groups. Equally rewarding has been the complete nature of my involvement from the songwriting and recording to the supervision of manufacturing, distribution, promotion, and ultimately live performance itself, when the songs and the fans come together. I have always run the band like a business, adopting long-term growth strategies and learning from the management decisions that have contributed to the successes and failures of other bands that came before us. This application of professional intensity to what would otherwise be a hobby, and transforming it into something enduring and impacting, has been extremely rewarding.

Within a year of forming, [Band A] entered a radio contest and won first place out of 200 groups throughout New England, and this taste of success inspired a vision of further accomplishments. Everything started with education and elbow grease. I buried myself in every book I could find on artist management and band development. I opened a bank account and kept detailed financial records. I read Billboard and Rolling Stone, and spent time with most bands that passed through town in order to learn from their successes and failure. I developed a business plan that incorporated these lessons as well as some ideas of my own. The plan emphasized long-term and short-term growth strategies applied to recording, touring, and management. I even phoned hundreds of college venues, metro rock clubs, and studios to put the plan into action. Our collective musical ability combined with my appreciation for problem solving, my drive to succeed, and my desire to identify and face challenges has given the band a distinctive edge.

Since college, we have survived ten line-up changes, traveled more than 500,000 miles performing more than 1,200 concerts in all 48 continental states, earned a recording contract with [Record Company A], recorded three albums with some of the top producers and mix engineers in this country, and our music is featured regularly in films and on national television. [Band A] has earned its success on the strength of two underlying principles: the development of a good product, and the importance of being aware and thoroughly involved. I strive to be involved with every aspect of operations from the studio to the stage, and from the radio to the record store. A holistic understanding of how all facets of the industry come together has been an essential part of our growth and development.

Working and performing with [Band A] has been uniquely rewarding. It has allowed me to pursue an ambitious dream that blends a diversity of gratifying elements including artistic expression, self-employment, and the development and management of a business. Beyond rehearsal and performance, my responsibilities have included book keeping, cash flow management, payroll, tax preparation, maintaining the mailing list, establishing and maintaining a product distribution network, booking tours, negotiating performance contracts, coordinating recording projects, securing product endorsements, coordinating charitable concert events, conducting interviews, and making other public appearances. I feel I have an aptitude and appreciation for management, and if recognizing management ability is the first step in assembling a career in management, the next step is discovering an appropriate application of that potential. To this end, I have three specific interests that I would like to explore in graduate school.

I want to consider applying my abilities to the non-profit sector as my grandfather did with [Nonprofit Organization A}, or my mother continues to do with [Nonprofit Organization B]. My personal and professional interests could be combined in museum management or involvement with an arts or social service foundation. Contributing to society and enhancing our culture by supporting the arts, in addition to helping an organization run more productively and efficiently, are important concerns of mine.

I also want to explore entrepreneurial opportunities. One of the most satisfying aspects of my tenure with [Band A] has been overseeing the evolution of the group from a college band into an enduring and financially viable entity. This was accomplished through hard work, a vision of growth and survival, and an appreciation for the ways in which the different elements of an industry combine. I would love the opportunity to foster this kind of development in another setting.

Finally, although my career in music has precluded further exploration of the international dimension of my personal and academic development, my appreciation of foreign cultures is great. I lived in France during my junior year of High School, backpacked through Europe for two months before college, and majored in International Relations at Brown. Adaptation, exploration, and communication in a foreign culture are one of the greatest challenges I have ever faced, and I look forward to doing it again. Babson would be an ideal environment for me to discover professional opportunities that are aligned with my interests.

I have enjoyed my career as a professional musician and artist manager, but I am ready for a change that would permit a more personally and financially stable lifestyle. The experience of completing Babson's MBA program would help me hone my general skills and interests into a specific field. It would enhance to my unique business background by proving to my future employers and peers that I am an experienced and well-trained leader and decision maker.

Critique

This essay demonstrated the need for business skill in an unconventional environment in a way that was believable, convincing, and persuasive. This student showed the admissions committee that although he had not worked in a large or even midsize company, his experiences could be linked to many business situations. The student demonstrated leadership abilities, teamwork experiences, and the recognized need to run his band like a business. The student's self-awareness of both skills and limitations gave the admissions committee a clear understanding of the candidate and what he would bring to the community: artistic creativity, outside-the-box thinking, flexibility, leadership skills, an understanding of running a business, and the experience of traveling throughout the country.

ESSAY #3

Question: a) What are your specific career goals immediately following graduation? b) What skills, competencies, and experiences do you have right now that will help you attain those goals?

In order to achieve my career goals, I have outlined my strategy for success by mapping my career goals at specific time intervals over the next fifteen years. In addition, my professional and personal experiences coupled with a Babson MBA will ensure my future professional success.

In three years, my career goals are to be a Babson MBA graduate, to attain a post-graduate entry-level position as an Associate in the credit derivatives group at [Bank A], and to begin to give back to my community by serving it. The completion of the Babson MBA program is the most critical component for achieving my career goals. As a newly graduated Babson MBA student, I will begin my new career structuring transactions in the credit derivatives group at [Bank A], as it is the number one ranked credit derivatives dealer in the world. My wife will continue to work for a few more years so that her income can allow me to accept a post-graduate entry-level salary. I know that the best place to start a new career is at a large bank with top-notch expertise in a specific area (credit derivatives). This will not only provide a challenging work environment due to high customer flow, but also will allow me to learn a new business from the best credit derivatives professionals in the industry. Additionally, to successfully attain my career goals, I need to ensure that I have the right balance with my personal life. As such, the next phase of my personal growth progression is to begin to serve my community during this time interval. My first priority is to raise money for cancer research. Initially, I will solicit sponsorship to raise money in cancer bike rides and also contribute separately from my own pocket. Also, as I was an underprivileged child without a role model at critical points in my life, I will begin my involvement as a role model for [Nonprofit Organization A]. to provide a source of guidance to children without fathers. Hopefully, I can guide a fatherless child to make the right choices by teaching him the lessons I have learned from my mistakes rather than having to learn the same lessons from his own mistakes. Also, as I am acquainted with the VP of Finance of another university from past business dealings, I will be seeking his advice (as he is well respected in his industry) on a proper strategy to gain membership to the Board of Directors or to a board of a similar university. I have a strong desire to freely lend my expertise to the VP of Finance of a university or university system to assist in minimizing interest costs and maximizing asset returns through the use of municipal debt and derivative products.

In five years, my career goals are to be promoted from Associate to SVP at [Bank A], to continue to nurture and grow my professional network, to continue my community service and to allow my wife to transition from her current career at [Bank B] to her new career as a full-time mother and part-time gymnastics judge/coach. By this time interval, I will be quickly promoted to SVP as I demonstrate my business acumen and leadership ability to management. As a SVP, I will be a senior member of the credit derivative group at [Bank A] and I will be positioning myself to manage the group in the near future. Also, I will continue to work hard to maintain and grow my existing professional network as it will be important to strengthen existing and to develop new professional allies. I will continue to be involved in raising money for cancer research and I will use my seniority at [Bank A] to make it an organizational priority to raise those funds. I will also continue to work on attaining the university board membership and to be involved with [Nonprofit Orginization A]. Most importantly, this is the time interval when my wife can choose to become a full-time mother to our children. In addition, I'll encourage her to begin the pursuit of her passion to become a gymnastics coach and judge.

In ten years, my career goals are to be promoted from SVP to MD of the credit derivatives group at [Bank A], to maintain and grow my professional network, to continue my community service and help my wife manage our family. By this time interval, I will be promoted to MD and will be managing the credit derivatives group at [Bank A]. I will continue the aforementioned community service projects and will have gained membership to the [University A] (or similar university) Board of Directors. Additionally, I will have a hands-on approach to helping my wife manage our family. I will be actively involved in every family member's life by providing encouragement, life guidance and friendship. I will be actively involved in my children's lives from their parent-teacher conferences to sporting events. I will continue to encourage my wife to pursue her gymnastics dreams.

In fifteen years, my career goals are to seek out a smaller investment bank (such as [Bank B] or [Bank C]) to change the direction of my career, to maintain and grow my professional network, to continue to provide community service and to stay actively involved in each family member's life. By this time interval, I will have excellent experience from a top-notch bank to leverage into a position at a smaller investment bank. I will strongly desire at this point to move to a smaller company because they tend to allow employees to place more emphasis on family and life balance. As such, I will be starting a new credit derivatives group or taking over the management of an existing credit derivative group (or another type of derivative group) at my new company. This new position will allow me to devote more time to my family and community service.

The work experiences that will help me to achieve my career goals have evolved from [Bank B], [Bank C] and [Company D]. At [Bank B], I had the opportunity to be a part of a municipal derivatives team of four professionals that consistently generated significant annual revenues and also improved the municipal derivatives market through constant innovation (for example, we were the first municipal derivatives desk to introduce a municipal bond option program called "MuniCHOPs"—municipal call hedging option program). From this experience I learned that I have the entrepreneurial spirit and can work well with a team under stressful circumstances. From my [Bank C] experience, I have learned that companies and employees may differ culturally. Upon my departure from [Bank C] to gain managerial experience at [Bank D], I assumed that [Bank D] was culturally similar to [Bank C]. However, I learned rather quickly that while [Bank D] was an excellent bank, it was also a conservative regional bank. In fact, [Bank D]'s conservative culture was the antithesis of [Bank C]'s entrepreneurial culture. As such, I realized that my entrepreneurial spirit and ambition were not appropriate for the culture of [Bank D]. This experience will remain with me because I have learned that companies, as well as employees, may be different and those differences must be recognized in the implementation of strategic managerial objectives. From my [Company E] experience, I have honed my entrepreneurial, communication, leadership and business relationship skills.

Also, my personal growth experience will help me to achieve my career goals. From my personal growth experience, I have learned that strong relationships are the most important component to my personal and family happiness. As such, the nurturing of strong professional relationships, thereby increasing my professional network is just as important to my professional success. As an experienced professional it is important to teach and develop younger professionals unselfishly, to foster a team-oriented environment, and to continuously maintain open lines of communication with former colleagues and business school classmates. Additionally, I have learned that balancing my life between my professional and family goals will contribute to my professional success as well. This will enable me to avoid both professional and personal regrets and pitfalls, thereby maintaining a high level of happiness. Also, as part of balancing my life, I am no longer motivated to professionally succeed by only the prospect of making money. But rather, I am motivated to succeed so that I can provide my family with the things that I never had as a child: family happiness, a comfortable home in a nice neighborhood, life guidance and a finer appreciation of life.

A Babson MBA will provide a diverse student body, an excellent selection of academic courses and the opportunity to begin a new career. The Babson MBA program offers a culturally diverse student body (38% international, 62% domestic, according to Business Week Online) that is similar to today's culturally diverse workplace. This prepares the Babson MBA student to learn how to understand and accept differences among culturally different group members under stressful circumstances. Hence, the Babson MBA student is better prepared to assimilate into a team environment at a culturally diverse company. Additionally, Babson is known for the entrepreneurship program. As such, I am interested in exploring the decision making process of the student that desires to be an entrepreneur. As one who has taken risk by starting a derivatives consulting company and worked (and will in the future) in a fast-paced entrepreneurial environment (but never had time to appreciate the moment) I want to develop friendships with those that have similar interests. Thus, I will have an opportunity to study the entrepreneurial spirit through the bond of those friendships.

Additionally, I am looking forward to formally learning finance from the Babson MBA program. As I believe that having a strong technical base is important, I look forward to scheduling Valuation (FIN 7000), Risk Management (FIN 7504), Portfolio Management (FIN 7530) and Advanced Derivative Securities (FIN 7550). Also, as I will be a senior level manager, I am interested in learning about leadership and organizational behavior. As such, Strategic Management (MOB 7000), Negotiations (MOB 7120) and Implementing Strategic Change (MOB 7500) are important to my interests in learning about leadership and management. Finally, my first elective priority is to ensure that I am scheduled for the Marketing for Entrepreneurs course (EPS 7574) so that I can meet fellow entrepreneurs.

It is of paramount importance to me that a wide variety of financial services firms recruit MBAs at Babson. As such, recruitment from various financial services firms will ensure that a diversified set of career paths is available. For example, as previously discussed, my targeted employer upon graduation is [Bank A]. However, if there isn't an opportunity to join [Bank A] in my chosen field (credit derivatives), then there are other potential employers that recruit at Babson that I can explore for opportunities in credit derivatives including [Banks B, C, D, or E]. Then there are smaller financial services firms that I can also explore career opportunities (in credit derivatives or another area of derivatives) at including [Banks F, G, or H]. At the moment, I do not have entree to a career outside of the municipal industry at any of these financial services firms.

As I have been in the municipal industry since I was a junior in college (13 years), I have a strong desire to grow professionally by beginning a new career in a different segment of the financial services industry. However, due to my longevity in the municipal industry coupled with an undergraduate degree from [University F], I have found it difficult to break-through to a new career in a new industry. As such, the prestige of the Babson MBA program, the success of Babson's alumni and my successful track record will be, in combination, the mechanism that allows me to shatter the glass ceiling that I have encountered.

My carefully planned career path and professional/personal experiences in combination with a Babson MBA will ensure that I am successful in my next career.

Critique

This essay, although too long by normal standards, covered a lot of information for the candidate. It is a good example of a student with clearly defined career goals, a plan of how he intends to achieve those goals, and clear articulation of how the Babson MBA is going to assist him in attaining those goals. Due to the fact that this student had a unique situation with regard to his work and prior education, degrees of latitude were afforded with regard to the length of the essay. This is not a strategy I would recommend for candidates; try to stay within the recommended word limit. This student clearly did the necessary research and was able to weave certain details of the program that supported his goals into the essay. Again, I advise caution in taking this approach; the last thing the admissions committee wants to read in an essay is what's in their course book. However, the relevance of what is stated directly supported the student's goals and made a clear connection.

Case Western
Reserve University
Weatherhead School of Management

The Weatherhead School of Management at Case Western Reserve University is a model of innovation and diversity. From our cutting-edge, Frank Gehry-designed building, to eighteen areas of concentration, including Bioscience Entrepreneurship and Nonprofit Management, the school is noted for being 'forward-thinking' and innovative in its approach to management education. The admissions committee, therefore, keeps these hallmarks in mind when reviewing and admitting candidates to the full-time MBA program.

"The committee purposefully constructs a class profile that mirrors the school's innovative and diverse nature, considering nationality (45 percent of the class is international), gender, ethnicity, work experience, and educational background. However, beyond the rudimentary demographic information, the committee also considers the 'gray area': What makes one candidate stand apart from the others? What qualities has this person demonstrated that guarantee involvement in activities outside the classroom? How do you know this person will be effective in the numerous team settings? It is through the essay questions that the committee is able to 'see' the candidates—not just for what they have done academically or on a standardized test, but for the people they are and that they wish to become."

Essay #1

Question: Describe your motivation for pursuing an MBA degree. How does it fit with your short- and long-term career goals?

My earliest impression of community service may have been the pins my grandmothers received for giving blood. My desire to help others was embedded by my family and manifested itself through a combination of three things: 1) my public policy education at [University A], 2) an introduction to the nonprofit sector at a seminar in D.C. through [Nonprofit Organization A], and 3) an internship at the [State A]'s 4-H Office. These experiences solidified my desire to work in the nonprofit sector.

My career thus far has entailed a rapid assumption of responsibilities. [Nonprofit Organization B], a national advocacy organization, hired me as a Development Assistant, and soon I was promoted to the newly created position of Prospect Researcher. As such, I was responsible for identifying and qualifying funding sources and setting up a "research shop." At [Nonprofit Organization C], a five-hospital system with numerous ancillary services, I conduct prospect research for twice as many Development Officers. I also have fundraising responsibility for [Program A], and I write grants for [Center A]. As a result of my career growth and increased responsibilities, my salary doubled in just under two years.

Three and a half years of nonprofit experience so far has exposed me to a variety of nonprofit organizations. Although their missions, size, and my role in them have varied dramatically, there are similarities that are current issues in nonprofit management. So focused on their missions, nonprofits often lack the qualities of a well-managed business. Some nonprofits walk a precarious financial tightrope, and others have significant human resource problems. These weaknesses compromise their effectiveness and their ability to tackle important social problems.

These kinds of administrative issues are almost always known quantities, but nonprofit managers often lack the skill sets and experience to know how to approach solving them. I believe the MBA from Weatherhead and a certificate from the Mandel Center will provide me with the unique background needed to balance the mission of an organization with its responsibility to operate effectively. The curriculum is the most comprehensive and practical of any of the schools that offer this combination, and I look forward to working with and learning from dynamic teachers and taking part in the Mentor program. Now is the right time to pursue my MBA because I believe am ready to contribute to organizational health in a strategic way, and business skills will equip me to move to this level and be effective.

With a degree from Case Western and the Mandel Center, I will gain a solid mix of business skills and understanding of the special issues nonprofits face. In the short-term I see myself as a Development Director or senior manager helping ensure both the fiscal and programmatic health of a community agency that depends on charitable dollars for its operating budget. In the long term I hope to work on the cutting edge of nonprofit management theory or become involved in the funding side of the equation as a grant maker or an advisor to high level donors looking to leverage their charitable dollars. The Weatherhead School offers me the best path to achieving the same satisfaction my grandmothers got from giving blood—helping nonprofit organizations help others more effectively.

Critique

Paragraph 1: The essay begins with a well-constructed introduction, which gives good insight into the candidate: focus on community service, importance of family, educational background, breadth of work, and internship experience. This paragraph gives a solid picture of the candidate in just a few sentences. It serves as a good foundation for the rest of the essay, which elaborates on the various facets of the candidate.

Paragraph 2: In detailing specific work experiences, the candidate is already highlighting the skills and talents she can contribute as a student in our program. Additionally, the assumption of new/different responsibilities and an increase in position and salary illustrate that her abilities are recognized and rewarded by the organizations for which she has worked.

Paragraph 3: Here, the candidate demonstrates her ability to analyze organizations with regard to basic business functions. This paragraph is also a preliminary introduction to the motivation aspect of the question.

Paragraph 4: This paragraph is the "heart" of the essay; it details the motivation for the degree, and it highlights aspects of the school program and how they fit with her goals. This paragraph has been perfectly set up by the three previous paragraphs.

Paragraph 5: This is an excellent essay summary that gives specific answers with regard to short- and long-term goals. The final sentence brings the essay full circle, back to the reference of how her desire for community service evolved.

Summary: This is a well-constructed essay that remains focused on the topic while giving the readers insight into the person behind the application. Specific examples of work experience and elements of the program that fit her goals give the impression of a candidate who has evaluated her own situation, set goals for her career, researched the options, and made an informed decision about what she is looking for in an MBA.

Essay #2

Question: How will your background and experiences enhance the quality of the entering class of Weatherhead MBA students?

Moving from rural Tennessee to suburban New York at the age of twelve was not an easy thing to do. Trying to blend in during this fragile stage of life was a challenge; "y'all" was not a part of the typical middle schooler's vocabulary in New York. However, this change in lifestyle at a young age laid the foundation for a passion to meet different types of people and experience various lifestyles and cultures. In college, I had several experiences that enriched me. From taking a class taught by Maya Angelou to scuba diving on the Great Barrier Reef during my semester abroad, [University A] provided the perfect slate for an undergraduate experience filled with meaningful experiences.

One of the most worthwhile experiences I have had, however, took place after I received my diploma from [University A]. Being chosen to serve my country for ten months in a [Nonprofit Organization B] program was one of the greatest honors I have received. Describing one of the projects that my team worked on will help illustrate the lessons I learned and the memories that I take with me into each new experience in my life.

My [Nonprofit Organization B] team, comprised of twelve individuals from eleven different states, lived for two months in a three-bedroom house that had been repossessed by [Nonprofit Organization C] after the tenants had violated the rules of living there. We lived in a neighborhood in which drug deals on the corner were common occurrences. We would build houses for [Nonprofit Organization C] during the day and return at night, exhausted and sore, to walk down the street to the community center and help the neighborhood kids with their homework. In this unique life experience, I literally lived among the people whom I was serving. I did not work all day and then return to a place of security, equipped with the amenities I was used to in my life. That was not an option.

Never before had I been so close in proximity to the very root of the problem that we sought to eliminate by building houses for the poor. No longer could I judge those on "the other side." I was one of them. They were one of us. I was reminded of the premise that Maya Angelou taught her class around—"We are more alike than we are different." Although she had made us recite that each week in her class, it was three years later when I was living it. She was more right than I had ever realized.

My background, shaped by these types of experiences, will add to the diversity of the class beginning this fall at the Weatherhead School of Management. Not only am I eager to share my own life experiences with others but I am also equally excited to be challenged by those who have had a very different past. The exchange between myself, one who wants to apply an MBA to the nonprofit sector, and another student, perhaps one who is ready to improve his managerial skills for the consulting field, has the potential to be outstanding. I know I would contribute to the diversity of a class of individuals, each from a different background with a different set of skills, all ultimately seeking the same thing.

Critique

Paragraph 1: The first sentence, simply stating a fact of her life, already draws the reader in to the essay—thinking of a twelve-year-old girl trying to "hide" her southern accent from her New York classmates. This reference point sets up nicely the following sentences, which exemplify her interest in meeting different types of people and discovering different cultures.

Paragraph 2: Here the candidate sets up the remainder of the essay. Also, as this experience is not one that many people will have shared, it reminds the reader of her uniqueness—in both pursuing the volunteer work and being selected for the program.

Paragraph 3: In describing her living conditions, the candidate speaks to her ability to be flexible and adaptive—twelve people in a three-bedroom house, living in a neighborhood far from her own life experience. The detail enhances the commitment to community involvement. She is not a "weekend" volunteer, but chose to live a lifestyle that would put her in daily contact with those she hoped to help.

Paragraph 4: This paragraph illustrates personal growth gained from her experience. The ability to enter a challenging environment, adapt to difficult surroundings, and appreciate the experience as one of growth and learning is exactly what an admissions committee would hope for with all candidates.

Paragraph 5: This summary paragraph brings the focus to the question at hand, with the candidate reiterating not only how the experience enriched her and will allow her to contribute to the class, but also her eagerness to learn from others with varying backgrounds.

Summary: The essay is effective in two ways. First, it demonstrates self-knowledge and personal growth—both of which are important for candidates to possess and embrace to fully take advantage of the MBA experience. Second, it details a nonwork experience. While the volunteer experience is certainly valuable (and valued by the admissions committee as they look for students to enrich our community), some candidates do not feel that they should write about nonwork accomplishments. They believe that because they are applying to business school, they should focus on business experiences only. However, most every school wants/expects students to have a balance between school and their personal life, so it is beneficial to learn about what they've done in the past.

Claremont Graduate University

The Peter F. Drucker
Graduate School of Management

Essay #1

Personal Statement: What special contributions do you believe you will bring to the Drucker School? Why is a Drucker School MBA important to you?

What special contributions do you believe you will bring to the Drucker School?

If this is going to be a personal statement, I might as well put "me" all over this statement. So, "out" with the generic and "in" with something a little different. I feel that I bring the following qualities and contributions to my Drucker experience.

Leadership

How do leaders become better? By learning from those who have been where you are trying to go. These leaders can show you the way, so you may lead others. I feel that Drucker provides those experienced leaders, both teaching the classes and sitting next to me learning. The exciting idea about graduate school is the fact that you are not merely gaining experience from internships and lectures, but the most experience will probably come from my study group members and classmates. As far as I know, there isn't anyone applying to Drucker from my company. So, my experience in the retail industry will probably enlighten my classmates, hopefully, for the better.

I've been involved in leadership opportunities most of my life. From co-captain of my basketball team to VP of my chapter of [Association A], leadership has taught me responsibility, courage, and strength. I know how it feels to have the entire weight of an expensive project on your shoulders. I feel that it is very important to have leadership experience in a program that relies so heavily on group participation. In every group, you are not always the leader. But after participating in these roles, I understand the role of a leader. By understanding, I believe that I can be more effective and cooperative in a group.

Resolve/Don't Quit Attitude

There have been so many times in life that I just wanted to throw my hands in the air and say, "That's it! I can't do it!" But I have always had that voice inside pulling me back together, telling me that I can make it. "Just hold on a little longer." I know for a fact MBA programs are not easy and Drucker is no different. But I know that I have the strength and resolve to pull through. Strength also comes from those around you. My "don't quit" attitude will definitely rub off on others, encouraging them that we can do this together. With all the group projects and study groups involved in the program, there is no choice but to pull for each other.

When I was eighteen, a car accident left me paralyzed from the neck down. Doctors counted me out from the first day out. They said that I would never walk again and would have to look at buying a more permanent wheelchair. I told everyone in the room that day; "I am walking back to school in the fall". When everyone counted me out, I decided then and there that I couldn't give up. Why attempt to do anything in life, if you don't think you can be successful at it? Regardless of how many times you may think you have failed, barring death, you can try again with the knowledge gained from the previous attempts. I have been told that a leg that has healed after being broken is stronger than it was before. Through relentless physical therapy and prayer, I carried my own books into my dorm room to start the fall of my sophomore year of college. Broken temporarily, but stronger indefinitely.

Creativity

With the current status of the economy, creativity will be a "must-have" in whatever industry you enter. I'm glad I have it. You have to think outside of the box to figure how you will first find your niche in the job market. Product development is the area of marketing I aspire to enter, once I receive my MBA. My creativity will flow into every aspect of my Drucker experience, from group projects to on-campus organizations.

As a member of my marketing association, I helped create our theme and exhibition for the national convention. Using items laying around campus, such as street signs, pieces of tarp, and plastic tubing, we re-created a construction site in a New Orleans convention hall. I do believe that I have the ability to make something from nothing at all. I enjoy taking a look at everyday items and finding methods of improving upon them.

Sense of Responsibility to self, family, and community

Accomplishments are not simply for you. When you gain a degree, you have a responsibility to your family and community also. I feel a great need to use my knowledge to help others around me. There are so many underprivileged youth in Southern California that could use the encouragement of people like me to inspire and show them the path to greater aspirations, beyond simply sports and entertainment.

While at Drucker, I plan to participate in numerous community service activities, [Nonprofit Organization B] and [Nonprofit Organization C]. But I must use my added knowledge from a Drucker MBA to go back to those communities that gave so much to me, in South LA and Compton. I do not want to be the only person to benefit from my degree. I want the world to receive the wisdom and kindness that was passed down to me.

Sense of the Big Picture/Ability to bring people together

Have you ever met a person that could enter a conversation and understand where everyone was coming from? I feel that I have the unique ability to view issues with an open mind and relate to someone's opinion without sacrificing my own. My belief is the key to communication, in a community as diverse as Southern California, is listening. Being able to hear exactly what someone is saying and why it is being said, in the tone/fashion they are presenting that idea.

International students, statistically, dominate the graduate school arena. You find this highly affirmative in the state of California. With the diverse backgrounds and languages we come from, it is imperative effective communication is present to bring about common understanding. The Drucker program is passionate about group work and participation. I know that I can come into a group setting and be productive. Looking beyond language/cultural barriers to see the big picture, both in class and in life, to bring us all together.

Charisma

The first time I heard the word "Charisma" was watching Earving "Magic" Johnson of the LA Lakers. Sports broadcasters were amazed at the way "Magic" could begin to speak and everyone would listen. Yes, I know. I could have used great leaders of the past or present, but "Magic" was different. Outside of his great basketball ability, he was an average guy. But, even after basketball was over for him, he could lead in political, economic, and social issues with the same passion and following. That's charisma. And I believe that I've got it. When it's time to take on a project, I can light the spark within and ignite those around me. Just like "Magic".

Why is a Drucker School MBA important to you?

Importance of a name vs. UCR

When I attended college for my undergraduate studies, my priority was to attend a school that I could afford. [University D] provided me with a reputable education and a full four-year scholarship. But [University D] was one of the lesser known of the [University System] campuses. I felt that it cost me some exposure to opportunities that might have been available if I attended a more prominent school. That's where Drucker comes in.

To me, Drucker has the name and national attention that I was not able to receive in my undergraduate years. In 2001, Drucker was ranked in the top 20 of MBA programs nationwide, in US News and Reports. The opportunity to have a MBA that means a lot to Fortune 500 companies, combined with your Claremont, Ca. location, makes Drucker a very desirable place to be.

Small school—make a BIG impact

If you throw a rock in a lake, the ripples are not quite as large as if you were to throw a stone into a small pond. I believe the previous analogy suits the effect of a counselor, a professor, and especially, an active student, in a small school environment. Given the opportunity, I think that I could both impact, and be impacted, by an education here, at the Drucker School of Management. A smaller school gives all those included greater means for interaction and learning. Simply from comparing the information sessions I attended, Claremont appeared to care more about the quality of their students and the integrity of the management program.

Coming from a small school, such as [University D], I appreciate the extra time and effort campus faculty and staff had to offer. I realize I have grown far more than my counterparts that attended larger school systems, like [University E] or [University F]. I have learned that within a smaller school lies a great opportunity to participate in multiple organizations. But when participating in those organizations, it's not just attendance in meeting or paying dues. It is not large and non-productive. You can actually accomplish projects and make an impact in the community.

Not just a Drucker MBA, a CGU graduate degree

Here's the clincher for me. I am delighted that you are able to take courses at other schools within the Consortium of Graduate Studies. Business is a field that, I believe, encompasses all other areas of study. Psychology has always been a field of study I felt was important to further my understanding of human behavior. If I could better understand human behavior, I could then determine marketing strategy based on possible consumer behavior. By taking classes in psychology or economics, I feel I could gain a more global idea of marketing and strategy. My MBA would be enhanced by the chance to not only learn from Drucker, which is great in itself. But, I can also participate in seminars and courses within the entire Consortium.

Investment with a strong return

All in all, I would be an excellent candidate for the Drucker MBA program. I possess the drive, intensity, and endurance to withstand the rigors of a semester system at full speed. Community service and social integrity are, and will always be, very important to me. My MBA degree will be part of a long journey, full of people that taught me many great things. The rest of my journey will be spent implanting my knowledge into others that can follow our lead of creating change in boardrooms and classrooms.

I want [my] focus [to] begin in marketing with product development at a consumer product corporation. Later, use that knowledge to help struggling Los Angeles areas in community development projects. For, I believe that the two areas deal with the same thought process just different outcomes. I want to motivate more corporations to invest in their communities to spark a chain reaction of social consciousness at the business level. I hope that Drucker is the school that can help me on my way.

Critique

The Drucker MBA Academic Committee found that this personal statement accurately portrays the "real" student, who has a personal approach. Since the Drucker Graduate School of Management offers a very personal approach to educating future ethical business leaders, it is important to create a mutually beneficial match between student and classroom, and to be able to gain a sense of an applicant in the personal statement — something that gives the "between-the-lines" type of information that cannot be obtained in an application for admission.

This student portrays his knowledge of the Drucker School and its ideals as well as how he will personally contribute and adapt to the culture of the school. Through abstract traits, the student defines what those qualities (leadership, attitude, creativity, sense of responsibility, big-picture concept, and charisma) mean in the world of business. He then elaborates further to explain how, through specific examples, he will contribute those qualities to make the classroom a well-fostered learning environment.

The Drucker MBA Academic Committee is interested in knowing what strengths and skills a student will bring to the classroom, as much of the Drucker curriculum is integrative and interactive among other students and faculty. It should also be noted that as an academic committee we strive to enroll students who will not only bring much to the classroom but also gain much from the classroom. This student gives a very clear picture that his admission into the MBA program would be mutually beneficial to himself and the Drucker School.

Additionally, through his response to the importance of a Drucker MBA, it is obvious that this student understands the value of brand recognition by acknowledging the name and reputation of the Drucker MBA. As an academic committee, we want students who will be proud of their efforts during MBA course work and who will take that pride into their leadership business roles. We want alumni who will support the school in more than monetary ways. Alumni can play key roles in public relations, recruitment, and overall advancement of the Drucker reputation. This student appears to understand that we are "A Different School of Thought," and he believes those differences will be worth the investment of his education.

Essay #2

Personal Statement: What special contributions do you believe you will bring to the Drucker School? Why is a Drucker School MBA important to you?

What do I bring to the Drucker School?

As an undergraduate, there was a schism between humanities and business majors. We were completely polarized into either the pre-professional group or the liberal arts group and the most common response to hearing that my major was Comparative Literature was the question, "What are you going to do with that?" Even then, I felt strongly that the pursuit of humanities was worthwhile because, through it, I learned about life and about people. I was introduced to interdisciplinary education through [University A's Honors Program], and then was drawn to an interdisciplinary major that emphasized critical thinking. It took some time working to really answer the looming question of what I was going to do with my degree. But, after a few years, I was able to make the connection between business and my humanities education and realize that it takes a good understanding of people, as well as an interest in them, to be a good manager and effective leader.

Another challenge of this system is that there is little regular employee evaluation, which is compounded by our president living in New York. I have taken a leadership role in addressing many of the human issues, from showing appreciation to employees and customers, suggesting actions to help employees grow and develop and mediating disputes, while trying not to violate our structure and philosophies to administering benefits. Recently, we completed a job at a university in Utah in which we applied our technology to a new market for the first time building a specialized lab for an electron microscope. The timeline demands and scheduling, plus the stress of the learning curve on a new project, created a dispute between two employees who happen to be brothers. One, uncharacteristically, left the job completely and came home early, while the other finished the job. When they each came to me to tell their side and get my support, I was able to listen and be empathic without taking sides, and then suggest that they think about what they could change to make to prevent the situation from reoccurring. I was happy with how I handled the situation, and how they handled it. They have made some adjustments for subsequent jobs and I have made some suggestions for each of their continued development.

I am very proud of the manager I have matured into over the last several years. In my early twenties, I believed that career advancement was best achieved by moving around every couple of years and trying new things. More recently I have come to believe that real personal growth is achieved more by staying and putting down roots, than by moving. In a sense both perspectives are valid. By moving around and trying different positions, I gained great technical skills and an understanding of many different industries and departments. By staying in a position that offered little external structure, I learned to motivate and manage myself and to build solid relationships. Ultimately, it is the combination of technical skills with personal skills that will determine my success as a manager. At this point in my life, I can say with confidence that I have developed both skill sets and am ready to pursue a degree in management.

Why a Drucker MBA?

My interest in a Drucker MBA originated from personal recommendations of people I have greatly respected. I had initially heard of the Claremont colleges in high school. The teachers and administration of the private academy I attended strongly advocated Claremont because of the personal attention and focus on teaching. Later, when working for [Company B], one of the managers who happened to be an alumnus encouraged me to consider the program. Most recently, I consulted my boss' wife who is an Executive Vice President of Strategic Technology at [Company C]. Of all of the schools I was considering, her strongest support went to the Drucker program. I found that especially surprising since she herself had earned her Executive MBA at [University D].

After I began researching the Drucker program for myself, I was drawn to interdisciplinary approach and the concept of business management as a liberal art. I believe the philosophies of the school closely fit my own, as I do not believe that business can be successful and ethical when isolated from the human elements. Quite early in my career, I went through layoffs with three different companies. One company distinguished itself in my mind by continuing to hire up until the day prior to the layoffs with no regard for the effect on the employees. Since then I have been fortunate to work at companies such as [Company B] that took great pride in their management skills and philosophy, even when faced with difficult decisions.

Because of my liberal arts background I feel much more at home with the Drucker Program than with some other programs I have investigated. Even through the application and information gathering process, the experience has been much more personal than with other schools. The core philosophy mixed with distinguished faculty and thoughtful support programs makes the Drucker MBA program very rich. Possibly the biggest point of differentiation, and thus the biggest attractor, is the focus on leadership and management. These skills are so absolutely timeless that whatever happens in the economy, whatever changes arise over the next twenty years, they will be excellent preparation. Accounting or marketing practices may change over time, new technology comparable to the internet may emerge, and the investment to acquire leadership and management skills will still have been well worth the investment.

Critique

The academic committee is able to gain a sense of the student's personality from this essay. It is critical for the Peter F. Drucker Graduate School of Management to enroll students who are pursuing an MBA for reasons greater than increased salary and career advancement. Because the Drucker MBA has a liberal arts approach to management, the school aims to graduate students who are socially responsible and have goals of becoming leaders and managers. The Drucker School is a school of management, not just business. The student who wrote this personal statement is clearly focused on becoming a better manager, not just advancing her career or salary.

This student comes from a nonbusiness academic background but has worked in business for ten years. With this type of background, the student can bring a different perspective to the classroom that will increase its diversity and perspective. She understands the importance of building business skills to complement her nonbusiness background. The academic committee also notes that this student has given very specific examples of goals she has set and of ways she has practiced her personal leadership skills. It is valuable that she realizes that rectifying the weaknesses in her technical skills can make her a better leader and manager. Thus, the classroom will lend itself to teaching those technical skills and will give opportunities for her to practice those skills. The Drucker MBA program is a highly integrated team atmosphere both inside and outside the classroom. This student shows that she works well in a team environment by giving specific examples.

Time management is a critical skill for part-time students who also work full-time. Based on personal examples of things this student manages in her career, we recognize that she can successfully handle the demands of working full-time while attending school part-time. Additionally, she explains her understanding of the Drucker School and why we are "A Different School of Thought." This is imperative because students who enroll in the Drucker MBA program need to understand that we educate future business managers and leaders. We take a different approach to education by providing a small, personal environment taught by world-renowned faculty. Students who understand and appreciate this approach reap incredible benefits from their Drucker MBA.

DARTMOUTH
TUCK SCHOOL OF BUSINESS

Note: The four Tuck essays included are each in response to this question. See page 44 for detailed information.

Question: Please respond fully but concisely to the following essay. Although there are no restrictions for the length of your response, most applicants use 1,000 words or fewer. Your response should be typed and double-spaced, with your name on each sheet. There is no right or wrong answer.

A well-known, multinational mining company has a long-term contract to extract precious metals in an impoverished region of a developing country. Over the past decade, the operation has proven very profitable to the company. Recently, there have been peaceful, but highly disruptive, protests by members of communities adjacent to the company's property. The ruling military dictatorship has been unresponsive in meeting the local communities' needs. The local communities are now demanding a share of the mining operation's profits in the form of approximately U.S. $8 million to provide clean water and basic sanitation for the surrounding villages.

You have recently been promoted and sent to this country as the expatriate general manager responsible for the operation. The mine is assessed U.S. $20 million in annual taxes by the local government. This year you will show a U.S. $50 million after-tax profit if you elect not to address the request of the local community. Your team has worked very hard this year. A U.S. $50 million profit is the minimum level to ensure that your team meets its bonus plan.

- *Provide an analysis of your options.*

- *Describe what you would do.*

- *Discuss the rationale for your choice.*

- *Address your plan to communicate with any constituent affected by your decision.*

Essay #1

"Argue for your limitations and they're yours."—Anonymous

A great leader possesses two indispensable traits: the ability to recognize his or her own limitations, and the ability to recognize the motivations and competencies of others that can help exceed these limitations. Coupled, these traits provide a powerful capacity for problem-solving. As the manager of a mining operation in a developing country, my problem-solving skills are now challenged.

MINING OPERATION—SITUATION ANALYSIS

Assumptions

To better define the parameters within which I am working, I make the following assumptions. My team is composed primarily of ex-patriates in management, with local citizens comprising the balance of the workforce. The bonus plan allows managerial participation only. The dictator is concerned with holding onto power, and maintaining his $20M tax revenue. We are nearing the end of the fiscal year; therefore, I can forecast that the $50M minimum profit will be achieved, if unforeseen costs are not incurred. Finally, the $8M demanded by the community has been confirmed as the amount required in order to meet their priority needs, which are, in fact, basic sanitation and clean water.

Business Strengths

The operation is productive enough to achieve $50M in after-tax profit this year, allowing us to benefit from the bonus plan, which enhances management's productivity incentive. Ties to the surrounding community exist through local employees. The government is a stakeholder via its tax revenue. My team possesses managerial and cultural experience specific to operating in this community.

Business Weaknesses

The community sees relatively little benefit from the operations of this profitable foreign corporation. This inequality, combined with government disinterest, has led to operational disruptions. The government is unconcerned with community needs, yet we pay $20M in annual taxes. The bonus does not benefit most local workers, hence, they have little productivity incentive. Although they represent a tie to the community, this is not currently leveraged. A lack of clean water and sanitation results in chronic illness amongst employees, detracting from productivity. Finally, the company lacks technical knowledge and experience in community development.

Opportunities

Several significant opportunities exist. Creation of a profit-sharing plan to include the local workers could create incentive and provide added economic benefit to the community. My company is also afforded the opportunity to exercise social leadership—by making a real difference in citizens' lives. This could conceivably increase productivity through improved employee health and morale. In addition, protecting the government's tax revenue could act as leverage to induce positive government action.

Threats

Protests grow in frequency and severity, disrupting business operations. Community illness continues to threaten productivity. Bad publicity surrounding the situation leads to poor employee morale and decreased value in the eyes of shareholders. A looming threat is the potential precedent set by paying the full $8M. In this scenario, the bonus plan goes untapped, and assuming full corporate responsibility leads to further demands, by the same communities, and by different ones—in my company and in others. My operation's potential profit would already have decreased by 16%. Similar events throughout my company and others would be financially unsustainable. It could present insurmountable obstacles to doing business in developing countries, that is, if limits are not set.

Resulting Elements of Plan

—Sustain and even increase productivity by:

  • Rewarding management this year with the bonus.

  • Creating a profit-sharing plan to provide added incentive for local workers (contingent on increased productivity and the resulting profits).

  • Improving health and morale through community development efforts.

—Decrease the risk of further operational disruption.

—Share accountability for community development amongst different stakeholders, not solely the company.

A SUSTAINABLE SOLUTION

I propose a partnership of different parties that will share accountability for addressing community needs. A pilot program will be implemented, to identify and address the highest-priority need. The stakeholders in this program will be my operation, corporate headquarters, an NGO, and the government. The company will contribute funds, as will, if at all possible, the government. The NGO will provide technical expertise. My operation will aid in project management, in conjunction with community representatives and the NGO. The community will provide an in-kind labor contribution. In addition, a profit-sharing plan will be added for the employees, starting with the new budget cycle.

Importantly, the company's initial financial contribution should come from corporate, not the local branch. This is because the financial structure does not take into account these unforeseen costs, which are necessary to operate effectively in the country. A cost-benefit analysis should be provided, showing that this contribution can increase productivity and minimize costly risks such as operational disruptions, bad press, weak employee incentive, and poor morale—all of which lead to reduced operating margins. Another selling point is the publicity possible: our corporate collaboration with the social sector, working to improve lives in the communities in which we operate. This publicity could increase employee morale and shareholder value.

Corporate action takes time. The argument to decouple the "social costs" from the financial structure was made. If the change is not fast enough, my branch will provide the first installment for the pilot, from next year's budget. Any perceived time lapse will be made palatable to the community via the expansion of the bonus plan and through strong community engagement in planning for the pilot. Initial funds will also pay for NGO selection. Once identified, the NGO will be convinced to participate because of the benefit to the community, but also the unique partnership—an opportunity to tap into the private sector to accomplish its own goals.

My branch will act quickly on several fronts. Strong links to the community will be developed through local workers, who will act as community representatives, and help identify others from outside the company. Through these links the community will be engaged. With the NGO and branch management, they will prioritize what portion of the project should first be implemented and how. The sell to the community should be based on the fact that the pilot program is a necessary first step. The community will benefit from it and the proposed profit-sharing plan. If successful, further projects may be possible.

The government must be persuaded to provide partial funding. This should be presented as an opportunity to increase government popularity, e.g. security, and ensure its continued tax revenue. The story line: their lack of participation will make country operations increasingly difficult financially, and possibly unsustainable. Diplomacy (e.g. the local US ambassador) should be used to apply cautious pressure to the government using this stance.

In the long run, corporate can decide whether to expand the program. In this case, foundations and aid organizations could be contacted as potential donors. Implementing the pilot program gives corporate time to evaluate the issues, identify other donors, and reform the financial structure appropriately. Insight will be gained from the pilot, aiding their decision-making.

This collaboration creates value beyond what I alone could have created. Each constituency contributes different, but complementary abilities. Corporate social responsibility is acknowledged, but limited by sharing accountability with other parties. Profits are maximized by quelling operational disruptions, maintaining and expanding worker incentives, and creating strong employee and community morale.

CONCLUSION

The leaders of multinational corporations have the opportunity to enhance operations, and financial performance, by addressing social issues. Partnering with social-sector organizations can be an effective model for doing so. It is a way of exceeding corporations' own limitations and effecting positive social change. Those who do not address social concerns will increasingly find their financial concerns are at risk. Kofi Annan stated this eloquently, "Thriving markets and human security go hand in hand; without one, we will not have the other."

Critique

This essay presents a clear, thoughtful analysis of the situation, with a creative, compassionate, and mutually beneficial solution. This candidate's solution depicts a realistic situation of working with the corporate headquarters, a nongovernmental organization, the government, and local citizens. Throughout the essay, the candidate maintains a serious yet optimistic tone, often referring to the dilemma as an "opportunity."

Essay #2

My past experiences are surprisingly relevant in my analysis of this case. As a civil engineer, I am well aware of the importance of clean water and basic sanitation infrastructure. While on active duty with the U.S. Army, I worked as an officer in [Location A], [Location B] and [Location C] in positions that involved a significant amount of community interaction. In [Location A] I was an environmental advisor to the General responsible for all U.S. Army facilities. I managed environmental programs and responded to [Location A residents'] complaints about sewage runoff into local rivers, hazardous waste spills and leaking underground oil storage tanks. The U.S. Army hires many local civilians to supplement the active duty and U.S. civilian staff, so I received more than enough feedback from local sources. In [Location B], I worked as a construction equipment maintenance officer and frequently traveled to [City A, Location B] and [City B, Location B] to purchase repair parts, which taught me the importance of maintaining good relationships with local businesspeople. In [Location C] on a peacekeeping tour, I planned future road and bridge repairs, which were often restricted by U.S. policies forbidding nation building. Each repair project had to be justified by military patrol requirements rather than local community desires, although projects that met both needs were definitely the most rewarding.

As a student of cultural anthropology, I've studied the mechanics of societies, hierarchy of needs, issues of globalization and perceptions of wealth, poverty and happiness. Although specific cultural details in this case are not presented, a relativistic analysis of the situation would yield some explanations for the conflicting views of the mining company, the local community and the dictatorship, all of which are worth considering before making any decisions. And as a current resident of [Location D] and former resident of [Location E], I've become accustomed to living and thriving in multi-cultural environments.

The following are the potential courses of action I would consider as general manager of the mine. Some are mutually exclusive while others could be performed in unison. I've divided these courses of action into three categories: those involving the company directly, those focusing on the local people and those involving outside agencies.

Company Options

- Pay for the infrastructure work directly as an operating expense. Charging the $8M as a direct expense will only decrease bonuses by 10%, given a revised pre-tax profit of $62M, therefore the monetary impact is not as severe as it initially appears. This option will give me the most control over how the money is disbursed, who gets the construction contracts and how quickly the work is accomplished. Future profits should pay back the $5M expense many times over. Conversely, this action could lead to future community demands that are increasingly outrageous.

- An extreme option is to withhold $8M in taxes and use it to fund the local community's infrastructure projects. This will most certainly enrage the country's dictatorship with potentially dire consequences for the mine, but it may also force the country to re-evaluate how its citizens' needs are being met.

- Shut down the mine temporarily or even permanently. This option will demonstrate the mining company's resolve to avoid being subjected to extortion. The obvious disadvantage is that future potential profits will be forfeited. But the ethics of the company will not be comprised and the locals may decide to work with, rather than against, future multi-national entities.

People Options

- Coordinate a meeting between local community leaders and my management team. Listen to the local leaders first and consider their ideas, but also explain that it is not the company's direct responsibility to provide for all community needs. Past company leaders may have been ignoring community complaints for years so listening now may lead to a lessening of demands. A risk is that the locals may become more frustrated, disruptive or even violent.

- Increase the wages paid to local employees of the mine so they are well above the average local wages and establish a management-training program for the best local employees. Assuming a significant percentage of the mine's labor force are local nationals, this should help placate them by injecting more money into their community and by increasing opportunities for advancement. A disadvantage is that the increased labor costs may erode profits in both the short and long term.

- Institute a community partnership initiative. Beyond basic infra-structure — schools, police forces and small business enterprises could also be improved through the mine's support. Although this option is the most expensive, it would certainly reverse the public's sentiments and will help create a new generation of qualified and cooperative workers.

- Hire a civil affairs expert to work with the local media and press agencies. Although this may be considered propaganda to some, the local community has likely not been given enough relevant information about how the mine operates. This may help the disgruntled locals to consider why the mining company cannot be expected to provide for every need.

Outside Agency Options

- Assuming the mine is owned by a parent company in the United States, I could contact the U.S. Embassy to ask for assistance from organizations such as the U.S. Agency for International Development (USAID) or the State Department's Office of Commercial and Business Affairs. These organizations could exert pressure on the dictatorship to allocate a portion of the $20M in taxes to local community projects or may be able to obtain outside funding for these projects. The potential disadvantages are that embassy bureaucracy may prove to be too slow and the organizations may be restricted by political or policy constraints.

- Coordinate for the infrastructure upgrades through donations to a nongovernmental organization (NGO). This will satisfy the community's needs, while providing oversight of the project by outside agencies. The collaboration of the for-profit mine and non-profit NGOs is a win-win situation for both. Sanitation and clean water directly impact the health of the local labor pool so this investment the community's health will also lead to increased future productivity.

- Contact the local military defense attaché to ask if any foreign military construction units would be interested in performing the construction work as a training exercise, which can often be done if financing is available for the project. This would bring in a foreign military presence and allow less of the $8M to be siphoned off by potentially corrupt local nationals.

After deliberation on the above options, I've decided to pursue the following four-step course of action:

1. Initially, I would avoid taking any action in response to the protests for as long as possible after my arrival at the company. Many newly appointed leaders decide to change procedures to demonstrate their authority before they are fully aware of the impact of these decisions. I would focus on reviewing all incoming and outgoing correspondence relating to the local community and would also meet with subordinate managers and the community leaders to determine the history of partnering between the mining company and the local community.

2. Since the mine has been operating for over ten years, I would evaluate the global market for the precious metals being mined and review the mine's ten-year plan for future production. Is this a high, low or average profit and revenue year for the mine? If the market looks grim and the productivity is declining, it may be a good time to suspend operations. I would also need to confirm that company bonuses do not represent a significant percentage of total compensation, because a 10% decrease in a bonus that is half of an employee's income is much more significant that a similar decrease in a bonus that represents only a quarter.

3. After gathering the above information, I would seek advice from the corporate level of the mining company, and advise them of my plans described in the next paragraph. As part of this action I would research all company, host country and international regulations that relate to this situation so I am aware of any legal constraints.

4. Assuming the above research does not yield any surprises, I would authorize the $8M infrastructure expenditure and charge it as an operating expense. The $70M profit would be reduced to $62M; the dictatorship will be paid only $17M in taxes while the mine keeps $45M in profit. Although the military and NGO construction options are valid, in this case, with disruptive protests occurring, I think these options would be too cumbersome. Therefore, I would hire a construction manager to supervise the construction contracts from within the company.

My constituents are the mine's employees, corporate executives, stockholders and directors. I would explain to them that my decision was based on thorough research and analysis of many alternatives. No company works in a vacuum, or can afford to focus solely on maximizing profits at the expense of the corporate reputation. A local population without clean water and sanitation infrastructure is not in the company's best interest, as the spread of disease will lead to decreased productivity locally with negative publicity impacts that are potentially far greater.

Bonuses are incentives that vary based on economic and social trends, and the performance of the company, but are rarely guaranteed. The biggest immediate concern for many employees will be the 10% decrease in bonuses, resulting in negative feedback and maybe even some resignations. Based on my analysis, a confrontational rather than cooperative solution to the protests would have resulted in a greater than 10% impact on future profits and bonuses. I would strive to make this clear to all constituents.

Depending on the actual success of the infrastructure improvements, I would also propose to the corporate marketing executives that our resolution of this problem be highlighted in future marketing campaigns to demonstrate the company's attention to human welfare issues. Similar campaigns by other companies have increased market share by adding intangible value to the companies' products.

Critique

This essay utilizes the candidate's skill and experience in engineering to develop a realistic, thorough, yet simple solution. The analysis demonstrates a careful and thoughtful consideration of the pros and cons of each action from the viewpoint of the various constituencies. The essay demonstrates a keen understanding of the writer's responsibilities, but doesn't downplay the needs of the locals, validating that they affect the company's success.

WHEN BAD ESSAYS HAPPEN TO GOOD PEOPLE

The following pages contain samples of real essays submitted to the Tuck School of Business that answer their killer long question. Sometimes it's easier to learn from one's mistakes. For that reason, two of the essays we offer you are poor examples of how to respond to this question.

Essay #3

Notes from the flight over:

- Analysis of my options.

Positive negotiating tools:

We have the Long-term contract as an asset.

Local government receives 20 million in taxes from mine.

Local workers comprise a meaningful percentage of local residents.

Undesirable issues:

Local communities want $8 million for clean water and basic sanitation.

Local communities protesting disruptively (assume that protests affect earnings).

Military dictatorship unresponsive to local community needs.

Option 1: Do nothing

Results: Company makes $50 million

          Team hits minimum level for bonus

          Locals still unsettled

Option 2: Bribe the Dictatorship

Actions: Pay the military to crush the protests

Results: Potentially improved profits (provided that new profits exceed bribe).

          Real problem still exists, but exacerbated by force.

          Dangerous precedent of graft.

Option 3: Negotiate w/ local gov't

Actions: Taxes aren't progressive, offer them a 1-time cut of profits above 50 mil. This would be in exchange for an up-front payment to community for water, along with a percentage of the taxes going to the community for water.

          Do some goodwill PR w/ the community (not related to the water). Keep the local government identified as the source of the clean water to avoid setting the precedent of having to pay for municipal improvements.

Results: If local govt and community play along, protests subside, and after-tax profits increase. Run the risk associated w/ the precedent of paying a higher tax rate.

What's an ex-pat GM to do?

Looking back, there was so much I didn't know at the time. Yes, of course I knew our business, and I earned my promotion. I was even fairly well versed in a pseudo-expatriate lifestyle. Still, it was a situation that required a good deal of metered guesswork, instinct if you will.

I was busy fighting my way up the chain of command in the States, and I ran into an obstacle. Nepotism can be a bitch. When you lose the opportunity for up, out starts to look pretty good. I started to fish around for opportunities elsewhere, and the board caught wind of my new direction. They slapped together this package for me, what I now refer to as the Heart of Darkness deal, and sent me on my way. Jumping to General Manager created a world of new challenges, and removed any permanent obstacles to internal ascension. The expatriate element of the deal even sounded sexy at the time.

I was on a plane with my family before I could research the new locale. I was told that my predecessor had left for personal reasons, and needed to be replaced immediately. I later determined that he had been too closely tied to the country's military dictatorship, and the board wanted him out. When I grabbed the reins, my division was finishing up Q3 and getting ready to head into the home stretch. They were on path to hit the $50 million minimum level for their bonus plan, but they had been working like dogs to get there.

Local communities had been peacefully protesting for the bulk of the year. Those protests reduced the number of able-bodied workers that we had in the mines, and restricted the daily flow of material. It was clear from the start that the division had been running at 110% of their normal efficiency in order to hit 85% of their financial goal (the minimum target for bonuses). If I would last as their GM, I would have to sweeten the pot—to reflect the work that they had been doing.

When I first analyzed the situation, I came to the following conclusions: On the positive side of the table we had a long-term contract on the land, and the local community depended heavily on us for their survival ($20 million in annual taxes, and jobs for a large percentage of the population). On the negative side we had the local community protesting for $8 million of spending in cleaner water and basic sanitation, and an unresponsive military dictatorship running the state.

On the plane flight over I hashed out three basic plans on how to approach the situation. The first and simplest idea was to stay the course. Without any change in direction, my division would hit the minimal level required to receive bonuses. The protests were of a peaceful nature, and it was unlikely that the protesters would attempt any form of local coup with the national, military dictatorship in place. While this approach was the simplest to accomplish (bearing in mind that I still had a division to run), it did nothing to address the limited bonuses that my employees would receive, or the quality of water and sanitation in the local community.

My second idea was really just a childish whim. It wouldn't take much to bribe the military dictatorship into crushing the local protests. Besides my own personal compunction against using force to quell peaceful protests, there was the slippery slope of providing graft to a military dictatorship. It was not an option. I mention it only because, as I later discovered, a similar idea was the cause of my predecessor's downfall.

After more serious thought, I came to the realization that I would never find incremental success with a company that was perceived as an outsider to the local community. While the vast majority of our workforce was comprised of local workers, very few locals were employed in managerial positions. This was a reflection of the dearth of college-educated people in the local community, but nonetheless branded us as a foreign operation.

I believe that intelligence thrives in many forms. While the local community did not have many citizens with the hard quantitative knowledge that I would need for group managers, I was certain that there would be a healthy selection of locals who could positively assist the division in relations with the community. I tasked the division's management team to find a handful of entrepreneurial and politically savvy workers, and hire them as cultural liaisons between the division and the community. At the time I didn't realize how critical this decision would be.

While I was waiting for my team to hire the new liaisons, I progressed onto what I thought would be the ultimate plan. The structure of our taxes to the local government was simple. The $20 million tax was a flat fee, levied as a form of lease payment for the land that we used. I presumed that I could dangle a progressive tax carrot in front of the local government to change the rules of the game a little. My plan was to ask the local government to front the $8 million needed to improve the water and sanitation for the local community. In exchange for that up payment, I would give them a healthy 10% cut of all after-tax profits in excess of $50 million until they received a total of $10 million. I intended to have our liaisons focus on improving the community's opinion of the company, while maintaining the view that the local government paid for the improvements. I didn't want to set the precedent of our division paying for capital improvements to the local community, for fear of an annual conscription being dedicated to that cause.

All I can say is; I am damn glad that we hired those liaisons before I put the preceding plan into action. I completely misjudged the characteristic of the local environment. My liaisons keyed me into a few pertinent facts. For starters, the local government did not have the $8 million to take care of the improvements that the community was requesting. Secondly, regardless of the wording of the deal, the local government would have balked if we started progressive tax payments one year and then tried to rescind those payments after the $10 million goal was reached. Finally, without having any association to the sanitary improvements, the local community's opinion of our company would not improve at all. I would have removed the temporary obstacle of the peaceful protests in exchange for higher taxes, and we would still be viewed as outsiders.

I spent a week trying to immerse myself in local culture and customs through lunches and dinners with our newly hired liaisons (time was short). While I didn't consider myself an expert on traditional rituals or history, after that week I had a much better appreciation for how our division could work in harmony with the local government and community.

The plan that we created went as follows: Our liaisons were personally connected with many officials in the local government. Through their personal relationships, we learned that the government would respond quickly to a public challenge to match funds for the sanitary improvements. Since the local government did not maintain surplus funds from taxation, the plan was to ask for matching funds in the form of a tax cut to the corporation. Our division would then spend the matched funds on local improvements (in the name of the government). While the liaisons assisted our PR department in crafting a local campaign to issue the challenge, I worked with our accountants to free up some assets to back the challenge.

The prior year's assessment of our physical plant had revealed that much of the capital equipment in our mining process was decades old. At the time, we used an archaic effluent treatment procedure to separate waste material from rocks potentially containing valuable ore. This outdated procedure was 70% slower than modern techniques, and dumped a considerable amount of silt into a local river. While the silt was harmless to humans, it had an aesthetically undesirable muddying affect. There was also the long-term issue of the silt collecting in the river near our plant.

Every three years we would have to have the river dredged just so we could continue operations.

Replacing the old process with a modern solution would cost $20 million dollars and take several years to fully implement. No one in the chain of management that preceded me had a long-term commitment to this division, and therefore, they applied capital improvements to areas that would yield faster results.

With the end of the year rapidly approaching, I realized that we could publicly commit to this capital improvement without booking any of the charges to the current fiscal year. By tying this capital improvement to the fund-matching challenge, we could get the local government to free up some of our tax money for other sanitary improvements. Best of all, the investment would increase our productivity, and the amortized cost could be spread out over a 10 year period.

Our liaisons helped us to design a powerful publicity campaign to chide the local government into the fund-matching plan. The liaisons knew the right tone to take with each local medium (e.g. TV, radio, newspapers, and community meetings). Within an extremely short period of time, the local government was making counter proposals publicly to call our bluff. The timing was perfect, as we had just received approval for the new effluent treatment plan. The rest is history. We presented the new effluent treatment plan to the public, and the government followed through with the matched funds (in the form of a tax cut).

The protest quickly subsided. My division was able to pull their numbers up to 92% of goal, which resulted in a healthy increase in bonuses. Within three years, the new process was fully implemented and the group was running a full 30% more efficiently than with the old process. Our relationship with the local community and government improved dramatically. We had created a precedent for reduced taxes and community improvements. Since such a large percentage of the local community worked for us, it was often possible to find ways to improve our infrastructure while benefiting the community. In the end, we had a more profitable and more stable division simply by becoming better integrated with the local community.

Of course now that everything is running smoothly I am starting to look for new places to grow. My kids are getting old enough that I want to bring them back to the States for school, and my success here has opened up some new opportunities at the head-office. I will probably move on to a new post soon. Looking back, I see what a great learning experience working in this environment was. I hope that whatever path my life follows next will prove at least as challenging.

Critique

I read this essay and wondered if it was a joke. The essay attempts to craft the answer in a fictional narrative, but instead depicts the writer as insensitive and thoughtless — the antithesis of the characteristics that Tuck is seeking. The fact that this candidate mentions "pay the military to crush the protests" as a potential option offers a window of insight into his character. Other tongue-in-cheek, colloquial expressions such as "nepotism can be a bitch," "sweeten the pot," and "call our bluff" are apparently meant to be humorous, but instead depict the applicant as immature — somewhere between not serious and ridiculous. This candidate's solution for the mining dilemma is based on forming a liaison with the local government to "chide the local government into the fund-matching plan" — not a very realistic or creative solution, and one that shifts the negotiations from the GM to the liaison. The essay concludes with the message that now that the problem is solved, he will be moving on, likely back to the United States and a new, advanced post. Throughout his essay, this potential candidate presents himself as not serious, vulgar, flip, arrogant, and uncommitted.

Essay #4

Business leaders often come across different situations with an ethical dilemma being involved. Successful leader should be able to find or to create a new choice not obvious at first sight. Besides, leader should consider ethics as a part of the equation, as an aspect of the management process.

First of all, we should identify the stakeholders. They are my team, local communities, ruling dictatorship and my company shareholders. My ultimate goal is to find an ethical and mutually beneficial solution.

In general, I see the three variants of possible action:

My first variant is to address the needs of local community by giving the money required for satisfying their needs. In this case I'm giving up the interests of my team. In fact, our excellent results this year became possible only due to our team spirit and emotional momentum built. In other words, I should do my best to satisfy my team. In fact, an esprit de corps is at stake. Besides, there is a great risk that talented employees left without appropriate incentives will leave the company for job that pays better probably in another country. This in its turn will lead to lower profits next year.

The second variant is to ignore the interests of local community and pay the bonuses to the team. But our business cannot exist without local community that is the source of workforce for the company. Moreover, our company is the part of local social environment. Ignorance of the local needs will break the harmony of our business "ecosystem." Tension will grow and our operations will become less efficient or even impossible as a result.

My third option is to decline the tax imposed by the government or to dispute the amount to be paid. However, these solutions may turn out to be dangerous both for me and for the company's property. In this case, the ruling military dictatorship is likely either to cancel the contract or to hamper the progress of our business.

To make the right decision and elaborate an action plan as well as plan of communication with all parties involved, let us consider all pros and cons.

It is usually very difficult to change the rules of team compensation in a large multi- national company. For instance, [Company A] in Russia alone profits more than U.S. $50 million per year, which is less than 1% of the company's total net profit. Certainly, nobody will change the corporate compensation policy if local team doesn't meet the goal. Having U.S. $8 million paid to communities, I can try to save the team bonus but company management will hardly compromise with me. Though there is a small probability of such an outcome. Anyway, there are two options: either team receives bonus or not. Keeping in mind my strategy to avoid dilemmas, I have to retain the profit level required for the bonus to be paid. If all this fails and my efforts turn out to be in vain, I will resort to the company's management so that the problem could be approached as an exception to the company's rules.

With just bare figures in mind, not paying money for the local needs looks very attractive. In Russia for instance, corporate management style today is far from ethical. As recently as two or three years ago there was a miner's camp in front of Russian Government House. In such a way mines workers protested against delays in wage payments which exceeded twelve month. This particular example shows that ethical dilemmas in Russia are often being resolved not in favor of ethics. Being a well-educated and intelligent person I understand very well that such social unconsciousness is one of the main problems of developing Russia. I don't want to seem cynical, but probably being ethical pays back and no doubt gives chance to sleep better. That's why I need to do my best to satisfy the demands of local community because that's my duty as a member of prospering society.

Turning back to our problem, I want to emphasize that there are lots of ways to be socially conscious without paying U.S.$8 million right now. People have been waiting for help for a long time why won't they wait for one more quarter? The good idea is negotiating with community leaders the donations plan that will assume not lump, but monthly or quarterly payments effective from the next quarter. Acting this way I'm securing my team bonuses and achieve ethical balance and harmony in the business "ecosystem." At the same time it is crucial to persuade management and shareholders that local communities should be supported to provide an effective business process of an enterprise.

To rebel against draconian taxes is not as absurdly as it may seem at first sight. Actually it is the local authorities that should take care of the people. I don't want to say that tax should not be paid, but it is necessary to discuss the purposes of the subsequent spending of the money collected. In fact, such close interaction with the government should be a part of our integration into the local social life. Being a part of the area infrastructure that gives jobs and contributes to the country's budget we have the right to influence the funds allocation. In developed countries this right is usually exercised by lobbying but under military dictatorship the only way to do this is to make a deal with the dictator.

Satisfying the local needs by the government is the most desired outcome. We have killing argument to use in our speech: we can raise the dictatorship's reputation. All we have to do is to declare that the dictatorship demonstrates exemplary social consciousness with respect to its people. This declaration will be heard as we have an authority recognized in the World community.

To summarize all said above, I see the following action plan:

First of all, I'll try to convince the government to take financial responsibility for local demands using the arguments discussed. Partial compensation of local needs is also good deal because it'll give us time—at least couple of quarters. If it fails, I will resort to the second step.

The second step is negotiation with local leaders aiming at postponing of our financial help. I can also propose different "indirect" compensations for local community. I can create more jobs for local people by opening new departments, for instance, local company for our mining machinery services. I can found joined committee for local area development that will be financed not only by our company but also by the government, and different international funds. I can implement new technologies of water and air purification for the region using the experience of our other branches worldwide.

If all this doesn't work, I'll try to obtain the bonus from the company on exceptional basis assuming that we are giving the money to satisfy the demands of the society.

After all, if all my efforts are in vain I'll pay the bonus to my team because first of all I'm the leader of the team and its normal functioning is my responsibility given by my management and shareholders.

Critique

This essay suffers from a host of problems. The candidate demonstrates an unrealistic assessment of the situation and his abilities. If the writer's initial plan, which involves delay tactics, doesn't work, he states, "I'll pay the bonus to my team." Statements such as "keeping in mind my strategy to avoid dilemmas," "not paying money for the local needs looks very attractive," "probably being ethical pays back and no doubt gives chance to sleep better," and "People have been waiting for help for a long time why won't they wait for one more quarter?" present a character who is incapable of solving problems, unethical, and insensitive.

MASSACHUSETTS INSTITUTE OF TECHNOLOGY
SLOAN SCHOOL OF MANAGEMENT

Essay #1

Question: Please give us an example of when you exhibited creativity in a personal or professional setting. Please describe your thoughts and actions. (500-800 words)

"We have a perceptual problem around efficacy," said the packaged goods company president. It was my first day on a new assignment for their hair thickening product, and he was explaining that their launch had been followed by a year of flat sales. "Although the product has clinically-proven efficacy, centuries of snake oil salesmen have created incredible skepticism in the market." His challenge: redefine efficacy to distance ourselves from "potions and lotions" and increase market share.

After a month of brainstorming ways to convey efficacy, we conducted one-on-one interviews to test our ideas. Man after blading man expressed angst over his hair problems, but none of them had done anything more advanced than the combover. "You see, we need to convince them there's a product good enough to warrant doing something," the president said.

I was not convinced. The more we tweaked the message to stress clinical efficacy, the more we had to caveat it to satisfy the FDA; the more we touted real results, the more we sounded like a late-night Infomercial. In my mind, we were just undermining our own efficacy message. We needed to find another angle to attack this problem.

While the client continued testing messages, I took a week to reflect and explore. Looking for insights, I studied [Company A]'s success, learned the psychology of plastic surgery, and read a history of hair color marketing in The New Yorker. It was in the article that I found an inspiration, for it described how [Company B] refocused its marketing on emotional rather than physical benefits—hence the tag line "Why? Because I'm worth it!" Reflecting on this example, it occurred to me that perhaps we were focused too much on what was going on top of men's heads, and not enough on what was going on inside them.

Curious to explore this further, I recruited a psychologist specializing in body image to review the interview transcripts with me at my office. What we uncovered was surprising—almost all men have high levels of concern when they first notice their hair thinning. However, over a short period of time, their concern fades due to internal acceptance, external reinforcement of worth ("honey, I love you just the way you are"), and general aversion to appearing vain. As a result, most men are resigned to their fate before they have time to do any serious exploration of options.

With this information, I reframed the question from "how do we redefine efficacy" to "how do we get men to act before apathy sets in." To answer this question, I used existing research to develop a quantitative, visual description of how men flow through the entire decision process. Along with the decision steps, I showed the most frequently mentioned reinforcers or blockers of action at each step in the process.

Although this system dynamics approach is typically used for complicated industrial problems, it was perfect for this puzzle. First, it made it simple to see the apathy cycle we had identified. Second, it highlighted that men who broke the cycle most often did so because of the encouragement of a friend, not the existence of effective products. Third, it showed that the overwhelming benefit to men who had acted was a sense of control—regrowing hair was an aspiration, but taking control was their inspiration.

These findings suggested three important steps. First, we had to reach men before they became apathetic. Second, we had to assure them it was "normal" to do something about hair thinning. And third, we had to emphasize that taking action was taking control. To bastardize [Company B]—"Why? Because it beats sitting back like a defeated old man!"

When I shared this new interpretation with the president, he understood my earlier skepticism of the efficacy dilemma. Within two months we replaced the efficacy-focused advertising with a new campaign emphasizing the importance of acting early to treat thinning hair, and the associated feeling of control it creates. In addition, we adjusted our media purchases to hit younger men who were early in the recognition to resignation cycle. Finally, we developed a program encouraging existing users to share their experiences with friends.

Through creative approaches to the problem, I drove significant change. At a product level, within a year sales grew by 18% and the average customer age dropped from 33 to 28—a good indicator that we were driving men to act sooner. At a company level, I introduced new tools and disciplines which have been successfully applied to other tough marketing problems. And at a societal level, I helped thousands of men find a better hairstyle than the combover!

Critique

This one was fun to read and is a great example of working smarter, not harder. The student's task seemed like a typical consulting engagement, but he was able to look at an old problem with new eyes. As he phrased it, he "reframed the question."

Creativity is often thought of as a moment of inspiration; in this case, the candidate accompanied that moment with some impressive follow-through. He hired the right kinds of experts, modeled the decision process of the customer, and adjusted strategy based on his findings. Intuitive leaps are important, but so too is the ability to implement, and this student showed both. Wouldn't you want him on your team?

Essay #2

Question: Please describe an impact you have had on a group or organization.

I joined the Board of Directors of [Company A] in 2001 for a two-year term. [Company A] is a non-profit treatment, education and research center that provides traditional Chinese medicine health care to approximately 700 people each month. Most of the center's clients are low-income or homeless and suffer from life-threatening illnesses such as Hepatitis C, HIV, AIDS—and Cancer. The medical attention that people receive at [Company A] supplements the traditional treatments they receive and allays the severe side effects that accompany such treatments.

When I joined, [Company A] was in a dire financial situation. California's budget for AIDS research had been slashed and the public funding that had provided 45% of the organization's budget in 2000 would only cover 20% in 2001, at the same level of operation.

As a Board member, I focused on development, with the goal of ensuring the organization's long-term success. My first action was to identify and cultivate individuals and foundations capable and likely of meeting the organization's operating expenses in the short-term. After developing a list of potential investors and in collaboration with the Executive Director and founder, I developed a three-year $400,000 proposal to the California Endowment to fund ongoing initiatives.

As is the case with many community-based nonprofit organizations, the staff and board at [Company A] were unaccustomed to tailoring a pitch for their programs and had an opportunistic approach to fundraising. They had never had the bandwidth to aggressively seek funding and were unable to communicate about their work with people who weren't already familiar with Chinese medicine. With little background in the subject, I was especially sensitive to this tendency and set out to remedy it. I led an informal media and communications training for the Board to help them craft the pitch for their work and develop the proposal for [Endowment A]. The training

I conducted generated incredible momentum around fundraising and jumpstarted the Board of Directors. If the proposal we developed is approved, this funding will support [Company A] after my term has expired. I f not, the process of developing a pitch and creatively raising funds will still have sparked action on the part of Board members who had long since stagnated in their roles.

At each Board meeting, I update the Board on fundraising progress and lobby for a stronger focus on fund development in this difficult economic climate. Ancillary conversations with individual Board members have ensued and I finally am seeing the results. Raising funds has become a focus for the board and long-term funding strategy has become a reality during my tenure. Since I've given them communication tools and encouragement, the Board has taken on aspects of fundraising from which they had previously shied away. Surprisingly enough, the work has become more fun as well—we have rallied around the common goal of raising money for [Company A]'s important work. In this situation, I am most proud of the fact that my impact is going beyond the immediate task at hand and is actually affecting behavioral change.

My work has also led to bringing back to life a nascent Cancer support program. The staff at [Company A] had never developed a long-term project with measurable impacts and needed guidance in order to sustain a fledgling program. I coached the Executive Director, presented a strategy to the Board, and created a map for a program that now serves cancer survivors in two low-income San Francisco neighborhoods, Bayview and the Mission, where residents have some of the highest rates of Cancer in California and the lowest rates of health care access. To date, the program has served almost 100 people and is receiving significant recognition and support from the Western medical community.

With state funding evaporating and demand for services skyrocketing, [Company A] still is in a difficult situation. I believe that strategically raising funds and developing programs are critical to surviving this challenging time and I've made it my mandate to communicate these priorities to the Board of Directors. Despite the fact that I only recently joined the Board and that my experience with Chinese medicine is minimal, I've succeeded in making the organization more financially viable and effectively managed.

Critique

This essay is a wonderful example of how people can highlight leadership and organizational skills outside their work environment. So often, applicants think of community service as a box to be checked rather than a chance to really show their stuff.

It's clear in this essay that the applicant cares deeply about the work of the group, but she doesn't spend a lot of time just talking about that; she takes us through a compelling situation and describes how her actions had an impact. We always ask ourselves, Would this situation have turned out differently if the applicant wasn't there? The answer in this case is an obvious yes. She also does a very good job of focusing on the context of the situation—the challenges faced by the organization, the ambiguity inherent in cross-cultural situations—without being accusatory. This is impressive.

I'd ask all applicants to look at how succinctly this candidate describes the situation and how much time she devotes to articulating her process. Our job as admissions officers is to search for the "how" behind the "what," and this student made the "how" very clear. You can easily imagine her leading another organization to enhanced success.

Rutgers—The State University of New Jersey, Rutgers Business School

ESSAY #1

Question: Describe an ethical dilemma and how you resolved it.

Within the past year I faced a situation where I had to quickly decide whether to compromise my ethics to aid my company in its attempt to win a much-coveted new business pitch. My decision not only impacted me, but also my colleagues, and could, quite possibly, have impacted my company's reputation and revenue.

An understanding of the context and pressures involved best sets the stage for my quandary. My healthcare communications company performs project-based services for pharmaceutical clients. As such, we often participate in new business pitches where our team will present our thinking, strategies, and concepts to the potential client with the goal of winning the business. Preparation for these pitches is intense, involving many hours spent researching the product and its market, analyzing the competitive landscape and unique product issues, brainstorming strategies and tactics to meet the identified needs, crafting creative concepts, and rehearsing for the presentation itself. All the above are typically done within two weeks leading to a one- to two-hour pitch. In essence, a pitch is a high-intensity event where my team is challenged to create the most innovative solutions and present in a way that wows the client, outclasses the competition, and secures additional income for the company.

I discovered competitive intelligence at a pitch purely by chance. While the client took a break and we set up in the room, I discovered our two competitors' pitch binders on a chair. Pitch binders traditionally include a company's strategies, tactics, and, more importantly, a proposed budget for the client's consideration. Herein lay my dilemma.

My quandary was this: should I a) quickly peruse the competitors' pitch binders, allowing me to then tailor my own team's presentation, thereby gaining a competitive advantage, or b) leave the binders untouched, ignore the opportunity availed, and trust in my team's strengths to win the pitch and beat the competition? With my colleagues shortly aware of what caught my attention, the temptation and pressure to peruse the competitive binders heightened.

I faced a dilemma in a situation that did not afford lengthy consideration. I had to make a firm decision quickly and convince my colleagues of the ethics of the decision, whichever path I chose. In the end, I determined to act upon my basic instinct that it was unfair and ethically wrong for my team to review the competitors' pitch materials. I made a decision I was ethically comfortable with and my faith in our capabilities and strategies for the client won over the temptation of an easy assist. With my internal ethical conflict decided, how then to convince my colleagues not to peruse the binders themselves?

My next challenge was to state my own personal stance and call upon the ethics of my teammates to make similar decisions. Not only was I one of six presenters, but I was also not the most senior individual. My superior could have made a different decision, which would carry more weight and sway my colleagues. I therefore determined to convince my superior of the merits of my decision to create a strong voice with the team. By acknowledging the temptation, yet clearly stating my thought process and the questionable ethics, I successfully convinced my superior and the rest of the team followed our lead and concurred. I left the binders where I found them, reassured the team that we could and would win the pitch unaided, and proceeded with the presentation as planned when the client returned.

In the end, my team prevailed in winning the business—without the assistance of a peek at the competitions' materials. I have never questioned my decision, and aspire to adhere to my ethics in the future as well as I did in this situation. Had we not won the business, I would still be confident that my actions and those of my team were both ethical and fair.

Critique

The Rutgers Business School graduate admission process does not, in general, require an interview. Therefore, the essay takes on an even greater importance by providing the admissions committee with the opportunity to obtain a sense of the applicant's writing and critical thinking skills. At the same time, it offers the applicant an opportunity to showcase those talents.

The term "business ethics" was once considered an oxymoron. In today's business environment the exact opposite is true, and companies, as well as graduate programs, are looking for individuals with strong ethical and moral character. Our essay topic is by choice very broad. We are looking for not only the identification of the ethical dilemma, but also the candidate's reasons for choosing this particular example and the resolution of the problem.

The candidate in this example faced the age-old dilemma regarding the potential acquisition of competitive intelligence. In business, does the end always justify the means? Is winning the only important criterion, regardless of the cost? Clearly, for this individual, the answer was no. In making that decision, she also exhibited a strong faith in her product, her company, and the presentation skills of her colleagues and herself. This is particularly important to our program, which demands team presentations and cooperative efforts throughout the MBA.

The applicant also offered a glimpse into her leadership skills, another area that we consider important in the review process. After making her own decision as to the proper way to proceed, she also had to convince her senior colleague and the rest of her team to follow suit. This took courage and conviction, strengths that will serve her well in our rigorous program.

We also evaluate the writing skills of the candidate. Business communication is an important skill and a required element of our MBA program. This individual wrote succinctly and on-topic without overembellishment, abilities that will be appreciated by both professors and employers.

Essay #2

Question: Describe an ethical dilemma and how you resolved it.

One of the first lessons I learned as a consultant is to maintain the integrity of the client-consultant relationship. The relationship is a fragile one, with the client revealing the inner workings of their operations, politics, and strategies to perfect strangers. While client confidentiality rules are most times clear cut, maintaining client integrity becomes a bit more complex when the client is your own firm.

Upon graduation from [College A] in 1998, I sought to apply my economics degree and math minor in a challenging business position. I accepted a position at [Company B]'s Economic Analysis Group (EAG) in [Location C], the global headquarters for [Company B]'s transfer pricing practice. Transfer pricing is the economic principle that exploits differences in global corporate tax rates to maximize profit within multinational corporations. My role as a research analyst was to assist in justifying the prices charged across borders among subsidiaries of large multinationals and maximizing global corporate profits within the rules of global tax laws.

The EAG was a relatively small group by [Company B]'s standards, and communication was very open among the 40 professionals. It was tradition to circle the large boardroom table every Friday morning during staff meetings to share tales of complex transfer pricing issues. Most managers and partners paid little attention to the analysts as they described their projects. Six months into my tenure, however, the managers and partners began to look up from their scribbles and notes and pay close attention when it came my turn to speak. They all knew that I had been assigned a highly sensitive and "secret" project—one that directly affected their compensation.

I joined [Company B] at an interesting time in the firm's history. [Company B] and [Company D] had already announced their split, but the corporate divorce had only recently made it into arbitration. [Company B] was looking to get as much money as possible for grooming [Company D] into the firm that it had become. I became part of that unique firm history when I was assigned my most delicate project—valuing the historic split between [Company B] and [Company D].

The project itself was not much different than other transfer pricing studies that I had performed. What was different, however, was the secretive nature of the assignment. Only one manager and I knew the details of the engagement in the [Location C] office. I was instructed by the legal department in [Location E] not to discuss the matter with anyone, especially the partners within the firm.

The [Company B] partners had a personal interest in the outcome of the split. One global partner in particular, [John], was extremely interested in the effect of my research on his compensation. I had worked with [John] on multiple projects before, and by nature he was a challenging and persistent individual. During informal meetings in his office for client work he would make a passing joke or question about my secret research. For the most part these comments were easy to brush off. That all changed, however, once we left the office for a client trip.

Soon after I was assigned to the [Company B] split, I was asked to go on a client visit with [John]. Our goal was to visit the headquarters of a new client, a pharmaceutical delivery systems manufacturer in [Location F]. The client's transfer pricing issues were challenging and included valuing and shifting ownership of their intellectual property to a lower tax jurisdiction in [Location G]. This was my first on-site client trip and our goal was merely to collect facts from top management as we started the valuation process.

The train ride to [Location F] was pleasant enough. We conducted our business at the client and the interviews went extremely well. [John] even complimented me on how prepared I was and how I handled myself. Halfway through the trip home, however, [John] cornered me on the firm split, directly asking me about the details of my special research. My face turned bright red and my stomach dropped.

I initially ignored his question and tried to change the subject. He persisted and asked me to be a "team player". I responded firmly, "[John], I am not allowed to divulge client information ever, regardless of whom the client is. You know that. If you have any specific questions about this research, please ask [Mike] (the director of the tax practice in [Location B]).” He was a bit stunned, but sat back and was quiet the rest of the way home.

I was nervous about how terse I had been with a partner. I was still relatively new to the firm and was already working with [John] on several projects. Upon my return, I spoke with the manager whom I was working with on the split. She shared with me [John]’s persistence in questioning her on the same issues. She commended me on my response and told me not to worry about [John]. Her counsel turned out to be true. [John] didn’t get any easier to work with, but he did cease the constant pestering regarding my research on the split.

Looking back, I am proud of how I handled myself in that difficult situation. I set my own ethical precedent that integrity is essential in my professional life. Overall, this challenge has helped me mature and develop strong interpersonal skills in difficult business situations. I continue to build on this lesson in my interactions with clients and internal consulting teams.

Critique

The essay often plays a key role in the application review process. Applicants have the opportunity to showcase their skills in both writing and critical thinking. A well-written, well-conceived essay that both stays on point and offers a unique story can clearly enhance the applicant’s potential for an offer of admission.

Our essay topic asks the candidate to define “ethical” from his or her own perspective; determine whether a particular incident or experience was, in fact, a dilemma; describe the thought processes that were used in resolving the issue; and identify that final solution.

The applicant in this example was faced with a number of challenges and articulated them very well. He was young and relatively inexperienced when this incident took place. However, despite his youth, he was in a position of access to sensitive, confidential information that was desired and of great personal importance to more senior members of his firm who could have a direct impact upon his future with the company. Should he use his newly found “chip” to better his own position and cross the ethical line, or should he maintain his own level of ethical behavior and risk a professional backlash?

In a concise, well-written, thoughtful essay, this candidate clearly described the thought processes he utilized in making his decision and the options that he considered. The ethical boundaries that the applicant maintained in a challenging situation identified him as the type of individual who would be a very successful MBA candidate and the type of future business leader needed in these uncertain times.

Essay #3

Question: Please submit an essay describing what you learned from your experience as a member of a team whose project was not completed successfully.

I took the job of Chief Technology Officer with a growing investment firm, as opposed to one that is fully established, in order to take part in the design of the business. With the company in its nascent stages, many processes were still developing, and my newest undertaking was no different. My task was to design an efficient procedure for creating "Wealth Plans." These plans are the trademark of the firm, and remain its best sales tool. At that time, however, they took up to a month to prepare, and each one was different in content and design. These factors made the recognition factor negligible at best, and made the design a start-from-scratch process with the commencement of each and every plan.

Having seen these plans convince clients that our firm was their best choice, I recognized the value of their prompt and thorough completion. These plans are expansive; covering everything from the clients' investment profiles to their tax and insurance needs, and the majority of developmental delays stemmed from a lack of organization and permanent design within these modules. I would take the best parts from all previous plans, put them together in an intelligent format, and streamline the process. Looking back, it seemed simple at the time.

Originally, I had started the project on my own, and, quickly, I realized that my skills alone would not suffice. My talents as Chief Technology Officer were up to the task of programming and spreadsheet design, but I learned that expertise is not valuable in a vacuum. Without assistance from other professionals, the plans would be quite lacking in terms of content outside of my proficiency. If each module had been complete, my earlier assumptions of fast closure would have been justified. Unfortunately, not only the content as a whole differed in each instance, but the actual formulas and design of individual modules changed almost randomly from plan to plan, as well. I noted the content and flaws of each module, prepared a summary and an action plan, and took them to my supervisor.

We assembled a team consisting of a CPA, a portfolio manager, an MBA, and me (a Microsoft Certified Systems Engineer) for the task of establishing plan design and protocol. Our first meeting produced a schedule for completion, an outline of what we thought would be appropriate content for each module, and the decision that would ensure our failure—our steadfast focus on function over form. By concentrating fully on the function of the plans, we ignored the pitfall of oversophistication that would have frustrated most clients.

We progressed quickly as the members contributed individually to the overall proposal and directed the design of any modules that fell under their bailiwick. As the technology guru, it was my duty to translate the ideas and needs of each section into workable spreadsheets and programs. Though intricate in design, each instance would be simple to complete and identical in order and design to the plans of other clients. While recommendations and exceptions would always be unique to a specific client's situation, the majority of the plan now only required simple data entry on the part of our employees.

With the finished program loaded on our server, we were ready to present our accomplishment. However, wanting to recoup time spent in development of this project, we decided to take it directly to our firm's sales team for use. Upon completion of the first plan (finished in five hours instead of a month), I had been ready to celebrate our success amid smiles and a few free beers. To our surprise, we were met with the sales team's look of confusion.

We failed to remember that these plans are first and foremost a sales tool. The plan itself was flawless, and we showed everyone the amazing leaps in creativity and utility that had been made. But, unless you had been working on it for a month with the experts who devised each module, I truly doubt you would be able to comprehend it. To the sales team, this was 20–30 pages of overly analytical, unnecessarily complicated material that would confuse our clients instead of closing deals. We had developed the plan with our own needs in mind and had ignored its true audience.

Stepping outside of the confines of a project, job, or even an industry is essential to true progress and a proper perspective. The sales team and I spent another two weeks enlarging the fonts, rewording jargon, and adding a bouquet of colorful graphs. We ended up with a plan that was just as technical, but far more suitable to our clients. I had thought our progress and teamwork to be remarkable, and, if we had originally focused them in the right direction, they would have been. While I learned that you need to keep your audience in mind at every step, another important lesson was that of goal setting.

We started with the objective of streamlining the production of plans. In hindsight, it would have been more intelligent to first finalize the design of the plans in terms of their end goal—bringing in new clients. Intelligent people who are willing to work hard and well are not enough to ensure success. Without a solidly thought out purpose, long term setbacks increase, and, without leadership, that purpose cannot be determined.

Critique

Identification of a successfully designed and implemented plan or project is generally simple for the business professional, faculty member, current student, or hopeful applicant. However, such a task can be difficult when asked to identify an experience that did not conclude as intended.

This essay question demands honesty and introspection. It also gives members of the admissions committee an opportunity to evaluate the applicant's attitude toward working on teams, an important component of the Rutgers Business School MBA program.

In a very readable and well-written essay, this candidate gives readers the opportunity to follow him as he assessed a new project, attempted to complete it on his own, and then realized the need to form a team of experts in order to bring the project to conclusion. We are then made aware of the steps that the members of this group took as they reviewed their new assignment, made preliminary evaluations, implemented action plans, and presented their results.

Throughout the essay, the applicant honestly points to errors in thought and process that ultimately lead to the initial lack of success. More importantly, he clearly identifies the new learning that took place and how it was immediately used to redesign the project and meet the needs of the populations for whom it was intended.

The admissions committee believes that the willingness to admit error, learn from initial mistakes, and take corrective actions, along with the critical thinking that also took place, are traits that will assist this candidate throughout the demanding MBA program.

TULANE UNIVERSITY

A. B. FREEMAN SCHOOL OF BUSINESS

FROM THE SCHOOL

"A great essay? Much like a great MBA candidate, a great essay is the right combination of excitement, interest, knowledge, focus, and ability. Essays are but one window into the person that will walk the halls of the business school for a couple of years and wear the distinction of being a Tulane alumnus for life.

"The Freeman School at Tulane is a very special place. Consequently, we are not looking for well-rounded candidates; we look for unique people that have special abilities. Here a group of about 100 students are divided into teams providing international representation from several geographies, different economic and political hemispheres, and different academic arenas. The interaction between these groups, combined with the academic challenge, is the foundation to the Freeman MBA. It is a core experience that will change the way in which one views the world.

"The Tulane MBA is all about changing the student's worldview, while equipping the individual to make decisions. Tulane students start the MBA program by learning great interaction and trusting skills.

"Tulane's team structure, in an intensive core program, builds on the diversity presented in the MBA class to shape a unique MBA experience. I bring up this point because it is insight into how one can deal with other people, cultures, and ideas that the most recent Freeman School essay considers:

Describe one person that has made a profound impact on your life. What skills did that person possess? How did others react to this person? What has been the outcome of your experience with this person?

"This is not your typical 'tell me about yourself' question. We enjoy a lot of information about the applicant including resume, references, and transcripts. Frankly, we could probably tell applicants a lot about themselves that they don't know. However, the point of an admission application is to assure that you will benefit from the experience and that the group (peers) will benefit from your presence.

"We look for an applicant that can learn from the experience of another. Central to learning from another individual is the ability to recognize strengths, skills, and weaknesses. Interestingly, these skills also translate to management skills as one seeks to understand the needs of an organization—and build a coalition of people to achieve success."

Essay #1

During my tenure at [Company A], I had the opportunity to work with and learn from the company's senior executive, [James]. Inside the structure of a small firm, I was able to work closely with [James] on a daily basis and experience his management style.

[James] and I have very similar backgrounds and a similar outlook towards life. Although I am younger than [James], our lives have followed a very similar path. We both grew up in the same town, attended the same high school, and both went to [College C]. From our similar background and outlook, I was able to capitalize on [James's] management experiences and learn a management style that suited my own values and utilized my attributes.

Three principles from [James's] management philosophy have had a great impact on the development of my management abilities. The first and most frequently stressed principle was the necessity to never allow oneself to lose sight of the larger picture. The second principle was that a manager's success depends on how well they are able to utilize their colleagues' strengths and talents. The third principle was that in order to excel, you must consistently reinvent and improve yourself.

While working at [Company A], I dealt daily with the analytical side of commercial mortgage backed securitizations. In my role it was very easy to become overly focused on the technical side of a project and forget the project's overall purpose. Early in my career I had a habit of becoming too focused on a particular issue in the securitization process and would not be able work past the issue until I had it solved. After a few frustrating weeks of spending nearly all day and night in the office in order to meet simple deadlines, I met with [James] to discuss my dilemma. [James's] approach was simple and quickly became part of my decision making process. His approach was to step back from the technical dilemma, look at the project as a whole and ask, "Does this provide value to the client?". This simple question helped direct me toward the issues that mattered the most instead of wasting time on the details that were insignificant to the outcome. [James]'s big picture outlook also stressed the importance of a proper work/family balance. Even while committing himself to running the company, [James] never forgot the importance of quality family time. With the proper balance, he was able to spend significant time at work and still devote himself to the raising of his family. The family values that were demonstrated at [Company A] showed me that it is possible to find the delicate balance between work and family time.

Another one of [James's] strengths was his ability to draw from his colleagues' strengths and talents. There were multiple ways that [James] utilized his employees' talents, but there were two ways that I found particularly valuable. The first was his belief that there was only so much that could be learned from training and watching others. Under [James's] direction at [Company A], employees gained a substantial amount of authority very early in their career. His belief was that after a certain level of fundamental training, the best way to truly learn the process was to go into the field and implement the process for the client. He had a theory that if he hired good employees, they would be able to figure out the details on their own as long as he taught them the fundamentals. The [Company A] employee had substantial authority over client interaction and the final product sent to the investors. The second belief was that in order to create a stronger company, he needed to make his employees well rounded. He wanted to expose his employees to as many different situations as possible in order to find out where their talents lay. If you were interested in a different part of the securitization process, [James] tried to let you have as much exposure to it as possible. For example, when I told [James] that I would benefit from more exposure to the investment banking side of the securitization process, he contracted me out to a client in New York. He rented an apartment in [Location B] and I spent a winter working with a large investment bank learning how a deal was run from a banking perspective.

The third principle that I learned from [James] was the need for continuous self-improvement. His theory was that self-improvement was a critical factor in being successful. At [Company A] there was typically a week or two of downtime when work was slow after the end of each quarter. [James] devoted these four to eight weeks per year to training. He implemented case studies. Employees were expected to run through difficult business deal scenarios in order to sharpen their skills. Employees were encouraged to enroll in real estate training classes via the Internet. On a one to one basis, [James] enjoyed teaching employees about different aspects of the industry and about the results of his most recent revelation. No questions were considered too basic to be asked and he made sure that there was always an atmosphere where employees felt comfortable enough to walk into his office to ask a question.

[James's] patience and professionalism earned the respect of both clients and employees. His ability to give employees substantial authority and recognition resulted in a stronger team that produced a high level of success.

Both my work related and personal decision making skills have benefited from my time with [James]. Whenever I face a decision, I am now more thorough in my analysis and pay special attention to how the situation fits into the context as a whole. As a result, my decision-making abilities have not only improved, but I find myself wasting less time on insignificant details and I have gained a more macro level viewpoint. I have been able to employ a similar employee development strategy to [James's] when I was put in charge of training new analysts in the [Location D] office. The result of the strategy was that the analyst spent a significant portion of their training in the field and was able to gain a much more practical understanding of their role. Finally, I have tried and am currently trying to follow [James]'s example of consistent self-improvement. I held the same principle of self-improvement before I worked for [James], but my time with [James] certainly helped it to grow. Under [James]'s example of self-improvement I have been able to improve both my personal and work related skills. When I wanted to improve my financial skills by enrolling in the Chartered Financial Analyst program, he encouraged me by allowing me to stop traveling for the month prior to the level one and two exams so that I could both work and study out of the [Location E] office. I am fortunate to have had [James] as a mentor. The skills that I have learned from him will forever impact my personal and business life.

Critique

Getting it right: This essay illustrates some very strong writing skills, conveys a clear message, and articulates attributes that we look for in a Freeman MBA candidate. The candidate recognizes some clear traits presented by the individual he admires: "never allow oneself to lose sight of the larger picture"; "a manager's success depends on how well they are able to utilize their colleagues' strengths and talents"; "consistently reinvent and improve yourself." Wow—any of these lines would be fitting captions for a motivational poster!

The applicant also recognizes where he fails to measure up to the behaviors presented by the individual—"I had a habit of becoming too focused"; "importance of a proper work/family balance." The applicant recognizes the perspective of his peers when dealing with them professionally and socially. He further articulates the skills he has learned as a result of his relationship with this person.

While this essay is clearly structured around a person that has shaped the applicant's professional life and attitudes, it does an excellent job of conveying the applicant's ability to recognize some core skills that will be very useful in an intensive MBA experience like the one offered at the Freeman School.

Essay #2

One person that has made a profound impact on my life is my former manager, [John Brown]. I had the opportunity to work with [John] as he preferred to be called for fifteen months; and his personal and professional skills made a huge impression on me. I adopted him as my mentor. [John] holds a Bsc. in Electrical Engineering, and an MBA from [Country A].

[John's] tenacity of purpose and determination to succeed against all odds saw him overcome an earlier setback of three failures, before passing the entry examination into the university for his undergraduate studies. [John] taught us to take failure as a learning experience. [John] was honest in his dealings with both colleagues and subordinates. He was continuously seeking the welfare of his subordinates much to the annoyance of his colleague managers.

[John] had excellent negotiation skills, and was very adept at bringing others to his point of view. He had an extraordinary level of drive and energy—devoted equal time to the minutest detail; he have memo drafted several times to correct all the mistakes. [John] always considered various options before making a decision—he always explored the "what ifs" of all alternative decisions. His final decisions were ultimately guided by the interest of the company with an eye for the bottom line. Occasionally, he would invite us to dinner or lunch after a very stressful working time. He made it a point to know each person's family members by their names and will always inquire about their welfare. He advised us to be innovative and take decisions in his absence, but made it a point to give him the feedback at the earliest opportunity.

Most staff held him in high esteem, and treated him with a lot of dignity and respect. His opinions were highly respected by top management. It was not surprising that all requests he recommended to top management were approved.

One of the outcomes of my experience with [John] has been my decision to pursue an MBA. He always talked about the impact of MBA experience on his life and career—he fueled my desire to have the MBA experience. I have also realized that hard work, determination, and honesty pay off in the end. Most importantly, I now see failure as a learning experience—it is easier to take risk.

Critique

Short but sweet: One essay submission to the Freeman School requires the applicant to provide a true Reader's Digest version of the topic. In business school, students spend a lot of time learning about the executive summary—a short statement that contains only the pertinent facts. This international student conveys several important management skills in this essay. Equally important, he responds to the essay question completely.

ESSAY #3

He was born in a small town, in a small country, [Country A], in the 1920s. In those days, the locomotive could still stir excitement among the people, the extended family was still the most important social network, and farming was a way of life. Those were also turbulent days. Once again, civil wars and local generals who vied fiercely for power plagued the country. The [military] would come in and try to impose order, then they would leave, only to come back and leave again. Out of this turmoil emerged the National Guard and its controlling leader, [General B]. Between 1936 and 1979, the country remained under the thumb of the political dynasty established by this general. Civil and political liberties were violated, public graft was practiced with impunity, socioeconomic injustice increased, and in spite of all this, the economy grew and even attained a degree of modernization.

The small town boy, [my grandfather], grew up in this environment. But he grew up to be an honest man of renowned integrity and bravery. He defied the [ruling] dynasty and for this he paid a heavy price, enduring imprisonment and humiliation at the hands of his jailers. Gradually, as it became clear that opposition was futile, he turned away from politics and threw himself into his private work, gaining a reputation throughout [the continent] as a talented administrator and banker. He rescued from ruin some of the largest corporations in the country and made them thrive. He then went on to serve in the upper ranks of the [regional banking authority], helping make the region's common market a success. As his own professional successes accumulated, he was invited to join the leadership staff of [an international bank], where he played a key role in bringing developmental assistance to [the region].

I am his first grandson, and he is my role model. His shoes are too big to fill, but I will at least try to follow in his footsteps. No other individual has had a more profound impact on my life. I grew up watching this man make difficult choices that others might have avoided because they were too risky or costly from a personal perspective. In 1979, he became involved in the national struggle to overthrow the oppressive [ruling] regime, and soon thereafter left his position at the [international bank] to join the government of the [new political party]. He served as the Revolution's first president of the [government bank], later became a member of the [leading political party], and later still served as [my country's] ambassador to the United States. He shared the revolutionaries' desire for socioeconomic process and justice, but he rejected their political authoritarianism. Acting on principle, he left the [new (leading) political party] government, and returned to development banking. I respect and admire that.

By 1983 there was much discontent with the ruling government within [my country] and there was international pressure for the [new (leading) political party] to hold free elections. My grandfather was chosen to be the presidential candidate for the opposition, which was fully backed by the United States. As the campaign began, so did negotiations with the [competing party] for free and transparent elections, something my grandfather had always dreamt for [my country]. The more he campaigned around the country, the larger the masses grew and the faster his popularity rose. He also became a serious threat for the ruling party. The [competing party] sabotaged his campaign by inciting violent mobs wherever he went. His supporters would attempt to fight off the mobs to no avail, and on one occasion a mob leader managed to injure my grandfather by throwing a sharpened rock at his forehead. And yet, he pressed ahead in the face of such adversity; and continued to demand conditions that would prevent fraud on Election Day. When these conditions were not met, he decided to stand on principle yet again. He left the race. As a consequence, the [competing party] was victorious at the polls. I respect and admire that.

My grandfather returned to politics when an armed opposition movement formed to overthrow [this] regime. Known as the [opposition], this movement needed a person with integrity and public support. My grandfather was that person. He believed in the cause of freedom and accepted to be a member of the [opposition directorate]. But he soon grew disenchanted with the [opposition] leaders, whom he found to be intolerant and whose methods he found questionable. "Abuse of power," he often would say to us kids "is wrong, no matter who the abuser is whether is the [new political party] or the [opposition]." He resigned from the [opposition directorate], knowing full well that many would criticize his decision and that some would even malign him. I respect and admire that.

At every critical point, my grandfather could have had power and wealth had he chosen to play along, but instead he chose to do what he felt was the right thing. Countless times during his career in business and politics, he was offered the chance to blur the line between the two for personal gain. He resisted, and kept them separate. And countless times, people who had no power or influence appealed to him directly or through intermediaries for help. He always found the courage to give voice to their grievances. Market women who were left holding worthless currency, political prisoners doomed to rot in jail, poor farmers who had been dispossessed of their tiny plots, mothers whose sons had been wounded in battle and had no prospect of rehabilitation for lack of resources, they all knew him as the man who would listen and respond.

I often meet strangers who, when they realize [who] my grandfather is, tell me how much they relish having met him, or how grateful they are that he helped them without even knowing who they were. When I was younger, I used to wonder why every time my grandfather visited [my country], the media would seek him out and people on the streets would rush to embrace him. Now I know.

Now I also understand that my grandfather's difficult choices are his legacy to me. In a world filled with political and corporate scandals, I carry this inheritance with deep satisfaction and pride; and in my heart and mind I hear his voice, encouraging me to pursue great professional accomplishments but never at the expense of my own humanity, principles, or honor.

These days, long after the locomotive has been retired to the museum, my grandfather is using a computer to write his political biography. If this book turns out to be only half as powerful as the conversations, the advice, and the stories he gave me when I was growing up, it will be a great book indeed. And when I give this book to my children, I will tell them that I am trying to live according to the standards set by its author. I will tell them this was my grandfather, your forebear, a man who was great yet humble, brave yet wise. I will tell them that we are all at our best when we affirm that such men can still be made.

Critique

Missing the mark: It is terribly important to read the question—not only for the idea but to see what the admissions committee is asking. We purposefully imbedded some key words in the essay question to hint at the direction an applicant should take. We wanted "profound impact," "skills," "reaction," and "outcome" to be articulated in the essay response. This essay was a wonderful exposition on a clearly interesting individual; however, the focus of the essay was to convey the life story of the applicant's grandfather. It is not until the third paragraph that the reader encounters the applicant's reaction to his grandfather's actions: "I respect and admire that." The essay—although beautifully crafted—failed to provide a clear insight into skills that the applicant has learned as a result of his encounter.

University of Chicago
Graduate School of Business

Essay #1

Question: If you were a character in a book, who would it be and why? What do you admire most about this character, and how does it relate to you personally and/or professionally? (300 words maximum)

Atticus Finch, as portrayed in Harper Lee's To Kill A Mockingbird, most accurately exemplifies my beliefs and my code of conduct. He embodies a strong moral compass with a composed and firm disposition. Although Atticus seems mellow and even old-fashioned, many of his beliefs are quite revolutionary. He is a hard worker who is an active parent with his children as well as an active member of the community. Raising his children with his own strong sense of morality and justice, he is a strong believer in family. A lawyer by trade, he is a teacher of both his children and his community. Atticus sees people as individuals, regardless of race and background, maintains an open mind to new ideas and thoughts, and teaches through reason rather than force. He is a patient and consistent man. The code of conduct that he maintains for himself remains constant and disciplined no matter how awkward or uncomfortable the situation. His objective is not the pursuit of money and fame, but justice and truth. I respect Atticus Finch for his keen mind, his instincts, his eloquence, and his willingness to stand up to social oppression regardless of overwhelming opposition in what may seem to be a hopeless and futile situation. He is very deliberate and erudite in his actions and knows how to maximize the resources at his disposal to achieve his goals. I admire him for his courage to test the social paradigm and for his willingness to stand up for what he believes is right. Passionate, yet collected and composed, I conduct myself with beliefs which parallel those of Atticus in many respects. Using the resources at my disposal and proactively developing my skills, I work in a calculated manner to attain my future goals professionally and personally.

Critique

What makes this essay so effective is its simplicity. Within the first two words of the essay, the reader already has a positive impression of the writer. By identifying Atticus Finch as the literary character he most admires, the writer chooses someone who is easily recognizable and who is known for his strong moral character and social ideals. Before completing the first sentence, the writer has already created a strong impression in the reader's mind, and the rest of the essay serves to strengthen the association. Remember that this type of essay is designed not to educate the reader on the applicant's literary knowledge but rather to allow the applicant to create a strong association that illustrates who he or she is as a person.

ESSAY #2

Question: If you could pick three guests for a formal dinner, who would they be and why would you choose them? (300 words maximum)

If I could pick three guests for a formal dinner party, unconstrained by chronology and mortality, I would pick Theodore (Teddy) Roosevelt, Winston Churchill, and Steve Irwin, "The Crocodile Hunter". Teddy Roosevelt and Winston Churchill have always intrigued me, because apart from their enormous accomplishments in public life, they led fascinating lives beyond the realm of politics—Roosevelt the big game hunter, conservationist, and hero of San Juan Hill; Churchill the soldier, war correspondent, and Nobel Prize winning author. My third guest, the zoo director and television personality Steve Irwin, strikes me as the ideal foil for the two elder statesmen. As an Australian and non-politician, he would strike a balance between these bastions of American and British public life and focus the conversation on the personal experiences that make Roosevelt and Churchill so fascinating. Additionally, Irwin, with his cheerful self-assurance, would not be easily overwhelmed by Roosevelt and Churchill's domineering personalities.

With this triumvirate, I imagine the conversation moving from Teddy's tales of his wild game safaris in Africa and the spectacular beauty of the American West, to Winston relating his great escape from the Boer prison camp and his experiences in the British Raj, with Steve Irwin trying to one-up them as he recounts the origins of his various scars and expounds on the art of crocodile wrestling.

While the political careers of Roosevelt and Churchill can, and do, fill volumes, it is impossible to capture on the written page the passion and energy with which these men lived their lives. With this dining combination, I would hope to catch a glimpse of it. I can't think of a more interesting or remarkable evening than to be regaled by tales from these three exceptional men.

Critique for Essays #2 and #3

This essay and the essay that follows effectively answer a pretty common essay question. What makes these essays so effective is the way the candidates illustrate one or more elements of their personalities through the people they choose. In both instances, the reader finishes the essay knowing something about the candidates that might not have otherwise been evident in reading their applications. Steve Irwin, Teddy Roosevelt, and Winston Churchill illustrate the first applicant's thirst for adventure, while the second applicant's grandmother, political science professor, and John "Buck" O'Neill convey his strong sense of social conscience.

Essay #3

Question: If you could pick three guests for a formal dinner, who would they be and why would you choose them? (300 words maximum)

Guests at my formal dinner would be Robert Booth Fowler, John "Buck" O'Neill, and Harriet Marks. Professor Fowler is a political science professor at the University of Wisconsin—Madison who specializes in the intersection of religion and politics. He was the most passionate, creative, engaging and charismatic instructor that I have ever had. He continues to inspire me to be passionate about what I do, to act always with a determined vigor, and to devote much of my free time to the teaching and training of others.

My second guest, John "Buck" O'Neill, is a former Negro Leagues baseball player and manager who later entered the Major Leagues first as a scout for the Chicago Cubs (signing, among other players, Ernie Banks and Lou Brock), and later as Major League Baseball's first black coach (with the Cubs, in 1962). He is almost uniquely qualified to provide living testimony regarding the intersection of sports and the history of American racial relations, both of which interest me greatly. If you saw Ken Burns's documentary on baseball, you undoubtedly recognized Mr. O'Neill and his affable, gracious style, as being the show's truest star.

Third, I would invite Harriet Marks. Mrs. Marks is my grandmother, who is recently widowed and seems a bit lonely. Although she has never expressed an interest in religion and politics or in American race relations—and has little understanding of baseball—I know that she, more than anyone else, would appreciate the invitation.

Essay #4

Question: What are two attributes of your character that make you unique? How do you expect these traits to make an impact on Chicago GSB and your classmates? (300 words maximum)

Incident number one: it was a sultry August morning in Manhattan. From the 27th floor of the [office] building, the downtown skyline sprawled before us. It was the [Company A] analyst training program, and I was surrounded by a group of highly talented, driven peers from some of the best colleges in the world. We were listening to managing directors tell us wild tales about multi-billion dollar deals they had worked on.

Suddenly the words echoed in my ears. "Have any of you ever been to the god-forsaken state of Iowa?" The room of 250 was silent. My retort practically fell out of my mouth. "Yes, I'm from Iowa!" A huge explosion of laughter and applause. The speaker, a famed "deal maker" from our Mergers & Acquisitions group, turned red. "I am now removing my foot from my mouth," were his exact words.

Incident number two: I was in my senior year at [University B]. It was mid-December, and Wall Street recruiting season was in full swing. I trudged through the snow along 56th Street to interview with a major securities brokerage firm. To this day, I can still hear my interviewer as he took a final glance over my resume. "[Jenna], you're very qualified for this job. But one question remains in my mind: what's a nice girl like you who plays the cello wanna do on a trading floor?"

I have lived as a transplanted Iowan in New York and London for over six years, and I do play the cello. Through all the jokes and befuddled reactions I've received, I've learned that the most stimulating traits I can bring to a community are a well-rounded background and an open mind. This includes an appreciation and understanding of the rural and the urban, the domestic and the international, the artistic and the mundane. In gaining this appreciation, I've realized the overlap between these seemingly antithetic worlds and have come to understand the value of interactive diversity.

Critique

What made this essay effective was the candidate's use of the narrative. Most essays I have come across on this topic read like a laundry list: "My years of consulting experience have provided me with the tools to be an effective team player"; "My years in public relations have really strengthened my communication skills"; and so on. There is no reason to spend time further illustrating things that are already covered in detail in the application. This writer was effective because she decided to focus on two seemingly insignificant parts of her life—playing the cello and being from Iowa. As a reader reviewing her essay, I may have noticed these two things about her, but I certainly would not have associated them with her open-mindedness. By effectively using some simple narratives, she left a lasting impression of what being from Iowa and playing the cello can contribute to an MBA program.

Essay #5

Question: Why are you seeking an MBA or IMBA at the University of Chicago Graduate School of Business? What do you hope to experience and contribute? What are your plans and goals after you receive your degree?

"[Jenna], you must go to the U of C. The faculty, the campus, the whole environment...," raved F.H., one of my senior associates who happened to attend the GSB at the University of Chicago.

"I know," I replied. "I've been thinking about it for a long time."

You have some very convincing alumni. However, I do not need much convincing. I have known for quite a while exactly why I want to attend the University of Chicago. Let me begin by providing you with a bit of historical context in which to better understand my motivations.

For the last several years, I have worked as a financial analyst at [Company A] in New York and London. By all accounts, I have excelled in my job. I have been consistently ranked and compensated in the "star" category, was one of only a handful of second year analysts globally to be promoted to a third year position in our London office (most were laid off), and the only analyst in the global investment bank this year to be granted a third year position in our fabled fixed income division. I have also been advised that I am a "shoe-in" for promotion to the associate position. However, I am opting to seek a place at the University of Chicago GSB rather than pursue further promotion within my firm. Why?

As an undergraduate at [University B], I majored in mathematics and reveled in the theory I learned. I subsequently became interested in finance, however it was not part of [University B]'s undergraduate curriculum. I then went to work on Wall Street, but always felt there was a gap in my education. That gap has grown in my mind to the point that I do not want to continue my career without firmly grounding myself in theoretical finance and the other business disciplines.

Given my math background, I want—and indeed need—the analytical rigor of Chicago's curriculum and the practical and theoretical understanding of finance that it can provide me. While there are many other MBA programs out there, none can match Chicago's combination of prominence in economics and finance, its legendary faculty (past and present), the flexibility of its curriculum, and its location in a city that is an international business center that has as much to offer culturally as any other in the world.

I am eager to gain exposure to a very diverse and international group of classmates at the University of Chicago, as well as their insight on the industries in which they have worked. I look forward to sharing a dynamic and thought provoking classroom environment with them.

I can offer my classmates a culmination of my solid investment banking background, well-trained and analytical mind, and genuine desire to learn by working with them and forming lasting friendships.

I owe it to myself to continue to seek rewarding challenges in thoughtful and intense environments. I hope to use the knowledge I will have gained at the University of Chicago to go into corporate bond research. That is my future ambition—and an MBA education from the University of Chicago will provide me with the foundation that I need to get there.

Please accept my thanks for your time and consideration. I hope that you will enjoy reading my application as much as I have enjoyed writing it.

Critique

This essay demonstrates an effective answer to the "Why an MBA?" and "Why here?" questions. The most common pitfall that people experience when answering this question is that they do not do an effective job answering the "Why here?" question. Applicants need to keep in mind that a university admissions committee wants to know that you are interested in that university specifically and not the five other programs to which you are applying. Convincing the committee that their institution is the best fit for you is critical to answering this essay effectively.

A less common problem is not providing a clear focus for your MBA. A common response I have seen is "An MBA is the next logical step in my career." A statement like this does not answer the question. Have a clear purpose for why you want an MBA now. How is an MBA going to help you achieve your specific goals? Be clear about your purpose; speaking in generalities is the kiss of death.

The writer of this essay was effective because she was thorough and enthusiastic about why she wanted to go to the University of Chicago, and she was specific about the reasons she thought an MBA was important for achieving her goals. Providing an effective answer to this question is not a complicated procedure as long as you can be specific!

UNIVERSITY OF IOWA
HENRY B. TIPPIE SCHOOL
OF MANAGEMENT

FROM THE SCHOOL

"The admissions essays serve several purposes in the application review process at the Tippie School of Management. Of course, they tell us something about the candidate's ability to compose an essay. More importantly, the essays help us to know more about the applicant as an individual and to answer questions such as: What really matters to this person? What life experiences will he/she bring to our program? What makes this person 'tick'?

"Our essay questions are quite straightforward, requesting information about the candidate's career objectives, purpose in obtaining an MBA, and leadership experiences. The best candidates use these questions as a springboard to provide a more complete picture of themselves. We recognize that not everyone writes like a best-selling author. However, we expect the admission essays to be concise, to be free of errors, and to address the questions posed.

"Two essays are required in our application. Each of the essays below was submitted as part of the application for admission to the fall 2002 entering class and are responses to the following:

Give an example of a situation or an action that describes your potential for success in a professional environment.

"We selected them because each reflects the candidate's personality, fleshing out our picture of them as a real-life person."

ESSAY #1

"You have three qualities that will allow you to be successful in life: persistence, organization, and people skills."

My mother told this to me when I was young and did not fully appreciate what it meant or why it was important. I just knew that I liked to set goals for myself, have a structured environment, and be around people. Now, after years of experience through work and school, I have a complete understanding of how and why these three things are so important. They will allow me to be successful in any of life's activities and, in particular, a professional environment.

While working for [Company A], I inherited a territory that was suffering saleswise. I knew that in order to make an immediate impact, I would have to focus my activity on the doctors and offices that would bring in the most business. One of my most important doctors, Dr. C., had a large population of patients with epilepsy in his clinic. It was my job to introduce him to the new anticonvulsant medication that I marketed and to convince him to keep it in mind for some of these patients. I knew my mission, so I prepared an initial call plan that included uncovering what his practice needs were at that time, combined with weekly visits and reminders.

At our first meeting, he took one look at me and walked the other way. After speaking with his nurse, I soon discovered that he did not believe drug reps brought value to his practice and, therefore, would not see them. At that point I knew he would be a challenge, and I was up for it. I devised a strategic plan to get myself in front of him. I decided to devote my time and energy to the "gatekeepers" by befriending the office staff and nurses.

Reverse psychology? It seemed the more attention I gave the rest of the office, the more curious Dr. C. became about me as well as my medications. Every week I would get to know each of the staff members and bring in candy or a lunch. I would always include full details about my product to prove the value I felt I could bring to the office, and also leave a friendly note for Dr. C. requesting he set aside a time for us to meet in person. The staff teased Dr. C. for not participating in my luncheon, and I believe the pressure from them (and from me) eventually broke him down. He finally invited me to sit down with him in his office to review all the details of the medication and discuss his needs at that time. The call went very well, but he did not make any commitments, so I continued with my original sales plan.

Over the next few months, I asked him to try the medicine with some of his patients. I offered examples and ideas of which patient types would make good candidates, explained the dosing schedule and potential side effects, reminded him of the numerous journal articles that praised the drug's remarkable efficacy, and kept him abreast of the competition. He remained hesitant to use the drug, but with my persistence he agreed to let me organize a conference call with a leader in the neurological community who was having wonderful results with the medication. It turned out to be a fun and educational occasion, and I felt that it afforded me the opportunity to increase my credibility with this very important physician.

Later that week, I was pleasantly surprised to receive an email from Dr. C. thanking me for the event. He said that he felt the conference was very worthwhile and that he appreciated my efforts to bring him the information. Because of this, he promised that he would try the product with the next patient who had uncontrolled seizures. It took about six months, but we were finally at a mutual understanding and able to grow the business relationship.

Throughout my life, I have discovered that knowledge and hard work will be rewarded. Add to these, determination, organized planning, and the ability to develop and maintain relationships with people, and it will make an individual very successful. It is my goal to always remember my mother's encouraging words and use these qualities in everything I do.

Critique

This candidate begins her essay with a quote stating the characteristics she demonstrates through the example provided—persistence, organization, and people skills. The level of detail she gives in her example is a little more than needed, but the essay provides insight into her approach to life that helps us evaluate her as a potential member of the Tippie MBA program.

ESSAY #2

The decimal point is a powerful little dot. With a mere step to the right or to the left, ten percent can change to one hundred percent, or to one percent. Who decided to give this amazing power to such a little speck of ink, a mere pixel on the screen? Honestly, I don't know. But if I could travel back to the time when Mr. Mathematician decided to use a small dot for the decimal, I would raise my voice and implore him to use an asterisk. Make it noticeable; make it stand out; make it BIG!

Instead, I sat on a cold metal grandstand at [Speedway A] in [City B, State B], in May of 2001. I was now in my twentieth month serving as the Systems Integration Director of [Team C]. [Team C] recruits ordinary college students, fuses them together, and challenges them to design, construct, test, and race a solar powered car across a continent. This day, the team was eagerly racking up qualifying laps at a 2.1-mile closed-course racetrack attempting to enter [Race D]—a 2,400-mile race that followed Old Route 66 from Chicago to Los Angeles. We were right on track. We had built the best car in the team's history; we had the healthiest list of sponsors the team had ever accumulated; and, we had a dedicated and eager team that had worked day and night and on weekends and holidays for almost two years to be a part of this great race.

But at that moment, as I suffered on that hard aluminum bleacher seat staring at my calculator screen, I realized that we were in serious jeopardy. The car wasn't performing like it had over the last two months during testing. The numbers just weren't adding up. My strategist murmured in my headset that things didn't look good and we should pull our driver into the pits to check things out. Ten minutes later, my fears were confirmed. It was the battery pack. We spent a full day at the track infield going over the numbers, but they all led to the same conclusion. Our battery pack engineer had made a mistake. Somehow during the design, in one of the specifications, in one of the numerous equations, a one-tenth had become a ten. Almost instantly the ability to win vanished from our dreams and we seriously doubted our ability to enter [Race D].

Just five weeks before this discovery, our battery pack engineer had developed problems in his personal life and had left the team. He was our only expert in the area. His ability and his experience were forever lost. And now, due to race regulations, the 154 laps driven out of 165 that we needed to qualify were also gone. Our $16,000 experimental battery pack was toast, and so were the hopes of every team member. The race was in five weeks.

Five weeks. I knew what had to be done, and I knew I would do it. There would have to be a new battery pack, and every team member's spirit would have to be relit. We would have to raise money, and we would need technology that had never existed before to appear, to work perfectly, and to be fully understood by our race crew. Our logistics team now had to plan for a car with unknown performance, and our public relations team had to keep our image high while still admitting the truth to our sponsors and to the public. These were the people I managed, and this was my challenge.

I volunteered to be the new battery expert, among other things. I bought French rocket launder batteries from a British company through an Australian product holder. My strategy team changed all their known values to variables; my electrical team completely redesigned the propulsion system. The mechanical design team re-built the battery enclosure. The race logistics team planned for the worst, and some key calls to compassionate corporations paid for the whole she-bang for a mere $20,000. Not a bad price considering that it took us two years to raise the other $730,000 to support the rest of the project.

We re-qualified, entered, and finished [Race D]. A mid-pack finish was more than we could have imagined. We were given the technical innovation award by the U.S. Department of Energy for our battery pack design, and our team won the award for Best Teamwork during the long stretch from Missouri through California. We were also presented with the award for best-looking vehicle design. And I am now referred to as "Captain" by my teammates. I learned to speak a little French, to become an electrical engineer, and to somehow lift high the spirits of thirty of my closest friends. For me, this was an experience of true leadership, that of bringing out the best in other people and succeeding in the common goal. If only I could just make the decimal point a little bigger.

Critique

This candidate's essay is an excellent example of a creative, interesting story that illustrates important characteristics for success in our MBA program and in business. His initiative, self-confidence, teamwork, and leadership in a unique situation come through clearly. These traits are all qualities we seek in our students. His writing style brings out his characteristics as part of an engaging story.

UNIVERSITY OF MICHIGAN
BUSINESS SCHOOL

Essay #1

Question: Describe your post-graduation career plans. How will your education, experience, and development to date support those plans? How will an MBA from the University of Michigan Business School help you attain your goals? (500 words)

I would like to pursue an MBA at Michigan in order to gain skills in marketing and corporate strategy for a career as a brand manager. Brand managers are the key link between the innovators in a corporation and the consumers in the marketplace. A broad knowledge of the firm, from Research and Development to logistics, is necessary in order for a brand manager to successfully develop a brand's strategy. My educational experience in economics and English has provided me with the quantitative and qualitative skills necessary for a career in brand management. From my experience as a management consultant, I have had the opportunity to work with a broad range of departments within a wide variety of firms, and I would like to synthesize this knowledge and build upon it with an MBA so as to eventually become a brand manager for a large food and/or beverage firm. My ideal specialty area would be in ready-to-eat food products because of my interest in branded food products.

Michigan is the ideal fit for my background and interests for several reasons. First, coming from [College A], I am a strong proponent for women in business, and I have continued my support for career women at [Company B] as a leader of the Women's Network in the Midwest and Canada. I highly value the Women in Business Initiative at Michigan. [Jane Doe], a fellow alum from [College A], a colleague at [Company B], and a member of the Women's Leadership Council at the University of Michigan Business School, has frequently lauded the dedicated efforts at Michigan to support women in business.

Second, my interest is to work for a large food and/or beverage company, and nearly all of the major food and beverage companies recruit at Michigan. Also, the school has produced a large number of leaders in food and beverage companies such as [Jane Doe] at [Company A] and [John Doe] at [Company B]. I would ideally like to complete a summer internship at a company such as [Company A, B, C, D, or E], all of which have actively recruited at Michigan in past years.

Third, I believe that studying business at Michigan would allow me to build upon my existing skills and enhance them with solid marketing and corporate strategy work that my liberal arts educational background lacks. The breadth and depth of courses at Michigan appeal to me as well as the exceptional faculty members. The classes which fascinate me within the marketing and corporate strategy disciplines include "Strategic Brand Management," "Consumer Behavior," and "Strategy, Technology, and the Management of Innovation." Professors for which I hold great esteem are [Professor A] in Strategy and [Professor B] in Brand Management. Lastly, I would like to get involved in the Marketing Club to learn from others with similar interests, and I would participate in the Consulting Club to share my knowledge and passion from my work at [Company B].

Critique

This is an excellent example of an essay that clearly let the admissions committee know the answers to three important questions about an applicant's background and career objectives: Where are you coming from? Where do you want to go? Why is Michigan's MBA program the most suited to help you achieve your educational and professional goals? This applicant clearly identified how she intended to build upon her liberal arts education and her professional work experiences to transition to brand management. In doing so, she showed us that she had a very good understanding of Michigan's general management focus as well as the school's relationships with recruiting companies and the prominence of our alumni in her chosen field. Further, she showed us that she has been involved in the women's network at her company and that her commitment would continue as a student by getting involved in our Women in Business Initiative.

There are several reasons admissions staff really want to understand the answers to these questions.

- Attending an MBA program is a big investment in yourself, in terms of both personal commitment and finances. We want to see how thoughtfully an applicant has approached this decision about his or her professional development.

- Your association with the business school you choose to attend is lifelong, and we want to ensure that you will gain maximum benefit from your experience in the MBA program as well as contribute to the Michigan community as a student and as an alumnus.

- We want to gain an understanding of your philosophy of management education, e.g., preferred learning style, goals for professional development, etc. Each business school has a distinct curriculum, values, and "personality," and we are looking for applicants that will be a great fit with our school now and in the future.

Essay #2

Question: Describe your post-graduation career plans. How will your education, experience, and development to date support those plans? How will an MBA from the University of Michigan Business School help you attain your goals? (500 words)

On completion of my MBA, I plan to continue my career in the investment industry by working as a buy-side discretionary trader for an institutional asset management firm. I would like to specialize in international equities, with a possible overseas assignment. Longer term, I plan to pursue a career in buy-side client portfolio management, leveraging my operations background and applying the increased knowledge of sound business theory developed through my MBA experience. More specifically, I would like to work in a senior-level business development/client service position that would allow me to utilize my cross-functional knowledge to evaluate, initiate and develop long-term sustainable relationships with large institutional clients.

My active involvement in college extracurricular activities supplemented my education by focusing on two areas of interest. I pursued my interest in asset management through my involvement in the Student Foundation as a member of the Board of Trustees, where I oversaw the investment of our club's $500,000 endowment, and through my internship with [Company A] as an assistant buy-side trader. I gained international exposure through two study-abroad experiences, minors in international business and affairs, and extensive international travel.

My work experience reflects a logical progression in an investment industry career. Working for [Company B] gave me a "big picture view" of asset management and an opportunity to discover which path I wanted to pursue. I discovered my strengths in leadership through project management, in sales through client service and sales support, and in quantitative application through research and performance data analysis. Working for [Company C] has given me invaluable experience in buy-side trading and a clear view of my near-term goal. My experience managing several significant trading relationships, ability to remain calm under pressure in a hectic environment, and confidence in trading $444 million on a daily basis will serve me well as I enter a more senior level of trading.

My education, work experiences and development to date have all prepared me well for my next challenge—that of obtaining an MBA. Six years of working in asset management has limited my exposure to other areas of business practice, and I believe a well-balanced MBA curriculum will significantly improve my knowledge base of different functional areas and provide me with essential business management skills. Michigan is my first choice because of its reputation of building deep expertise in every business function and maintaining a truly global perspective throughout the MBA program, addressing my primary goals in pursuing an MBA. I am particularly impressed with your faculty and especially look forward to taking Finance 640 with [Dr. A]. I find his research on the correlation between weather and stock returns intriguing. Michigan also demonstrates a strong commitment to providing a global education through its curriculum and international opportunities. I would like to participate in both The Global Project Courses and the William Davidson Institute summer assignment. I believe these are incredible opportunities, enhancing my education through "real world" team projects and international business experience.

Critique

This is a good example of an essay that describes the goals of someone who wants to return to the same industry after graduating from an MBA program. Most MBA applicants intend a career switch of some type, and the breadth of the MBA education allows them to make that transition. For those who want to return to the same industry, it is helpful for the admissions committee to understand why an applicant believes that getting an MBA will enhance his or her career in that industry. After all, why couldn't the candidate just progress from position to position in his or her firm without further formal education? Additionally, since Michigan's MBA curriculum is built upon a general management philosophy, the admissions committee wants to ensure that the applicant does not have too narrow a focus and will appreciate and benefit from the range of course work. For example, many MBA alumni wish they had taken more organizational behavior classes instead of those extra finance or marketing classes.

This applicant provides a very detailed description of career goals—more detailed, perhaps, than most applicants could. That is not the most important aspect of this essay, however. This applicant uses the essay to show us how her interests, skills, and goals have developed in the past few years and then describes how the logical next step is an MBA and, more specifically, a Michigan MBA.

- Extracurricular activities in college provided her with the first experiences of managing investments, trading, and international interests.

- The first career experience out of college confirmed her interest in asset management.

- The second career experience offered significant responsibility and provided her with the confidence to progress to senior levels.

- Throughout the essay, the applicant succinctly describes skills gained and then acknowledges other functional areas of limited exposure.

- The applicant describes in a detailed way, not a cookie-cutter, right-out-of-the-brochure way, the value that Michigan's MBA program will bring to her development.

University of North Carolina at Chapel Hill

Kenan-Flagler Business School

ESSAY #1

Question: You have recently been brought in by the CEO of your company to act as the new project lead for a high-profile team charged with bringing a new product to market. The team has become dysfunctional and risks missing the project deadline. How will you go about turning the situation around? You have one month to make the deadline. (Answer must be no more than 2 typed pages, double-spaced.)

As a project lead brought in by the CEO to lead a dysfunctional team charged with bringing a new product to market within a month, I would attack each of the following tasks to make sure that the project is completed in a timely manner and within the expectations of management:

Meeting with Management: Define Expectations

Teams can become dysfunctional due to a poor understanding of their goals and how those goals fit into the overall corporate strategy. My first task as the project lead in this situation would be to work with management to define their expectations of the team beyond the project deadline.

- *Define Purpose:* What is the purpose of the product launch? Where does this product fit in to the overall corporate strategy?

- *Define Values:* What values should be used in making decisions for the project? For example, what is more important, quality or quantity, safety or efficiency?

- *Define Consequences:* What are the consequences of the team's failure to meet its goals both for the company and for the team?

- *Define Scope:* How much flexibility do I have in requesting additional resources outside of the team?

Meeting with Project Team: Define Goals, Timelines and Roles

A team cannot function properly if there is confusion regarding the team's goals, a misunderstanding of each individual's role within the team, disorganized timelines, or poor motivation due to a lack of understanding of the importance of meeting the team's goals for both the company and the team. In order to combat these issues and get the team on the right track, I would meet with the team to organize and discuss the following:

- *Give the project context:* Discuss the goals of the team as expressed by management stressing the deadline for the project, why this deadline is important, how the product launch fits into the company's goals and the consequences of the team's failure to meet its goals both for the team and the company.

- *Define a Plan of Action:* Outline the items that have been completed for the project and which items are pending. Set a timeline for completion of the project within the one month deadline, determining exactly each task that needs to be completed, the dates each task should be completed by and which tasks are dependent on other tasks for their completion.

- *Clarify Role for Each Team Member:* Go through each action item and assign team members to each item as necessary. Where possible, ask for volunteers being careful that no one team member becomes overloaded and that tasks requiring specific expertise are assigned correctly. Give each team member the opportunity to voice any concerns over their own workload stressing that they should only volunteer for items that they can complete within the set time limits.

- *Create an "open door" policy.* Charge team members with the responsibility of letting me know about any problems that may cause project delays or reductions in the quality of work. Be sure that they understand my role as a facilitator of communication and resource allocation.

Project Management: Reinforce, Review, Reward

Projects that are not properly monitored by the project lead can quickly lose momentum. As the project lead, I would perform the following tasks on a continuing basis to be certain that each team member stays on top of their tasks:

- *Reinforce the project's goals and timelines.* After meeting with the team, communicate main points of the meeting in an email or memo. Be sure to include a detailed project plan with specific team member assignments. As appropriate, meet with the entire team or individual members throughout the project to make sure that the timeline is followed. Communicate project status and milestones to the entire team.

- *Review Team Member Performance.* Make sure that each team member meets his or her goals and timelines, reinforcing the importance of meeting management's expectations. Be flexible in changing assignments and requesting additional resources where necessary.

- *Reward Outstanding Performance.* Be sure to "give credit where credit is due" by praising those team members who display above average performance and passing on this information to management.

In the past eight years, I have worked on teams with goals as diverse as designing a global specialized IP management system for [Company A], re-branding a corporation to reinforce a position as a market leader and creating a new sick leave policy better suited to a growing company. The most effective teams have project leaders who act as facilitators by providing the necessary infrastructure so that the individual team members can effectively contribute to the overall success of the project. In my experience, teams who understand their goals and values, are organized and communicative and are empowered by management, outperform all others.

Critique

The layout of this essay immediately conveys a sense of organization, professionalism, and purpose. The candidate outlines her task by first prioritizing and defining the problem. Proper problem definition is necessary for proper problem resolution. The use of subheads is effective because the reader is drawn to the key points. It highlights how well thought out her approach is.

Her diagnosis and assessment is thorough. She considers the consequences of her action plan and the roles of her team members. This essay conveys keen business acumen and sensitivity to team dynamics. It reads like an executive summary, and an impressive one at that. In her last paragraph, she jumps out of her role and wisely tells us of her real-life experience in leading and working on diverse teams. We're convinced she'd be an asset to any team and to our school.

ESSAY #2

---

*Question: You have recently been brought in by the CEO of
your company to act as the new project lead for a high profile
team charged with bringing a new product to market. The team
has become dysfunctional and risks missing the project deadline.
How will you go about turning the situation around? You have
one month to make the deadline. (Answer must be no more than
2 typed pages, double spaced.)*

"Mr. [Smith], thank you for agreeing to introduce me to the New Product Development team. Effective leadership will bring this product to the market in the next month. As the new project lead, I believe that it is important to establish quickly my credibility, trust, and respect with this high profile team. By clearly defining my role and authority, your support will help ensure our success.

"However, before we meet with the team, I would like to review my action plan with you. First, I intend to triage the situation. I do not need to understand all of the reasons for the team's dysfunction, but it is essential that the team recognizes a problem exists. I want to hear from them, both individually and as a team, that we have hit rock-bottom and it is time to pull together. I want to see their commitment and know they are willing to put forth the extra effort. If necessary, the team members may need to be changed and I will consider that option when I review the project's resource requirements.

"Secondly, I believe that it is vital for everybody to be on the same page with respect to the scope and amount of work that must be completed in the next 30 days. In other words, our expectations must be the same. Since they are the experts with this new product, we will develop a strategy to meet the original deadline as a group. We will define new tasks and due dates. We will reconstruct the original timeline, establish new milestones and determine the critical path necessary for project completion.

"Given the workload, I will review our staffing levels and determine whether additional resources will be required. Assignments will be based on competence and area of expertise; responsibility will be delegated based on experience and performance. Some of the activities may be channeled to outside services or different teams, but I will try to keep the work in-house and the launch costs to a minimum.

"The re-organization process will take a few days. Once we are re-focused I will establish an improved system of communication. Effective communication can prevent unnecessary delays and stimulate team cohesiveness. Based on my past experiences, a visual system works best. People can quickly identify action items and response dates without spending extra time replying to emails or reading memos. I will develop charts, timelines, and a message board that will be displayed in my office and the team center. These visuals will also serve as good reminders for the team and they will be updated daily.

"Additionally, there will be a weekly review to measure progress and address new issues. The review will be brief, but highly focused. Each team member will be required to update the team on his or her activities, as well as provide feedback for the other team members. I will moderate the discussion to ensure that a healthy measure of creativity and collaboration exists. Often with high profile teams, this meeting becomes very dynamic and stimulating. You are invited to attend any one of the four reviews.

"Finally, throughout the week I will follow up with each team member to provide encouragement, motivation and accountability. I recognize that this action plan borders on micro-management, but until the team proves that they are capable of functioning together, or the deadline is met, I will monitor this project launch closely. You have asked me to bring this new product to market in less than a month. Thank you for your confidence in my abilities and our team. We will not let you down."

*The people and events described in this essay are more real than fiction. [Mr. Smith] is the President/CEO of [Smith & Co.], my current employer, and I was recently hired to coordinate activities between the New Product Development group and several manufacturing locations.

Critique

The art of telling a great story is, of course, in the way it is told. The wonderful twist to this essay is the ending where the candidate inserts a footnote that reveals that his well-scripted fiction is based on real events. It is all the more impressive that Mr. [Smith] is the CEO of the corporation and that the applicant is his direct report. As for the style of this essay, the use of fictional dialogue is fairly commonplace, so while it adds drama and interest, it is not standout.

Overall this essay communicates a strong sense of purpose, the ability to set priorities, and a keen talent for managing detail and execution. To ensure that the process is as rewarding as it is rigorous, the applicant also tells us that as team leader, he will emphasize creativity and collaboration.

It's particularly impressive that this applicant immediately sets the team on a constructive path forward. The past failures of the team, and any griping about those failures or past dysfunction, he establishes as irrelevant, thereby creating a team culture that is performance-based and not focused on placing blame. He then sets up a system designed to create results—an agenda that aligns team incentives so individuals are not working across purposes, clearly defined objectives broken into discreet long- and short-term steps, and resources appropriately matched to objectives. He outlines a remarkable plan for a team turnaround.

ESSAY #3

Question: You have recently been brought in by the CEO of your company to act as the new project lead for a high profile team charged with bringing a new product to market. The team has become dysfunctional and risks missing the project deadline. How will you go about turning the situation around? You have one month to make the deadline. (Answer must be no more than 2 typed pages, double spaced.)

I am very confident that my extensive exposure to team oriented initiatives during the course of my academic and professional careers will strongly support my ability to fulfill the expectations of the CEO and of the team itself in bringing the project back on track and with renewed enthusiasm, coordination and creativity.

The first move would be to acquaint myself with both the product and the team by calling the team together for an initial briefing to familiarize myself with their backgrounds and the progress that the project has made. I would seek to instill a sense of professionalism and confidence in our collective ability to overcome the encountered problems and to achieve a very rewarding goal in the remaining time.

My approach in speaking with my new teammates would tend towards the informal side, but I would remain firm in my commitment to bringing this product to fruition and to serving the initial goals of the company. I would assert an air of authority but equally let my team know that I am approachable and that open communication between us would reduce confusion and enable the greater sharing of ideas through brainstorming and a fair criticism and discussion of views.

I would spend a considerable amount of my free time to evaluate the remaining work to be covered and set a plan to evaluate the quality and success of work already completed. Time is of the essence and progress cannot be stalled while I familiarize myself with the team's, circumstances, but I would ask for more caution and interaction between team members to ensure that time was not wasted through rash decision-making. My plan would be make up for lost time through greater efficiency and cooperation between team members in the final weeks and I would break the team into its various divisions such as sales, marketing, manufacturing and logistics. By enhancing the team's knowledge of the importance of interaction between various divisions each member will learn about how their work interacts with one another and when to seek assistance from other divisions when matters concern them, instead of blindly making decisions that could be ineffective and undermine the work of other divisions with which they are unfamiliar.

Taking each division in turn I would swiftly assess its strategy to meet the goal of the project and its time plan and if necessary I would revise this through suggestion to the division leader. At all times during the project I would seek to maintain constant motivation over the team by praising initiative and achievement. I would invite advice and comment from all members and see to set aside some time each week for relaxation and to strengthen the interpersonal development between team members. I demand 100% commitment from my colleagues because the company expects and demands nothing less, therefore I would ensure that the individual goals for sales initiatives, delivery and logistics networks and marketing promotions were all reached to the highest standards. My experiences of product launches have taught me that human interaction and mutual respect and understanding are key to the success of such interdisciplinary endeavors and I believe that I have the capability to instill such a characteristic to this team initiative. My firm yet approachable leadership will, I am confident, bring about an effective, enthusiastic and innovative response from the team and lead it to a solid and professional conclusion within the deadline, therefore ensuring a commendable product launch.

Critique

This applicant focuses on the interpersonal dynamics involved in leading a team to success. A primary goal in his plan is to motivate his team members and build mutual respect. He proposes facilitating a series of informal discussions to create a culture of open communication, build sensitivity to different work styles, establish a collegial atmosphere, and establish common goals. He identifies himself as being an open and accessible leader, one who intends to motivate his team with frequent praise for achievement. Overall, he communicates that he understands the key conditions under which teams achieve optimum results. Since teamwork is absolutely critical in business school, the essay communicates that this applicant is the kind of person we want to bring into our community and who will distinguish himself as a leader.

Essay #4

*Question: What obstacles or major challenges have you
overcome to achieve your goals? How do these life experiences
distinguish you from other applicants? (one page maximum)*

My most difficult challenge has been overcoming the habits and behaviors which
were integral to my early successes but which ultimately were keeping me from
becoming a better leader.

The overwhelming success of my first five years at [Company A] left me to believe
that anything I touched would turn to gold. By the age of 25, I was a top engineer at
the hottest company in Silicon Valley, with a fortune in stock options and seemingly
limitless potential. My approach, which was echoed throughout the company, was
brash, arrogant, and very technically focused.

As the company started to struggle and I joined a group of co-workers to study the
root of our problems, I started to realize how the negative patterns in the company as
a whole were reflected in my own behaviors. We were so confident in our ideas that
we drowned out the quieter voices of our customers and non-technical employees.
My involvement in this group not only gave me the chance to help the company, it
gave me the chance to reflect on and change my own patterns. I learned that is just
as important to listen to the opinions of others as it is to express my own. Through
facilitation training, I learned how to be respectful and inclusive rather than aggressive and confrontational.

As a result of this transformation, I now possess a unique combination of skills I
believe will benefit my fellow classmates: on one hand, I have very strong analytical
skills and can present a strong case for my ideas. On the other, I have similarly strong
facilitation skills and am able to bring together the diverse ideas of both strong-willed
and less assertive members.

Critique

This is a wonderful example of an essay that runs counter to what most of us regard as obstacles to overcome in life: poverty, undereducated parents, broken homes,
illnesses, career setbacks, etc. In fact, this essay wows with the unconventionality
of the obstacle presented: the arrogance and ego of a twenty-five-year-old Silicon
Valley hotshot, whose style (and that of his peers) had begun to create what he calls
"negative patterns" of operation in his company. He writes of his transformation
into someone who becomes more sensitive to other's ideas and ultimately excels

at facilitation and consensus. The self-awareness demonstrated in this essay and willingness to admit to this committee that he was once brash and inward-focused are truly refreshing and genuine.

ESSAY #5

Question: Please describe your career progression to date, highlighting leadership and management positions and reasons for changing employers or career paths, if applicable. How will an MBA assist you in achieving your short- and long-term career goals? (Answer must be no more than 2 typed pages, double-spaced.)

Having been exposed to various science and math after-school programs as a young child, it came as no surprise that I would enjoy the challenges of engineering as an adult. After successfully completing undergraduate and graduate degrees in Electrical Engineering, as well as six summer internships ([Company A], [Company B]), I decided to join [Company C] in [Location D] as an optical networking system engineer. [Company C] was a company known for its innovation, creativity, and great work environment, all of which made it an ideal place for me to begin my professional career. As a system engineer, I designed and developed requirements for fiber-optic communications systems targeted at the growing demand for integrated voice and data traffic.

At [Company C], I contributed to the success of my team beyond the average system engineer and my efforts were quickly recognized and rewarded. As a result of my effective communication skills and technical contributions, I was nominated to become an International Standards Representative (ISR), representing the strategic interests of [Company C] and the U.S. State Department at international telecommunications standards meetings. In addition to being one of only 15 ISR's at [Company C], I also developed programs to aid the transition of new college graduates to the [Company C] culture and was nominated to the Corporate Review Board within our division.

After two successful years at [Company C], I had the desire to join an exciting start-up company, expand my leadership role, and return to the Bay Area, and thus I joined [Company E], an early stage optical communications company. At [Company E], I took on several leadership roles, including leading the system software requirements development, managing optical component vendor relationships, and becoming their U.S. Standards Liaison. I also was selected as one of their external technical conference speakers. Unfortunately, despite our team's efforts and achievements, the [Company E] optics program was cancelled due to 2001 telecommunications collapse.

Due to my strong personal network and motivation to continue my career development path, I was able to join another optical start-up in the Bay Area, despite the limited positions and intense competition resulting from the telecom downturn. I joined [Company F] as a system engineer and product manager for optical sub-systems. This role provided the unique challenge of serving as the lead system engineer as well as managing the product development of five [Company F] products.

Throughout my career, I have served in leadership and contributing roles at both large corporations and small technology startups. A Kenan-Flagler MBA will be of great value to me as I make the natural transition to become a consultant and private equity investor, specializing in technology innovation and value creation. This short-term goal will serve as a vehicle to achieve my long-term interests. System engineering has allowed me to apply exciting technology to solve fascinating problems, but it is my involvement in community programs, including teaching engineering to kids and sharing the joy of problem solving with others, that truly motivates me. In the long-term, I will use the skills developed during my Kenan-Flagler MBA, combined with my own professional and teaching experiences, to develop, own and operate an international network of technology consulting and learning centers, focused on exposing youth in underserved communities to potential careers in engineering and science.

The UNC Center for Entrepreneurship and Venture Innovation will provide an excellent curriculum that will prepare me for my future as a global entrepreneur and successful technology consultant. Kenan-Flagler will afford me the opportunity to share my own unique professional experiences as well as to learn from a diverse group of bankers, brand managers, entrepreneurs and consultants from fields in which I may have had limited exposure. In summary, the Kenan-Flagler emphasis on teamwork and practical experience, coupled with the opportunity to interact with leaders from around the world, will help me to develop skills for long-term business success.

Critique

Overall, this essay is written in a very positive, open tone. The writer's thoughts flow well and cohesively. There is not too much detail or business jargon. This essay also does a good job of giving insight into what has motivated the student's career to date. There is a nice summary (in the next-to-last paragraph) of his main theme or proposition to the committee: that he is a proven leader in both large-company and start-up business environments. Not only does he clearly communicate why he is a good candidate, but he actively and successfully answers the question "Why UNC?" He tells us that UNC is a fit for him because our Center for Entrepreneurship will provide the targeted education and resources he is seeking.

ESSAY #6

Question: Please describe your career progression to date, highlighting leadership and management positions and reasons for changing employers or career paths, if applicable. How will an MBA assist you in achieving your short- and long-term career goals? (Answer must be no more than 2 typed pages, double-spaced.)

While witnessing my father's fight against liver cirrhosis, I encountered many patients who were suffering, like he was, because they had been not been diagnosed early enough. These patients often relied on useless or even dangerous folk medicines, due to the lack of information they possessed about their illnesses. At [University A], I majored in pharmacy, and upon graduating, I decided to pursue a career in marketing so that I would be able to improve public awareness of illnesses and treatment options.

I began my career as a sales representative at [Company B]. My outstanding performance earned me a quick promotion to brand manager of a key schizophrenia medication. As the company's youngest brand manager, I worked with a sales team of twenty employees. Through focusing on the message that schizophrenics could lead productive lives if properly medicated, my team significantly increased sales revenues of our product.

My achievements attracted the attention of another pharmaceutical company, [Company C], and I accepted a position there marketing insulin, one of the company's top products. At [Company C], I worked to apply innovative marketing programs to raise awareness of diabetic diagnosis and blood glucose control, doubling the company's insulin sales in two years. Based on this success, I was promoted to the position of New Product Planning Manager, and am currently responsible for all aspects of new product launches, including analyzing the profitability and feasibility of new products, as well as checking the progress of clinical trials and submitting related documentation to the [Country A] Food & Drug Administration.

Looking toward the future, my short-term objective is to become a global marketing manager at a multinational pharmaceutical company, which would allow me to deepen my insight into the international pharmaceutical market. After spending several years working as a marketing executive, I plan to select a company producing new medications vital to the health of [Country A]'s patients, and become the founder and general manager of its [Country A] affiliate. Serving in this capacity would allow me to contribute to [Country A]'s healthcare system, provide patients with needed medication, and conduct campaigns to improve diagnosis and treatment rates.

Through my work at [Company B] and [Company C], I have accumulated extensive knowledge of sales and marketing; however, I will need to strengthen my understanding of essential business functions if I am to achieve my ambitious career goals. The MBA program at Kenan-Flagler Business School matches my career goals seamlessly, offering a world-renowned business curriculum that would allow me to acquire the theoretical fundamentals of finance, management, and marketing. Additionally, the school offers courses that match my specific interests, including Brand Strategy and Implementation, Data, Tools, and Decisions, and Marketing Issues. Participating in Kenan-Flagler's MBA program would enable me to build a foundation of business skills while delving deeper into issues concerning healthcare, on my way toward fulfilling my goal of improving [Country A]'s healthcare system.

Critique

This essay begins in an unusual and dramatic way, yet it is extremely effective in explaining the candidate's passion for her chosen career. Her words immediately captivate the reader. This essay very clearly communicates her unique heritage, background, and professional experiences. You leave this essay wanting to meet this person and learn more about her perspective.

This is an example of how a relatively brief essay can still be very effective. This writer makes her points clearly and effectively. Her story and interests speak for themselves. The goals are realistic, the style of writing straightforward. The overall result is very genuine.

Essay #7

Question: Describe your three greatest accomplishments. What does each demonstrate about your personality? (Answer must be no more than 2 typed pages, double spaced.)

I was born modest; not all over, but in spots.

—A Connecticut Yankee in King Arthur's Court

My three greatest accomplishments to date cover the three major areas of my life: my career, my relationships with others and my personal development. In my career, my greatest accomplishment has been my successful leadership of [Company A]'s Sales and Marketing Department. When I took over the marketing and sales department, morale on the team was very low. The former director had been very reluctant to try new marketing and sales strategies and the performance of many team members had stagnated. In the beginning, I had very little experience developing sales and marketing strategy, however I knew that I had a team with a great deal of combined experience and intelligence. I organized brainstorming meetings for the department often including senior members from other teams. The rich discussion and debate that these meetings provoked provided me with some of the best and most successful programs that I have undertaken as a director. Some of these projects include a re-branding effort that re-positioned [Company A] as the market leader, contract standardization procedures that improved communication of client customizations between the sales and programming departments, and suggestions for several new products as well as modifications to existing products. I learned that by getting more people on my team involved in these projects, they developed a sense of ownership of the corporate strategies and implemented those strategies more effectively in their day-to-day activities. I also worked individually with each member of my team to set specific goals and worked with them continually to help them meet those goals. As a result of these measures, many members of my team have expressed a greater satisfaction with their positions and have become better and more productive employees. I am most proud of the fact that every member of my team has shown marked improvement in productivity, quality of work and initiative during my tenure as director. In leading this team, I have learned the value of teamwork, initiative, strong management and leadership not only as a means to success for myself, my company and my department but also as a means of creating a pleasant and productive work environment for all concerned.

My greatest accomplishment in my personal life has been my development of strong and diverse relationships with family and friends providing my life with great meaning and depth. Each of these relationships with my mother, sister, two closest friends and my husband adds a totally different outlook to my life and experiences. Their openness and honesty as well as their unique intelligences and talents adds so much color and depth to my perspective, giving me the ability to be more tolerant and to empathize with people who lead lives very different from my own. I have had the privilege of supporting each of these individuals when they needed me and have learned how much joy can be gained by a life filled with such acts. I have also learned to lean on each one of them and gain strength from their support and confidence in me when I have needed it most. Each of these relationships has required a good amount of work to reach their current level. I have had to learn the value of compromise and flexibility and have had to swallow my pride more than once. However, the rewards have far outweighed the sacrifices and I cannot imagine my life without these people in it. I believe that these relationships say a great deal about who I am as a person. They demonstrate the value that I place on diversity, honesty, flexibility and tolerance as well as the importance of forming a strong network of people who you can count on and who feel confident that they can count on you.

My greatest accomplishment in my personal development has been my transformation from a shy and somewhat directionless young woman to a confident, happy and very focused adult. Growing up in suburban Louisiana, I never felt that I fit in. I was bright in a culture that did not value intelligence in girls and I felt constrained by my very insular and homogenous environment. Consequently, I grew up shy and very unsure of myself. I knew that I wanted to see what else the world had to offer and college was the perfect opportunity to explore. At [University B], I was exposed to some of the best and brightest people from all over the world and to many new ideas, both in and out of class. However, I was unprepared academically, emotionally and financially for the rigors of life at a large, highly competitive university and my grades suffered. When I started my undergraduate career, I had little idea of what I wanted to do with my life. I thought that I wanted to be a physician because, frankly, I thought that is what intelligent and ambitious people did. When I realized that I did not want to enter the medical field, I felt somewhat lost. I graduated from college with a degree that I was unsure that I would use but also with a larger view of the world, a sharper mind and an interest in technology that eventually led me to [Company A]. If was during my time at [Company A] that I really "came out of my shell" so to speak. My experience working with clients and later, acting as a manager and a company leader, gave me the communication skills that I needed to work in a team environment and succeed in each of my positions. This was also the time in which I formed stronger relationships with my family and friends and when my relationship with my future husband developed. All of this gave me confidence both in myself and in my abilities. The little girl who used to hide behind her mother's legs at neighborhood parties now feels comfortable mingling with 5,000 strangers at a business reception. At [Company A], I found that I had a real talent for working with teams, managing and motivating people and offering ideas that would lead to a company's success. In the last three years as Director of Sales and Marketing for [Company A], I have developed a strong interest in corporate and marketing strategy. This has given my career a focus that I have never had before. I finally know what I want to do with my life and I now have the confidence, the skills and the determination to achieve anything that I set my mind to.

Critique

This essay is particularly compelling because of the honesty and eloquence with which this candidate writes about her feelings and experiences. None of her accomplishments is extraordinary, but each is admirable. In each story of accomplishment, what resonates is her core character and perspective. She communicates that she is open, humble, honest, flexible, and self-aware. You read this essay and think to yourself, I'd like this person as a friend, as a classmate, as a colleague.

She also communicates strong business experience. In her first accomplishment, as head of her team's sales and marketing effort, the applicant shows an innate knowledge of how teams operate and progress to success. She has a solid grasp of brand marketing and management principles. That acumen combined with her interpersonal strengths leads her to a successful outcome and a great learning experience.

In her second accomplishment she chooses to focus on a personal experience, the relationships she has with her immediate family and two friends. In this case, her essay might have been better served with another example. Writing about one's family is so clichéd and overdone, it's hard to get an admissions officer's interest. The challenge is to express that what she learned from these relationships is genuine, vital, and most important, relevant. She clearly does this.

What is truly refreshing about this essay however, is the last example. The candidate gives us true insights into who she was and who she has become by sharing her background with us. Having grown up in a culture where she felt that women's intelligence was devalued, she reveals the personal hurdles she cleared to get where she is. She is not afraid to admit that she was lost and directionless, that she was shy and overwhelmed by college, and that her grades suffered. But she doesn't make excuses; she takes us on her journey. In the end, she communicates that she has emerged as an individual with a talent for team leadership and a strong interest in strategy.

University of Rochester
William E. Simon Graduate School
of Business Administration

Essay #1

Question: Describe your post-MBA career plans. How will a degree from the Simon School help you to achieve these goals? How does your past education and experience support your career objectives?

After completing my MBA I plan on pursuing a position as a buy side research analyst with the long-term goal of running my own fund. Spending the last few years analyzing the performance of client companies as an auditor has helped me to discover my passion of financial analysis. Auditing, however, does not provide the challenges that a career in investment management offers. The challenge of combining advanced financial tools with economic analysis for the purpose of making investment decisions motivates me to pursue a career in investment management.

Over the past few years I have worked to refine my interest in financial analysis and markets including recent coursework in Intermediate Portfolio Management at [University A]. This coursework, in addition to my independent research, has reinforced my desire to enter the field of investment management. I plan on further pursuing this interest by sitting for level I of the CFA exam this coming May.

My accounting education and career have given me an in-depth understanding of business transactions and financial reporting. However, I lack a detailed understanding of, and the quantitative tools necessary to perform, security analysis. Accounting has provided me with an understanding of the relationship between corporate performance and financial information. The Simon MBA program will help me make the link between financial information and security prices.

The majority of problems faced by business today require a collaboration of ideas from a variety of management disciplines. The economics based, cross-functional approach at Rochester will enhance my understanding of the fundamentals of business. The finance curriculum and innovative faculty will expose me to the latest developments in equity valuation and financial markets, while the core coursework will provide me with the broad foundation necessary to excel in today's business world. Access to resources outside of the classroom, especially the Investment Club and the Simon Meliora Fund, will provide me with further opportunities for growth and networking.

I am confident that the Simon MBA program can offer me the best business education and access to the greatest network of resources. I am incredibly excited at the prospect of studying at Rochester. Its exceptional finance curriculum, innovative faculty, and tight-knit community make the Simon School the perfect fit for me.

Critique

The admissions committee feels that this is a high-quality essay. The applicant paints a clear picture as to why he wants to pursue his MBA at this time given his past work experience and personal preferences. He states how a Simon MBA would help him achieve his post-MBA goals in both the short and long term. He also does an excellent job of tying in current business trends in his particular field of interest with Simon's economics-based, cross-functional approach as well as its strengths in finance, renowned faculty, and small class size. This clearly demonstrates that the candidate has done sufficient research to identify Simon as a strong fit for the type of MBA program that he is seeking.

ESSAY #2

> Question: Discuss three professional accomplishments that demonstrate your potential for a successful managerial career.

I set the goal of becoming a CPA during my undergraduate studies at [University A] because I felt that it would distinguish me as someone with the knowledge, skills and abilities to succeed in the business world.

After months of intense studying, I passed the challenging exam. Earning my CPA license proved my mastery of accounting and dedication to a career in business. With this certification, I am identified as an ethical person with a broad based business understanding.

Recently, I was assigned to lead an audit team at one of the largest steel distributors in the world. The prior year's audit was plagued with inefficiencies and as a result there was a significant delay in issuing financial statements. The client was left frustrated with the level of service received from the firm.

From the start of the engagement it was apparent that I would need to regain the client's trust. I was able to develop this trust by maintaining a high level of communication. By keeping the client continually informed of the progression of the audit, I was able to avoid the bottlenecks that led to the delays in the prior year.

The client was pleased that the audit was completed ahead of schedule. Additionally, the senior manager and partner recognized me for my efforts in rebuilding the relationship.

In less than three years at [Company B] I have been promoted twice. My last promotion, to senior associate, came despite an extended absence from the audit group.

In the fall of 2001, I made the decision to pursue a special project run by [Company B]'s Forensic Consulting Group at the site of the World Trade Center terrorist attacks. I chose to participate in this project despite the fact that my departure from the audit group would jeopardize my chance for promotion.

Upon returning to the audit group, I consulted with my performance manager to determine how I could better position myself for a promotion. With his guidance, I was able to secure a place on an engagement that would enable me to demonstrate my leadership skills. By excelling in this role, I was able to prove in a short period of time that I was capable of handling the responsibilities of a senior associate.

Critique

This applicant does a great job in highlighting his three greatest accomplishments. While obtaining the CPA is clearly a more academic accomplishment, he is able to successfuly tie this achievement to his ability to succeed professionally. He also gives an example of how he was able to take the initiative to successfully mend relations with a frustrated client by completing an engagement ahead of schedule through proactive communications. Finally, he demonstrates leadership potential through his successful promotion to the senior associate level.

Overall, the applicant has demonstrated his knowledge of the Simon MBA program and has shown that he would be a good fit within the University of Rochester community. His past experiences demonstrate his ability to succeed, and he has openly communicated how a Simon MBA would help him to achieve his future goals. Finally, he has clearly and succinctly answered the question asked, providing appropriate details while remaining within the standard essay length.

UNIVERSITY OF TEXAS
MCCOMBS SCHOOL OF BUSINESS

Essay #1

*Question: Explain how obtaining an MBA at the McCombs
School of Business will assist you in achieving your personal
and/or professional life goals. Why is now the best time for you
to pursue this degree? Your explanation should include, but is not
necessarily limited to, a description of both your intermediate
and long-term goals, as well as a current vision of your desired
employment upon graduation.*

I am pursuing an MBA for two reasons: to facilitate transition from the non-profit to the for-profit sector, and to earn skills that place me in an international corporation allowing me to work and live abroad. The realization that my career goals will be best facilitated by an MBA did not come easily, but the road I have taken makes me more certain that business school is the right decision, and McCombs is the right school for me.

I have worked in three industries: publishing, hospitality, and affordable housing. In each, I relished the opportunity to learn about a particular area of interest. However, intimidated by my own lack of technical skills in the business, I limited myself to entry level positions, but quickly discovered that my abilities and interests stretch farther that those opportunities could provide.

I recently left a job at a non-profit that provides below-market loans and technical assistance to nonprofits creating affordable housing. During my tenure at [Company A], the organization underwent a significant consolidation. Participating in this merger and the constant reorganization of our staff structure, I realized my passions for business run deep, and I perform best when large issues are at stake. At [Company A], we continually struggle to improve product delivery to our clients. At my publishing job, success frequently depended on the support of current legal issues, from bills passing legislature to protected access to public information. I taught myself to negotiate this access delicately but firmly with protective public information officers, then tailored that skill to fit my job in hospitality, mediating conflicts with guests or managers. In every case, I was happiest when calmly negotiating a contentious situation. Such cases, common during [Company A]'s merger negotiations, were rare in its return to everyday business.

In business school, I want to learn the environment and issues endemic to a larger corporation. Eventually, I would like to take these skills and use them in a return to the non-profit sector. This desire is similar to that of someone raised in a small town who is ready to see the city. The benefits of a close-knit community are many, but one is well-served by moving beyond this security to a larger city to see what it has to offer. In the city, the pace is faster, the options are different, the people are new and diverse. Eventually, one returns to the small town with skills, knowledge, and point of view that allow one to solve small town problems with big city solutions. This, for me, is what education is about: closing the gap between the bigs and the littles, the haves and have-nots.

A practical application of this theory could be working as a strategic management consultant in a large corporation in Mexico after graduation, then using connections I make through that position to start a nonprofit providing job training, placing participants in internships within organizations where I've worked. This plan would allow me to exercise skills I could learn in the Spanish Language Track and in such classes as Business in Latin America or Nonprofit Strategic Management, and use my experience to increase another's opportunities.

McCombs has demonstrated a strong commitment to global management education. As someone who will live in Mexico after I graduate, I'm attracted to a school that has a large and active Hispanic population and can support my desire to understand the business climate of Latin America. That McCombs was rated by Hispanics, and that UT Austin houses a stellar institute for Latin American studies, means the school takes my areas of interest seriously. McCombs's location in Texas, its Texas Plus and study abroad programs, and connections to businesses in Mexico provide the opportunity to apply what I learn in the classroom to a challenging internship and a suitable post-graduate position.

McCombs is a fast track to a high quality of learning, from more dedicated teachers, than I could find in any on-the-job training. I have the intellectual ability and curiosity to take a lesson and run with it; what I need now is the right lesson. McCombs can provide me with a framework for the business community: a standard of how things work and what trends are prevalent. In return, I can use those skills to manipulate that standard and create outstanding exceptions to it. I will succeed wherever I go to business school, but I believe that success will be greater if I can take advantage of all that McCombs has to offer.

Critique

In this essay, we appreciated the overall writing style and we particularly liked some of the comparisons drawn and the essay's creativity. It was clear and convincing, and it showed that the candidate did research about our school and how it fits with her professional goals.

Essay #2

Question: Explain how obtaining an MBA at the McCombs School of Business will assist you in achieving your personal and/or professional life goals. Why is now the best time for you to pursue this degree? Your explanation should include, but is not necessarily limited to, a description of both your intermediate and long-term goals, as well as a current vision of your desired employment upon graduation.

Sumimasen (excuse me), arigato (thank you), and konnichiwa (hello) were the only Japanese words that I knew when I first landed in Hiroshima, Japan, for a six-month work assignment. By the time I left, I had not only learned conversational Japanese but I also had a clearer vision of my career goals. My experience in Asia, combined with an e-commerce leadership position at [Company A], led me to realize the necessity of an MBA as I move toward my ultimate goal of creating a global corporation.

When I began my career with [Company A], I structured my assignments to develop both my engineering and business skills. The opportunity to develop these skills on a global scale presented itself in the form of the [Company A]/[Company B] [vehicle program]. During the vehicle development phase at the [Company B] Headquarters in Hiroshima, I served as a Powertrain Systems Team Leader. My primary task was to facilitate the issue-resolution process for the Powertrain Quality Team, a diverse group of engineers and managers from [Company B] and [Company A], as well as suppliers. For each of the numerous challenges our team faced, my tasks included leading the resolution process and presenting the solution to upper-level management.

My experience in Japan broadened my understanding of global business and led me to begin envisioning ways I could operate a company in the global marketplace. My assignment at [Company A].com further influences the development of my goals. This assignment unexpectedly catapulted me into a leadership position. When my supervisor suddenly left the department to join a joint venture ([Company C]), a huge chunk of his responsibilities fell onto my shoulders. My primary task was to lead and manage the [Company A].com "eMarketing Media Partnership Forum," a group of approximately 30 members. I conducted meetings with managers of various [Company A] consumer business groups to review prospective companies for possible partnerships. Restructuring the core Partnership Forum process, I helped achieve a

200% faster deal flow. I communicated with multiple emerging dot-com companies daily, who in each case claimed to have the best business model since sliced bread. This assignment made me realize how much I needed a business education to further develop my business acumen.

Working at [Company A].com helped me develop my long-term goal of managing a large-scale global company. With an eye toward this goal, I launched my own e-commerce company, [Company D].com in July of 2000, primarily as a means of learning more about the industry and how to manage a business. While my limited project management skills help me successfully launch this company, a business education would help me acquire the full array of business management skills I need to ensure that my company succeeds. My short-term goal after attaining my MBA is to work for a management consulting company. Understanding how different companies operate and strategize will provide invaluable experience to apply towards my goal of operating a large-scale company.

My engineering education alone is not sufficient to succeed in this fierce business environment. My experience in Hiroshima, for example, revealed to me the technical and business expertise required to lead and manage a multi-cultural team responsible for two vehicles that are manufactured on two continents and sold in 130 countries. Through such experiences I have started to develop the global management, technical, and interpersonal skills necessary to manage people and projects. To successfully overcome the challenges I will face in the global marketplace, I need an MBA.

McCombs' dynamic curriculum and international affiliations make it the ideal environment for me to develop the management and leadership skills required to lead an international company. I can develop these critical skills through innovative courses such as "Management and Marketing in the Global Arena." To achieve my career goal, I intend to specialize in entrepreneurship and to gain international experience, ideally through McCombs' affiliation with the Center for International Business Education and Research (CIBER) program. I attribute the success of such alumni as [Alumni A] and [Alumni B] (both '98) with their startup, [Company F], to McCombs' innovative faculty and international scope. I look forward to taking advantage of these opportunities at the McCombs School of Business to ensure that I develop the skills necessary to effectively establish and operate a world-class operation.

Critique

In this essay, we were impressed by the creative opening that is immediately relevant to the candidate's career and his reasons for wanting to go to b-school. Furthermore, the essay, while offering details about professional achievements, doesn't get too bogged down in those details. In the professional summary, the essay provides signposts (words like "tasks," "leadership position," and "my understanding") that really help the reader grasp the main points quickly. Many poorly written essays are missing these conventions, and hence it's sometimes hard to understand where the essay is going and why.

ESSAY #3

Question: All students bring a unique personal background to the classroom and study team that can prove to be as enlightening to fellow classmates as their professional skills. Describe what, outside of work, most distinguishes you as an individual and will most enrich the experience of your peers at McCombs from your background, life experiences, values, or interests.

As a brick crashed through our living room window, I quickly ran into the kitchen to get my mother. I can still picture the look on her face as she read the racist remarks written with chalk on the brick. The day afterward, our landlord gave us an eviction notice. I was six years old, and this was the first time that my mother had to explain to me how nasty and violent hatred could be. With a Caucasian mother and an African-American father, I received the hatred of whites who didn't like blacks and of anyone who didn't like to see the races mix.

Growing up in a multi-cultural family has allowed me to view society from many different angles. At a young age I found it extremely difficult to relate to either race. Both sides of my family expressed prejudices and hatred. Living in Detroit, where many neighborhoods are segregated, I didn't know how or where I was supposed to fit in. Not until my teenage years did I begin to appreciate my ethnicity. Over time, I began to use it to my advantage. My early life experiences as a racially mixed child have led me to look for ways to build bridges between people of different backgrounds, colors, and cultures.

My ability to reach across cultural divides was tested while I was in Hiroshima for a six-month [Company A]/[Company B] joint-venture work assignment. There, where I rarely came across other African Americans, I clearly stood out from the crowd. Given my color and my height (6'3"), some people assumed that I was a famous athlete, and they often asked me to sign autographs and pose for pictures. A few times I was even mistaken for MBA-star Grant Hill. To function in such an environment, I drew on my ability to overcome others' assumptions and stereotypes. I proved that I can smoothly integrate into any team setting. For instance, I recognized the need to build a relationship with both my Japanese and American team members in order to create a productive team environment. Unlike the average gaijin (foreigner), I learned and adopted the [Company B] working style (which included participating in morning calisthenics), followed by Japanese cultural practices (such as slurping Ramen noodles), and studied diligently to learn conversational Japanese. Being racially mixed has taught me the skills necessary in a multi-cultural setting. Applying this skill set to my professional life has enabled me to bridge cultural gaps and develop strong relationships with my colleagues, enabling us to become friends.

For the second phase of the [Company A]/[Company B] joint venture, our team relocated to [Company A]'s Kansas City Assembly Plant. Immediately, I noticed that my Japanese counterparts faced some of the same difficulties that I had faced while in Japan (ordering food, banking, etc.). Recognizing their struggles, I tried to help them bridge the cultural gap. One way I facilitated this process was by hosting "cultural exchange" dinner parties. I would prepare a "soul food", Italian, or American entrée for my Japanese and American teammates. This would be the first time that some of the team members would taste collard greens, risotto, or Salisbury steak. After dinner, the group would socialize while playing UNO or Yahtzee. The team began to genuinely enjoy each other's company and wanted to learn more about one another. The Japanese members also felt comfortable enough to begin inviting the team to their homes to share traditional Japanese food and to sing karaoke. Acceptance laid the foundation for friendships that we carried into the work place and have maintained well beyond the vehicle launch in Kansas City. My ability to create friendships that cross cultural gaps will, above all else, enable me to contribute to the McCombs environment.

The McCombs community consists of people from around the globe. What has attracted me to McCombs is what Business Week describes as "a strong cooperative environment." My experience has taught me benefits of cooperation among people with differing backgrounds and perspectives. I anticipate learning from my peers at McCombs—in the classroom; through clubs, such as the International MBA Student Association; and through activities, such as barbecues at my residence. I will do my part to help foster "cultural exchanges" among my peers, allowing us to develop a global mindset and enjoy the McCombs experience.

Critique

We appreciated the strong, eye-opening introduction to this essay that wasn't gratuitous, but sincerely relevant to answering the question. The essay had a strong structure and relevant connections to another essay in the application, which led us to believe it probably wasn't cut and pasted from another school's application. The third paragraph was particularly powerful as it demonstrated that the applicant took the extra step to understand the "learning" that took place. It answered questions such as: Why is all of this relevant? How did it change me? How will it contribute to my success at McCombs?

Chapter 11

ESSAYS FROM THE STUDENT SIDE

Now that you've read the critiques by admissions officers of anonymous student essays, it's time to critique the essays of ten profiled students who believe their essays made the difference in their b-school application. We have added this new section this year to give added insight to real candidates—their undergraduate schools, GPAs, their GMAT scores, their work experience. These applicants reveal all so you can see an essay in its true context. With this method of full disclosure, you have the chance to gain a clear picture of the whole candidate and what it took for each one to gain entry at a top business school.

These applicants wrote on a variety of topics, from living abroad to launching their own businesses, from rock climbing and ice skating to deciding to leave a beloved college due to poor undergraduate grades. They constructed careful answers to some of the toughest questions posed by business schools and shared stories of both success and failure. But most of all, the authors showed their human side. These essays tell a story of the applicant that goes beyond a resume-driven list of achievements to delve into the person as a whole. This might include why they made the decisions that they have or where they plan to go in the future. In creating the new class for an MBA program, admissions officers like to know the people behind the standard impressive list of accomplishments. And we believe these essays have made that possible.

Ideally, this section of the book will provide you with inspiration, organizational structures, themes, new ways of expressing yourself, and renewed confidence that your essay can indeed make the crucial impact that you certainly seek. Take note, however, that we are not touting these essays as perfect—if there even is such a thing. Many of these students did not make it into every school to which they applied, though all are pleased with the school they chose to attend. That's the reality of the application process for the majority of applicants. It's not unusual to be accepted at Yale and denied by Harvard, accepted to Darden but denied by Haas. This is all the more reason these essays paint a valuable picture of a candidate's quest for a matching school.

Just in case you're wondering why these students would allow us to publish their essays, test scores, grades, and personal info, here's the answer to that: They realize the intrinsic value of sharing their experiences. Many said they were honored to have been chosen for publication and to have the chance to help others, like you, who may follow in their business school footsteps. Best of luck to you with your essays and beyond.

ALEKSINA VICTORIA

Graduating from an American institution, although in Bulgaria, and at the same time working with European consultants on the SAP implementation of the largest Bulgarian telecom has made possible for me to bridge over different cultures and languages. I have been also a bridge between school children and their future as entrepreneurs as mentor in Junior Achievement initiatives. My goal as one of the few Eastern European people on campus is to build the bridge between different cultures.

Stats
GMAT score(s): 720
Undergraduate GPA: 3.38
College attended: American University in Bulgaria
Year of college graduation: 2003
Hometown: Plovdiv, Bulgaria
Gender: Female
Race: Caucasian

Admissions Information
Business school attended: Goizueta Business School, Emory University
Accepted: Goizueta Business School, Emory University
Denied: N/A
Waitlisted: N/A

How a degree from The Massey School will help me achieve my personal and professional goals

I love a good challenge. Being accepted by one of the ten best universities in the South is a good test of my abilities. To study in an MBA program in the USA was my purpose when I moved to Nashville from St-Petersburg, Russia eight months ago. Returning to college at the age of 28 was a crucial decision in my seven-year non-stop and so far fulfilling career. I have always valued projects not only offering a good challenge but also helping me to broaden my knowledge and advance my managerial skills. My experience as the director of a marketing department in one of the leading travel companies in Russia had been precious, but then I realized that I didn't possess the tools that would be necessary to achieve my personal and professional goals. My current objectives are to continue improving my general management skills and developing myself in an intellectually challenging environment. During my next two years at Belmont, I want to push myself forward and grow as a business leader, as a student, and as a person.

My experience has taught me that my strengths as a businessperson are strong self-motivation, the ability to collaborate effectively, and my analytical skills. Starting as a personal assistant to the President of the company where I worked before moving here, I learned a lot about the principles of operation of a large company with branches in 7 cities in Russia. In a year, I was promoted to Region Project administrator of one of the most complicated areas for the company. I learned to analyze huge amounts of information and make decisions based not only on quantitative forecasts but also on my intuition. The most difficult tasks were reforming personnel responsibilities, recruiting new staff, inspiring the existing personnel and building a new team. This experience gave me confidence in making decisions in human resources management. Having completed the tasks, I initiated the creation of a marketing department in the company.

My major at the university was in international marketing and, at that time, to lead a marketing department was my primary goal. I learned how to manage and motivate subordinates and promote new ideas among all employees of the company. One of my achievements of which I am proud was launching a new local brand and organizing an effective promotional campaign.

Now, I'm thinking of myself in the next level - working for an international company as an executive, whose responsibility will be to coordinate significant multicultural projects. In five years, I see myself in management consulting, because in this area I'll be able to apply my analytical and interpersonal skills as well as my ability to solve problems. I am planning to work for a firm focusing on management and strategy problems in any industry. On a personal level, I intend to deepen my creative thinking to generate new ideas and improve my abilities to persuade others and to work in a highly diverse environment. That's why an MBA will help me to get a deeper and wider knowledge of business processes and expand my skills.

Through all my work, I have dealt with people of different cultures: Finnish, English, Dutch, Greek, Turkish and Arabic. Persistent work on improving my communication skills helped me to succeed. I learned to value tolerance, open-mindedness, and respect for individual differences. I always try to broaden my horizons and the question of connection between culture and management is one of my interests. This past October, at a Tennessee Annual Student Conference for International Leadership, I made a presentation on the topic "how new leadership styles influence corporate culture in Russia". I was the first student from the Vanderbilt English language center to make a report at this conference. It gave me confidence for success as a foreign student and confirmed my ability to communicate with people from different countries. I'm convinced that focusing in management at Belmont will improve my assertiveness as well as leadership skills.

I believe that the MBA degree from the Massey School will assist me in attaining my goals in many ways. First, the MBA will give me the opportunity gradually to develop skills needed to achieve my goals through focusing on solutions for real business situations. Since it is an evening program, I expect that most of my classmates will be working professionals and the theoretical material will be supported by real-world examples and company related projects. The program also promises courses important for my career, such as "International Business", "Organizational Behavior and Management" and "Negotiating". Second, the Massey School will allow me to learn and to test myself in a new and demanding environment of an American university and develop me as a leader. I feel that living, studying and working abroad will be extremely fulfilling, both professionally and personally. At Belmont, I will have the opportunity to collaborate with American professionals as well as compete with them. I will contribute my expertise of working in a changeable Russian environment and bring the traditional Russian strong team spirit. Third, I am applying to Belmont because it is growing and improving rapidly. Every day I pass by the new impressive building of the business school and I like the well-groomed, cozy campus and I dream to study in such a place. I have met a lot of interesting people there, both students and alumni, and their opinions about Belmont have been uniformly positive.

I know that at Belmont I can improve my leadership skills plus obtain practical expertise and a deeper knowledge of up-to-date principles of business operation to achieve both my personal and professional goals. Adaptation to the real world in its program, a challenging professional atmosphere, and rising development of the university - these are three primary reasons why I chose the Jack C. Massey Graduate School of Business. And I look forward to being invited to be a part of it.

AMINA HARVEY

"My background was in retail management and buying with a heavy emphasis on profit and loss responsibility. This was a unique background that made me stand out among my classmates. I also attended a historically black college and was a business management major as an undergrad. My school and work experience was completely different from all of my classmates and I made a point to discuss what I could bring to the program because of my unique experiences. I had received a full tuition scholarship in undergrad and was also promoted very quickly in my jobs, achievements which were highlighted in my resume. I was also very active in community service activities. For the two years prior to going to business school I worked with underserved families, advocating on their behalf to get them the assistance they needed to get back on their feet."

Stats
GMAT score(s): 570
Undergraduate GPA: 3.34
College attended: Hampton University
Year of college graduation: 2004
Hometown: Lanham, MD
Gender: Female
Race: African American
Admissions Information
Business school attended: Freeman School of Business, Tulane University
Accepted: Howard University School of Business, Peter J. Tobin College of Business, St. John's University
Denied: Darden School of Business, University of Virginia, McDonough School of Business, Georgetown University
Waitlisted: Smith School of Business, University of Maryland, Kenan-Flagler Business School, University of North Carolina, Babcock Graduate School of Management, Wake Forest University

What are your short term and long term goals and why do fell like this is the right time to get your MBA?

I currently manage a multi-million dollar crystal business for Belk Department Stores. As an assistant buyer I am responsible for all aspects of my business including advertising, product selection, pricing, securing money from vendors, signage, and sales. In the four years since I have graduated from Hampton University I have worked for Bloomingdale's, a luxury department store, and Ralph Lauren, a luxury retailer. My experience at these companies has laid the foundation for my future goals. Working in the luxury market exposed me to a new niche, where regardless of the state of the economy the market continued to experience increases in sales and demand. The global luxury goods trade is now a $90 billion dollar business and the fact that this market is expanding from privately held family businesses to major conglomerates, opens up many positions for managers who understand the luxury world from inside.

My short term post-MBA goal is to work for Moet Hennessey Louis Vuitton (LVMH) as a Marketing Manager. LVMH is the largest luxury conglomerate in the world, with a portfolio of around 50 brands known the world over. As a marketing manager at LVMH I will be able to drive the execution of marketing strategies that will enhance the company's immediate revenue growth and long-term strategic positioning.

I am particularly interested in earning my MBA at this point because I feel that I am at a natural break in my career. In the retail industry there are certain things that you must accomplish to get a full understanding of the business. One is working in a retail store, the second is opening a new store, and the third is working on the merchant or the buying side of the business. I have been able to accomplish these three objectives and feel that remaining any longer in the industry will make a planned transition into a new field more difficult. Having an MBA will also speed my career progression, since I do not currently have a marketing background, being able to have a marketing concentration or take specialized electives will act as a substitute for marketing experience.

While I have mastered skills necessary to excel in the retail industry there are still some desirable skills that I need to gain in order to cultivate a career in the luxury goods market, and I plan to obtain these skills while attending business school. Having a global perspective is an intricate part in succeeding in the luxury goods market. You have to be able to think globally and be open to different cultures, customs, and ways of thinking. Attending a school with a diverse, international student body will allow me to be exposed to, and learn from people not only from different cultural backgrounds but also from different functional backgrounds.

I also need to be able to gain business skills not obtainable in my current position, such as finance and accounting. These are not functions that I use daily in my current position, but as I progress in a marketing career I will need to be able to understand all aspects of business in order to successfully manage brands and products. Since I have not managed a large group of people in a few years, participating in a MBA program will also allow me to refresh my soft skills. Finally, and perhaps most importantly I will be able to acquire the skills necessary to start and run a successful business, and tap into an alumni network that would otherwise be intangible.

After my tenure at LVMH I am going to start my own technology consulting firm that will focus on creating and managing websites for high end designers. The reason that there is currently a void of high end designer websites is because the image that the designer sees can often be difficult to duplicate online to someone who is not experienced in marketing luxury products. I will use my background as a Marketing Manager for LVMH, and the skills learned from my MBA education to manage distribution, sales, customer relations, logistics, and product for high fashion lines.

ESSAY PROMPT

What is the most challenging experience that you have had in your career?

One of the most challenging experiences I have had in my career was opening a new flagship Ralph Lauren store. The task of actually receiving shipments of goods, and getting them on the floor was exhausting, but the more complex task was training eight interior designers to be proficient on the point of sale and ordering systems.

The first obstacle to the training was the fact that the store grand opened the day before Thanksgiving. In retail the day after Thanksgiving is the busiest day of the year. This one day can determine if an entire company will make its year end financial plan, and shape the companies financial outlook for the next calendar year. At Ralph Lauren the entire staff had been working diligently the few weeks before the grand opening to ensure that the store was merchandised according to strict Ralph Lauren visual polices. We were all under constant pressure to get the store opened before Thanksgiving. This meant days of working 10 to 12 hour shifts, coming in at 5am before shipments arrived, and having at most one day off a week. When the store did open everyone was extremely tired from the hectic schedules we had been working, and the store was bustling with customers who had been eagerly awaiting the stores opening. As a result there was very little time for systems training. All of these factors created an atmosphere where everyone was high strung and anxious, two characteristics that do not complement a retail environment.

The second obstacle was that the staff was not especially receptive to learning the new systems. Due to the fact that this was the only Ralph Lauren store in the D.C. metropolitan area that offered a home store, only licensed interior designers were hired as associates. Many of the designers owned their own businesses, and had not worked retail in a number of years. While they had very strong customer service skills, they were not used to selling goods, and being reviewed based on sales. There was also a 25 year age range among the associates which further complicated the trainings, because some associates were very adept at working with computers while others were not very computer literate.

The systems at Bloomingdales were very similar to the systems at Ralph Lauren, so I was able to achieve proficiency very quickly. During the first month we were opened I began to realize that I was spending a majority of my day at the register or at the ordering terminal walking associates through simple procedures. It was very easy for the associates to call me to assist them instead of actually learning the system. I found that I was going over the same concepts with different associates and realized that there had to be a more efficient way to ensure accuracy when ordering, and prompt service when ringing up customers. I decided to organize bi-weekly trainings for the associates, not only the ones in my department but for the entire store. Since we did not have a training or human resources office in our store I contacted the corporate headquarters and worked with the training department there to create easy to follow manuals, and also quick reference books to be kept at the register. Before the trainings began I had the associates rank the issues so that the problems that would have the most impact could be addressed first. Associates came in an hour before the store opened and we would tackle one chapter a morning. For the associates in my department I set up one on one time during slower parts of the day so that they could learn the ordering system. With this system accuracy was particularly important because it was the system that processed customers' orders for custom wallpaper, upholstery, and furniture.

Taking on this project was not part of my outlined job responsibilities. It was not something that I had to do in order to be successful at Ralph Lauren, but it was something that I needed to do in order to make sure my staff was successful. A manager is only as strong as her weakest employee, I was able to see the weakness in my staff and encourage them to take action. I take pride in this accomplishment because within a month of the trainings being completed, sales in my area increased by 63% to the previous month. I like to think that a portion of that increase is due to the staffs' ability to better serve customers through more efficient transactions. I saw the challenges that were ahead of me, made calculated steps to analyze the best possible solutions, and executed those solutions for the betterment of my staff.

ANNE BREWSTER

"I believe that my entrepreneurial work experience in starting up and running my own small business combined with my other work experiences in marketing and logistics helped me get in to the University of Washington MBA program. My passion for my work, along with a strong GMAT score and undergraduate GPA, also helped me catch the attention of the admissions committee. Because of the quality of my application, I received The Neal and Jan Dempsey Endowed MBA Fellowship to cover half of my first-year tuition. This fellowship is awarded to 'top students in each year's MBA class, with preference given to... applicants with technology backgrounds or entrepreneurial experience... These fellowships are to help the UW business school attract and support MBA students who will become future leaders as managers or entrepreneurs.'"

Stats
GMAT Score: 690
Undergraduate GPA: 3.52
College attended: Tufts University
Year of college graduation: 2003
Graduate school attended: N/A
Hometown: Whidbey Island, WA
Gender: Female
Race: White/Hispanic

Admissions Information
Business school attended: University of Washington Business School
Accepted: University of Washington Business School
Denied: N/A
Wait-listed: N/A

Essay Prompt:

Goals Statement: Applicants with a plan for their future and with a good grasp of what is expected of them as MBA students are the most successful students in our program. We know plans change, and we know people often pursue an MBA to create new career options. Please tell us about your plans. Ideally, your essay should answer all the following questions: Why are you pursuing an MBA degree? What do you expect to do immediately after completing the MBA program? What is your primary lifetime career goal? How do your life and work experiences to date move you closer to these personal objectives? What specific things will the MBA experience contribute to your post-MBA and lifetime career goals? What unique aspects of the University of Washington MBA Program, if any, would contribute the most to achieving your goals? (750 words maximum)

A mentor once gave me this sound advice: to get where you want to go in life you must model the present on the future you desire. When I envision myself fifteen years from now, I see the owner of a successful apparel company and a business leader with strong ties to the Seattle community. At this point in my life, my challenge is to move quickly and effectively in order to transform my vision into reality; I view the MBA program at the University of Washington as the next step on the path to the future I see before me.

I was fortunate to be raised in a family where my creative side was nurtured by my mother, a seamstress, while tempered by the practicality of my father, a lawyer. I began to design clothing early on, and by age 11 started to sell my work to teachers and classmates, demonstrating an entrepreneurial drive that continued into high school. I found my niche in a college job as a costumer in the Tufts drama department, where I deepened my understanding of design, rounding out my work experience with summer jobs at a fabric store one year and an upscale bridal boutique the next. By senior year, I appreciated the value of my economics major to my future endeavors, but was eager to apply the concepts I had been learning in the classroom. My coursework and life experience up to this point culminated in the debut of my clothing line, Osorio, a month before graduation in an on-campus sales event. The sale was a success, and I expanded the framework of that initial project into a small business when I moved back home to the Northwest.

Since graduating I have sought out different experiences that would move me closer to my goals while building on my past achievements. Working at an ad agency, and then at a public relations firm, I learned valuable skills that I put to use immediately with Osorio, as well as long-term lessons that changed the way I viewed the business world. I felt like I was on the technical crew again in the Tufts drama department, helping run the show backstage. I was behind the curtain once more, meeting with clients and working with colleagues to develop new branding strategies and marketing campaigns. This exposure to business on a grander scale gave me additional impetus to pursue an MBA, both as a way to study how successful companies are run while learning business fundamentals in a structured setting.

Seeking a challenging, prestigious program with all the features I felt were necessary, I only had to look as far as my own hometown. The University of Washington MBA program's realistic and experiential style of learning speaks more to me than the one-dimensional academics I outgrew as an undergraduate, as well as the chance to personalize a flexible study plan. During a classroom visit I watched Jennifer Koski lead a class of completely engaged students and realized what a privilege it would be to work in this team-based setting, alongside such talented and passionate classmates, guided by intelligent and experienced professors. Outside of the classroom, the alumni network and mentoring program would be a valuable introduction to the Seattle business community of which I hope to become a member.

The career center might help me achieve my goal of a summer internship at Nordstrom, which, combined with my course work and program experience, might make me an attractive candidate for a position with the company. There, I could gain experience working for a major retailer in my desired industry and receive a grounding in the details of what it takes to succeed in the apparel business. Before I strike out on my own, I would have this career experience coupled with an MBA background to help me advance towards my long-term goals.

Now is the time to pursue an MBA, as I have reached a point where my business does not require the same input it did in its early stages. To take it to the next level I need the knowledge of business fundamentals, hands-on experience and ties to a business network of alumni and peers that the MBA program offers. In pursing an MBA at the University of Washington, I see both a means and an end: a logical and pragmatic step towards my lifelong goal of owning my own clothing business and an invaluable way to spend the next two years of my life.

Derek Leavitt

"I am just completing my undergrad in business. While attending college, I founded and managed an IT consulting firm which I just sold so I can complete my MBA. I am a fly-fisher, enjoy most other outdoor activities, and I am a musician, playing both guitar and piano. I'm hoping to get on a rowing team at Oxford."

Stats
GMAT score(s): 750
Undergraduate GPA: 3.95
College attended: Northwest Nazarene
Year of college graduation: 2010
Hometown: Melba, Idaho
Gender: Male
Race: Caucasian

Admissions Information
Business school attended: Oxford Business School
Accepted: n/a
Denied: n/a
Waitlisted: n/a

Essay Prompt

Derek used this essay in his application to Oxford Business School in response to the following prompt: Explain why you chose your current job. How do you hope to see your career developing over the next five years? How will an MBA assist you in the development of these ambitions?

I'm a musician. Not the kind that has taken lessons and learned to read notes, but the kind that uses his ear to detect the underlying patterns and rhythm and his heart to convey the harmonies that fill souls and encourage minds. I don't play just a single instrument--I play many. In fact, my ability to play a sharp staccato or to change keys seamlessly plays out in more than just music. In school and in business, and in life in general, I know how to read a situation, how to formulate a plan of action, and how to implement that plan seamlessly. I have used this approach to accomplish many remarkable things at a young age, and I continue to use these abilities to improve myself and the world around me.

In high school, by age 16, I had developed remarkable skills in computers and technology. I capitalized upon my abilities by developing relationships with local businesses. After school each day, I would spend my time consulting with companies and invoicing them at $75/hour. After two years of small consulting jobs and upon graduation of high school, I forwent attending college and took my technology skills to the next level. At age 18, I took out a small business loan, signed a lease on office space, and recruited a small staff. I founded a full-scale technology consulting company, and I have spent the last 5-years since then building my company, encouraging employees, and connecting with clients.

The first goal of my company was to generate adequate revenue to cover expenses. This took only one year. By the end of our second year, I had built a company that was turning a profit on over ½ a million in revenues. I took this profit and reinvested it in my own education. For the next three years, I continued managing my company while I completed my undergraduate degree. During this time, I accomplished many remarkable feats for someone taking on so much. In relation to my company, I led my consulting team in attaining contracts with many businesses and school districts through-out the western United States. In relation to my technical abilities, I completed Microsoft's seven-test, highest technical-level certification, the MCSE. In relation to my college education, I have maintained an outstanding GPA and will have completed a full bachelor's degree in just three years by going year round and consistently taking 15+ credits per semester. I want to continue to immerse myself in great challenges, and I have a dream in my mind for moving forward with my career. I envision building an online social network that connects business leaders with students. To me, some of the most rewarding experiences I have had have been opportunities where I have shared my experiences in business with young students. I want to help other business leaders have similar experiences through an online network. I want to use my technical abilities to build a social network that provides tools for business leaders to connect, communicate, and encourage students. I want to build an organization that focuses on long-term support where students and business leaders are connected at a young age, and where the connection remains for well into the student's upper-level education and career.

Perhaps better than most I understand how beneficial a business education is. I ran a company before ever taking a business class, and I know firsthand how hard it can be to make decisions without valuable financial and accounting tools. Even though my company has always been successful, there is no doubt in my mind things would have been much easier if I had gone to school first. For these reasons, earning my MBA from Oxford prior to taking on many of my future goals is a natural path. To accomplish my goal of creating a world-wide social network, I will need to best tools and the best classroom experience. There is no doubt in my mind that the diversity and history at Oxford will open my mind and give me the best insights and tools to accomplish my goals.

Derek used this essay in his application to Oxford Business School in response to the following prompt: Which recent development, world event or book has most influenced your thinking and why?

A war has been waging in my mind for some time. It's not a battle of words or bullets, or of anger or fear, but a battle of obligations and specifically of into what end am I to put my talents and time. It's simple enough to conclude that one should not just act as they please and that one has a certain duty to himself and his surroundings. But from where do these obligations come, and how am I to balance my own desires with the obvious needs of others. Shall I exist merely as an object in service, or am I justified in slight bits of selfish expression of internal fears, doubts, desires, and wants. If I do chose to serve, can I assuage my human insides by realigning my desires to be in harmony with the needs of my surroundings, or must this battle wage forever?

There exists a hidden nature of fantasy tales, one I believe most sense but few recognize. The genre's intention of telling a good story appears simple, however, for me the most insight into real life has come from stories that cannot be true. In J.K. Rowling's Harry Potter, Albus Dumbledore was born with incredible talent, and he wanted it to be known. In his selfish pursuit for fame and power, Dumbledore lost much but in the process discovered what was truly important. At this point in his life, Dumbledore made a choice to forgo his own desires so he could teach and help others. I cannot say, and the book does not elaborate, but the question of whether Albus was able to realign his desires, or whether he had to fight an internal battle of desires forever, is definitely posed.

I admire Dumbledore because his life mirrors a real one that I have observed much closer. I grew up observing a father as he regularly pushed himself beyond exhaustion to mentally and physically support not only his eight children but also anyone else whose need became apparent. At some point in his life, my father made a simple deduction: he recognized he was capable and that he had the strength, and since that day my father forwent his own desires to help others. Perhaps my dad would like to spend his time fishing for trout, a desire similar to my own, or perhaps at times, my father just wants to cry over the pain of endless days of little more than service and sleep, but he never does. He never cracks, he never breaks down, and he has never failed to support and encourage the many in need around him.

In terms of many of my favorite books, Dumbledore's and my father's characters are not so rare. Tolkien's Aragon didn't want to become king, but he accepted his duty to serve the people of Gondor even in their great state of dismay. Lewis's Aslan, the lion, offers his own life to save that of Prince Edmund. In perhaps the greatest story of all, Christ gave his life for the salvation of our world. Surely, these were not easy decisions, and surely, even up to the last moment and maybe after, these individuals were fighting an internal battle. My father's example, alongside those of the great characters of fantasy and history, has taught me one great lesson. In front of me stands a choice, a choice between serving my own selfish desires or serving the needs of others. I doubt there will ever be a day where I don't at least slightly long to be standing in a river looking for hungry fish, but I will accept the call as I know within my heart that my own needs and desires are nowhere near as dire as those of the people around me.

ESSAY PROMPT

Derek used this short answer essay in his application to Harvard Business School in response to the following prompt: What would you like us to know about your undergraduate academic experience?

I began my undergraduate experience after two years of starting and running a company. This made me an untraditional college student, and it has led me to insightful observations about undergraduate education. I began classes with a fair amount of experience in making decisions that depend on many factors. In class, while we learn business concepts, I often listen to students who do not have my experience as they make absolute statements about the quality of a principle. Further, assignments often require students to evaluate different principles or ideas without regard to the context in which those principles or ideas will be used within. Context is not ignored completely, and sometimes we look at cases, but context is not considered as much as I feel it should be. I know from experience that there is never an absolute situation where a single method or approach is called for. Everything is contextual, and for this reason, I wish we would focus more on practical situations as we learn. I have grown to think that maybe this is just how undergraduate programs work, but I long for more.

Further, because I started my company prior to attending school and learning important financial and accounting tools, I had learned to use my instincts to make decisions. I clash with many students in this regard, as my undergraduate program stresses the importance of weighing and analyzing decisions. I feel like the analysis approach can be a little bloated, and that nearly as much success in decision making can be accomplished using instincts alone. As I have taken more classes, I have come to realize the value of weighing and analyzing decisions, and in my mind, I have come to ask which approach is better. I have been gradually applying what I learn in class to my own company, and I have observed the good results of decisions that were made using information gathered from statistics and financial analysis. Even after observing these good results, I still feel like too much analysis can slow down important decisions and needed change. On the whole, I have come to believe that a good balance between using instincts and carefully weighing decisions is needed to be a successful business leader.

HARDIK RAITHATHA

I don't really think a single thing was responsible. It was really the entire package that clicked.

Stats
GMAT score(s): 740
Undergraduate GPA: 3.72
College attended: G H Patel College of Engineering and Technology
Year of college graduation: 2004
Graduate school attended: N/A
Hometown: Rajkot, India
Gender: Male
Race: India

Admissions Information
Business school attended: Goizueta Business School, Emory University
Accepted: Goizueta Business School, Emory University
Denied: N/A
Waitlisted: N/A

1. *The greatest lesson I have learnt is . . .*

2. *Of Goizueta's core values (courage, integrity, accountability, rigor, diversity, team, community), which value resonates most with you and why?*

The greatest lesson I have learnt is . . .

There are three ways to learn from life: suffering, studying and seeing. While ones sufferings are at times not in ones hands and studying mostly has to do with ones intellectual self, it is indeed 'seeing' that teaches greatest 'real' lessons of life. I was a part of the Earthquake Relief Team after the massive quake struck the state of Gujarat in 2001. Our team was responsible for providing relief material and assistance to the survivors in a village near Bhuj. On reaching the village, we were greeted with tears and broken hearts. There were collapsed houses and miserable faces. We were one of the first teams to reach the remote village and as expected the villagers attacked the supply trucks. People were snatching at everything, from shawls to food packets, but –they were especially desperate for water. Bhuj is located in the midst of a desert; water is the most valued resource. All 1000 pouches of water that we had brought with us were gone within the first minute. I spent the next 24 hours seeing the villagers struggle to save every drop of water.

Having been raised in a city, I had given little thought to the term 'shortage' until I went to Bhuj. Seeing those villagers desperate for every single drop of water taught me the importance of conserving natural resources, whether in form of water, wood, minerals or land. In some villages people walk 2-3 miles every day to fetch a single pail of water. In others, electricity is still unheard of. The more I travel in rural areas, the more I comprehend the need to educate people in urban areas about the careful use of natural resources.

Since my time in Bhuj, I have been spreading the message of conservation wherever I can. My blog, my tours through the Rural Reach Program of Infosys and other places where I can share my thoughts & influence minds – all carry the message of conservation of resources. Using natural resources judiciously is the greatest lesson I have learnt in life.

Of Goizuetaís core values (courage, integrity, accountability, rigor, diversity, team, community), which value resonates most with you and why?

When the Diverse members of a Team take Community as the foundation, Courage as the building block, Integrity as mortar and toil hard with full Rigor to build an edifice that is

Accountable not only to themselves, but also to their progeny – the result is nothing less than a Civilization. Of all the seven core values of the Goizueta experience, Diversity not of background, but of perspective, is what reverberates with me the most.

Although I belong to a common pool of professionals, my diversifying factor is the Jackof-all-trades attitude. It has had a cumulative effect on both my education and my career.

It all started in school when I was expected to work wonders in competition, even if I was a rookie. These expectations forced me to adapt to many roles and to engage in many activities. Soon this adaptability became a way of life. Either as team leader or as a team member, my desire to represent the unit or organization transformed me into someone who could be trusted for the most diverse of jobs.

From founding the band at Infosys, Hyderabad, to representing the district in the state level judo competition, to maintaining the highest GA for consecutive four semesters – it is this diversity which culminated in versatile interactions and experiences. I have often found that these are the activities that have made my life multidimensional and have encouraged my personal and professional growth. Thus, it is the core value of Diversity that I would draw upon to make the greatest contribution to the Goizueta Business School.

JENNIFER KHA

Extracurricular Experience: Model UN(President), National Honor Society (Secretary), Delta Phi Lambda (Inter-Sorority Council and Academic Chair), Project SHINE ESL Volunteer

Awards: Emory College Dean's List (3.8 GPA minimum), National Society of Collegiate Scholars, National AP Scholar with Distinction, St. John's Woman in Science Award, Butler Chain Preserve Scholarship, National Honor Society Scholar, DECA Marketing District Champion, DECA Marketing State Champion

---

Stats
GMAT score(s): n/a
Undergraduate GPA: 3.87/4.0
College attended: Emory University
Year of college graduation: 2009
Hometown: Orlando, FL
Gender: Female
Race: Asian
Admissions Information
Business school attended: Goizueta Business School
Accepted: Goizueta Business School (Emory), Stern School of Business (NYU), Warrington College of Business (UF), Georgia Tech College of Business
Denied: n/a
Waitlisted: Wharton School of Business (UPENN)

Essay Prompt:

Goizueta Business School's mission is to educate principled leaders for global enterprise. Leadership can move as many as an entire generation or as few as a single individual. On a separate sheet, in 500 words or less typed, please describe a situation in which you exhibited leadership.

Amidst all the excitement during orientation week to establish my niche in college, one particular volunteer organization, Project SHINE, or Student Helping In the Naturalization of Emigrants, immediately piqued my interest. As the first generation product of a family that immigrated to America as well, working as a teaching assistant for an ESL class would provide an excellent opportunity for me to not only share my experiences growing up in a multicultural home, but to also gain a better understanding of the tribulations immigrants face in adjusting to their new culture. As a SHINE volunteer, I would assist an ESL teacher and help students build their English skills in order to live and work in America.

When I arrived at classroom 117, however, my experience would prove to be a much greater challenge. I was greeted by some twenty enthusiastic students my first day as well as the discovery that the main ESL teacher would not be arriving because of a family emergency. As I nervously introduced myself and encouraged the students to follow suit, I began to wonder what I had gotten myself into. Many of the 'students' were at least twice my age, some even in their late sixties. Even after repeated attempts, I could hardly even communicate with many of the students, much less conduct their class for the next two hours.

Despite the situation, however, I could sense a spark of eagerness and passion among the students to learn and absorb their new culture. I was determined to utilize our class time to satiate their hunger for knowledge and use my skills to capture their desires. As I created grammar review skits and vocabulary spelling bees out of classroom objects, I was, in many ways, taught by my students. I fashioned my impromptu lesson and games according to the students' curiosity and inquiries. In other words, I played off my students' questions to formulate my own teaching. Through this experience, I discovered that leadership was not simply an act of directing, but being able to constantly adapt and learn. Together, my students and I used both our new and old experiences to understand our own individual difficulties and worked as a group to overcome them.

Although I may not have miraculously produced fluent English speakers that day, my first day as an ESL teaching assistant reminded me of the importance of a leader to function as both an active listener and constant learner. It was through my 'learning' experience where I garnered laughs from a tiny white-haired Swahili man during our action verb vocabulary game and managed to even coax a shy Hispanic mother into acting out a dancing skit about everyday chores. It was through my new students that I learned that the best leader is not someone who consistently knows what to do or knows all the right answers. Instead, a true leader is one who remembers that he is too a team member and his role is to capture the leaders in his teammates.

JOE HARDIE

"I was high school valedictorian, served as Student Council President for the 17th district of Illinois—a district which included over 42 schools, had over 300 hours of community service logged—[and I] worked in HR for a year and an accounting department for several months before applying to business school."

Stats

GMAT score(s): n/a
Undergraduate GPA: 3.77
College attended: Brigham Young University
Year of college graduation: 2010
Hometown: Lena, Illinois
Gender: Male
Race: Caucasian

Admissions Information

Business school attended: Brigham Young University Marriott School of Management
Accepted: Brigham Young University Marriott School of Management
Denied: n/a
Waitlisted: n/a

ESSAY PROMPT

Explain what you can contribute to the Marriott School from you past experiences through church service, work ethic, leadership, and community service.

The Marriott School of Management has a growing reputation worldwide for training leaders in ethical business practices. That reputation was not gained overnight, and neither was mine. Over time my reputation has become one of character and of a strong leader. As an applicant of the Marriott School, I will continue a pattern of excellence already woven through church service, work ethic, leadership, and community service.

Church Service:

Since a young man I knew that the LDS church would play a major role in my life. For example, I knew that I wanted to serve a mission, but my nineteenth birthday fell between graduation and my first planned semester. With study and prayer I knew the Lord wanted me to serve as soon as possible. Some thought that I was foolish for leaving scholarships I had just earned with four years of hard work. Still, I left as soon as possible to serve in Warsaw, Poland. As a result, I have learned that the best time to serve in the church is now. The time to help others and fulfill any calling extended is now.

Work Ethic:

I have a strong drive to work until a job is done. As an entrepreneur there is no one to push you to succeed or give you a raise when you have worked harder than anyone around you. I was an independent contractor installing signs on farmer's fields in five counties and three states. Through two long summers I learned the meaning of lonely travel and hard labor. I talked to farmers, found their fields, pounded the posts and erected the signs. From this experience I know the satisfaction of a job done well through constant struggle and perseverance.

Leadership:

I possess leadership qualities that cannot be easily taught. For instance, I have recently been hired in the Harold B. Lee Library Human Resources Department at BYU. While there were many qualified applicants, I was offered the job on the basis that my superiors perceived it would be easier to teach me new technical skills than to teach my personality traits to others. I believe a leadership position is not about giving orders – it's about taking an active role in group motivation and accepting challenging assignments. I am a leader for the good of the team, not for my own ego.

Community Service:

I have teamed with other school members to create two different service organizations. One was an adopt-a-grandparent group, and the other a Junior High tutoring organization. Each aided the community in attaining unity and understanding. From these particular examples of my community service, I have learned that a little thought and planning can help large groups of people come together. They can become friends and they can change lives.

The Marriott School of Management will benefit from accepting my application. I will represent and contribute to this school for the rest of my life through hard work, leadership and service.

KALIN ILYSE MCKENNA

"I tried to make my application as personal and interesting as possible. I wrote a lot about my experience in campaign politics, and about my time as an au pair in Italy. I think my success was due to the story I told over my actual experience."

Stats

GMAT score(s): 740
Undergraduate GPA: 3.8
College attended: University of California—Berkeley
Year of college graduation: 2005
Hometown: Lake Forest, CA
Gender: Female
Race: Caucasian

Admissions Information

Business school attended: McCombs School of Business, University of Texas—Austin
Accepted: Wharton School of Business, University of Pennsylvania, Foster School of Business, University of Washington
Denied: Haas School of Business, University of California—Berkeley, Columbia University, Graduate School of Business
Waitlisted: Yale School of Management

ESSAY PROMPT

Kalin submitted this essay to the University of Texas at Austin in response to the following essay prompt: "What are your goals, discuss career progression and why you are pursuing an MBA. Why a Texas MBA?"

As a student of history, I am fascinated by revolution, especially the social and industrial revolutions of the late nineteenth century. As I learned about different social movements throughout high school and college, I could not quench my desire to start my own revolution, to be a part of a movement greater than myself.

With this ideal in mind, I co-founded Mobilize.org my sophomore year at UC Berkeley. The idea was simple: Encouraging activism among our peers would create a political tipping point. To me, this tipping point was essential to creating a movement towards community-centered politics. Initially the non-profit model fit me perfectly. However, as with any start-up non-profit, funding our movement was difficult despite strong support. These funding obstacles provided an important education in the difference between a vision and practical solutions.

Mobilize.org taught me invaluable lessons. I learned how to pitch a product, create proposals, fundraise and manage staff. I participated in press conferences, recruited volunteers and planned promotional events. Additionally, I created Mobilizer's Guidebook, a startup manual for youth activists and community organizers. The guidebook furthered our goals of empowering youth while serving as a consistent source of income. Although these experiences were positive, I needed to pursue a greater challenge where I could realize my full potential.

After graduation, I sought a larger organization that would allow me to grow as a professional and as a leader. I wanted to manage my own office, so I signed on as a Citizen Outreach Director with Grassroots Campaigns, a firm dedicated to promoting campaigns from the bottom up while generating income to jumpstart new progressive organizations. Immediately, I was responsible for managing a thirty person office. The work challenged me, the causes excited me, but something was still missing. While I enjoyed working to benefit new non-profits, I eventually determined that corporate experience was necessary to truly expand my skills.

I accepted a position with TerraCom, a small public relations firm, as part of the event management team. In this position, I dedicated myself to further understanding the operational aspects of a small business, including proposal writing and development, budgeting, contracting, media relations, and basic accounting. I also took the lead on several projects, some of which extended beyond event planning. I enjoyed the flexibility of a small business and the attendant high level of responsibility. I felt I was finally achieving the professional goals I'd envisioned, but I missed working for the causes important to me. I found myself at a crossroad between the corporate and non-profit worlds. At this juncture, I believe it is essential to build upon my experience with a formal education in business.

Although I have been outside of academia for the last three years, my fascination with revolution has not subsided. I believe society is on the cusp of a revolution that will center on social responsibility and corporate sustainability. Ambitious, profitable business models and compassionate, non-profit ideals need not be mutually exclusive. I will use my McCombs degree to achieve my career goal of combining the efficiency and financial viability of a corporation with the social consciousness of a non-profit.

I aim to start my own social venture within five years following graduation. I want to build a business that offers a viable, revenue-building product in the public relations field while empowering disadvantaged women. I was raised by a supportive family who taught me my gender would never limit my capabilities or achievements. Despite their encouragement, I've consistently encountered resistance from people who are intimidated by ambitious women. While I have a strong support system, too many women in the world are left feeling defeated. In association with community organizations, I will identify women who possess strong leadership potential, but lack opportunity or encouragement. I want to mentor these women and ultimately give them the skills and experience necessary to achieve success. In addition I want my firm to challenge society's misconceptions regarding women through the campaigns we develop and the institutions we support.

In addition to beginning my own social venture, I am committed to an overall movement towards corporate responsibility and social enterprise. I believe the best way to create lasting societal change is to integrate social policy into corporate business practices. I believe the McCombs School of Business is the ideal place for me to expand upon my current skills and set the ground work for future success. Not only does McCombs have a strong commitment to innovation and community, but it offers a specialization in Social Enterprise. It also has a strong working relationship with the LBJ School of Public Policy, one of the best policy schools in the country. I plan on taking advantage of this relationship by taking classes at the LBJ School to supplement my business courses. Additionally, McCombs offers a flexible curriculum and allows students to start taking electives during the spring semester of their first year. This customizable curriculum in conjunction with McComb's commitment to hands on learning and collaboration makes it an excellent program for me.

I know a degree from McCombs will allow me to cultivate the skills and the resources necessary to start my own company, while deepening my commitment to social enterprise and responsible business practices. I look forward to learning from my peers inside and outside of the classroom and working within the Austin community to achieve my personal and professional goals.

Essay Prompt

Kalin submitted this essay with her application to the Yale School of Management in response to the following essay prompt: "The Yale School of Management is a community of individuals with diverse backgrounds and interests. What unique attributes would you bring to the Class of 2011?" She reports that she found this topic "very difficult."

When I was in the third grade I announced that I was going to be the first female President of the United States. My parents found this assertion mildly shocking, but I was raised in a political household so they took it in stride. Three months later I changed my mind. It was two days after the launch of Operation Desert Storm and I knew the President had given the final order. As an eight year old I was a fervent pacifist.

Although my aspirations have changed since I was eight, my commitment to politics has not. Throughout college I dedicated myself to registering students to vote, passing out voter information pamphlets and encouraging students to go to the polls on Election Day. The information I distributed was non-partisan; I found activism to be more important than ideology.

When I first announced that I was applying to business school most of my friends were shocked, not because they doubted my determination, but because they didn't see me conforming to a world of corporate greed. I was the one who organized political rallies in college, marched on Washington for women's rights, and co-founded a non-profit organization to encourage youth activism. After college I fundraised for progressive organizations and volunteered for the Hillary Clinton campaign. At one point someone asked me "Kalin, what is an idealist like you going to do in business school?" While I appreciated his concern, I was insulted that he thought I would compromise my ideals. I am going to business school to enhance my idealism, to build upon my skills so I can better contribute to my community and the world.

Months later, I attended an MBA event in Washington, DC. For a city that attracts so many idealists, it breeds a lot of cynics. As I was waiting in line, I overheard a woman talking about the policy classes business schools are integrating into their curriculum: "I do not understand what these schools are thinking. Everyone knows MBA students don't have souls." Although her words disappointed me, they were a valuable reminder that it is important for people like me to go to business school.

I bring a different perspective into the classroom. While it is inevitable that some students are driven strictly by profit motive, I am driven by my deep commitment to progressive policies and ideals. Through this perspective I aim to challenge my peers and classmates to look beyond profit and towards social responsibility and corporate sustainability. I believe that we have a responsibility as global citizens to give back to the greater community. While this can be accomplished through service and other traditional avenues, I believe integrating corporate practices with public policy will create more effective long term progress. My background is rooted in policy, history and political science, not finance and Wall Street. I no longer aim to be President of the United States, but I will work to change the world.

KENTARO TAKAHASHI

I believe my honesty helped me in the application process. Since my motivation is very specific and not typical as a prospective student to business school, I was not sure whether it would sound positive to the admissions office. Being honest, I could show where my passion was and how passionate I am, although it does not necessarily mean it sounded positive. One of the biggest challenges in writing essays is how to show your passion. People tend to write some textbook-perfect essays, but most of them are not attractive. Find any topic that can specifically and clearly explain your passion, even though it is not a successful business-oriented event. Show how you deal with it and what you learn from it, and it differentiates you from other prospective students.

Stats

GMAT score(s): 730
Undergraduate GPA: 3.4
College attended: Keio University
Year of college graduation: 2002
Graduate school attended: Keio University
Year of graduate school graduation: 2004
Hometown: Tokyo, Japan
Gender: male
Race: Asian (Japanese)

Admissions Information

Business school attended: Goizueta, Emory University
Accepted: Goizueta, Emory University
Denied: Harvard, Columbia, NYU Stern
Waitlisted: none

Essay Prompt:

List one of your most significant professional or organizational accomplishments. Describe your precise role in this event and how it has helped to shape your management skill.

The most significant accomplishment in my career is the policy innovation of the financing section to which I have been belonged. To put it plainly, it is the introduction of risk management. In Japan, business culture is still outdated and apart from global standard. The existence of risk is often overlooked even though Japan experienced economic bubble burst in the 1990s and lingering depression from that time. What I have done is very simple, recognition and diversification of risks.

For business in my charge which is cash flow management, excess fund concentrated in a particular kind of financial product. Credit risk was overlooked and bankruptcy was believed to disappear thanks to the recent recovery of Japanese business. In reality, risk exists in any business at any occasion and there is no method to eliminate it. Risk management is the minimization of overall risk of portfolio and thus diversification is required. I proposed to diversify the fund management methods, persuaded my supervisors, and bought several low-risk financial products such as commercial papers, Euroyen bonds, and deposits.

Many of my co-workers, including my supervisors, appreciate this accomplishment, even though the significance has not been recognized yet since negative factors such as default and bankruptcy have hardly happened in the recent years. What I have done is not only the diversification of risk, but risk management as a whole. Future prospects, not custom of the past, should be focused in business, and risk management is one of the core part of them.

In this accomplishment, I noticed the importance and difficulty of introducing something new. I had to explain what risk is and how it is different from uncertainty, since risk is what can be managed. To introduce risk management to the office, co-workers' understanding was essential, because risk also exists in any other operation, and I have to explain my policy and idea to foster the understanding. The explanation involved presentation, case study of other global companies, and external information such as rating of financial products.

From such experience, I learned that explanation capability is the decisive management skill as a leader. Nothing would get done all by myself and I always need to collaborate with others. In order to exploit the best performance of others, I have to explain the goal, the process, and their verification to others to promote their understandings. Such explanation is the beginning of communication and mutual understanding which enhance the synergy effect of the collaboration. I believe that this experience is critical in my career since explanation is required in any business.

Essay Prompt:

The person who has had the greatest influence on my leadership style is . . . because . . .

The person who has had the greatest influence on my leadership style is Chipper Jones, the leader of Atlanta Braves. He is the ideal leader for me because he leads the organization not only by on-field performance but also by the approach to the game.

For example, he accepted the change of positions twice, even though he could have refused them. He does not hesitate to preach his teammates when he finds it a rational method to win the game. Even though he has several injuries, he works hard to overcome them and endures the pain to play as much as possible.

From his approach, I have learned the prerequisites as a leader. First of all, leader should be modest enough to accept something undesirable to achieve the goal. Members always look at the leader's behavior and they would devote themselves to the organization if the behavior motivates members. No matter how influential the behavior is, leader sometimes should use words to tell something important to members. Words are more direct and precise method of communication. Last and most of all, leader must be the model of the organization. Leader sometimes should put business ahead of personal issue.

Of Goizueta's core value, team resonates most with me because this is what I hope to do in my career. When I will be the general manager of the Japanese baseball team, which is my long-term career goal, the organization as a whole should function as a team, i.e. the output of the team is greater than the sum of its parts. In order to win championship, players, coaches and managers, scouts, staffs, and I should share the same goal and have the mutual understanding which is composed of respect toward each other among the members.

In professional baseball team, the goal is profit maximization. For that goal, winning championship is assigned to general manager, and the general manager creates plan and gathers players and other members who fit the plan.

In my experience both as a leader and a member in my life, functioning as a team is the most important factor in business. Leader should explain the concept of the business to motivate all of the members to the goal and there may be various different motivations. Each member has his or her own potential, and the motivation should not be equivalent as long as the role is fulfilled. Any business has its plan, and the leader divides the plan into the members' roles which fit their potential. All the members have to respect and collaborate each other in order to function as a team.

Essay Prompt:

What do you expect to accomplish in the Goizueta Business School MBA program? How will your participation in the MBA program fit in with your experiences and responsibilities as well as your short and long-term career goals? (Please limit response to two, double-spaced, typed pages.)

My long-term career goal is becoming general manager of professional baseball team in Japan and winning the championship. In order to achieve the goal, I have to have the working experience in the front office of major league baseball team, understanding of Japanese business culture, and global-standard business skill which I would like to accomplish in the Goizueta Business School MBA program. Most of the industries in Japan are still immature from a global point of view, and so is sports business including baseball. My responsibility is to improve the sports business in Japan and enhance the fan satisfaction level of the Japanese professional baseball by using global-standard business skill I will learn from Goizueta and working experience in the United States.

I hope to find a place at the front office of major league baseball team upon the graduation of Goizueta, and this is my short-term career goal. This is the opportunity to learn how the overall operation of world's most advanced sports business is done. It should be major league baseball team, because its management techniques are much more sophisticated, logical, and rational than those of Japanese professional baseball. I expect this experience will tell me how to fix the flaws and improve the operation of Japanese professional baseball and sports business in Japan.

After working in the United States for several years, I plan to head back to my mother country Japan. In order to introduce global-standard business skill and make a revolutionary change, especially in Japanese professional baseball to attract fans, understanding of Japanese business culture is indispensable. This is the reason why I am at the current position. In Japan, manufacture is the only industry that leads the global market and retains Japanese inherent business culture. NGK INSULATORS, LTD. has developed for more than one hundred years in Japan and currently leads several global markets. In other words, NGK is a successful global company although it still relies on the outdated and often much-criticized Japanese business customs, and one of the best places to learn them.

To conclude, MBA program is the essential step in my career plan. As relaxation of regulations is pushed forth, Japanese business will be more open and get close to the global business custom. Global standard business skill based on real working experience in the United States, combined with understanding of Japanese specific business culture will be needed in any businesses in Japan. I will perfectly match the new phase of business scene several years later in Japan.

NAJEEB YASER

"The major thing that helped in getting my acceptance was the essay that I have attached. I also sent a copy of my CV to the university with my application to explain my work experience. That experience includes executive manager of the largest and most prestigious restaurant in both Palestine and Israel, and working in the treasury Department of Cairo Amman Bank as a foreign exchange dealer—buying and selling foreign currency, margin trading, foreign investment, deposits and overall bank money transactions. While there, I took a training course at bank headquarters in the stock market and foreign exchange."

Stats

GMAT Score: 460
Undergraduate GPA: 3.02
College attended: Birzeit University, West Bank, Palestine
Year of college graduation: 2000
Graduate school attended: N/A
Hometown: Palestine, Israel
Gender: Male
Race: Middle Eastern

Admissions Information

Business school attended: University of North Carolina—Greensboro Bryan School of Business and Economics
Accepted: University of North Carolina—Greensboro Bryan School of Business and Economics; John Brown University MBA Program
Denied: N/A
Wait-listed: N/A

Essay Prompt:

Submit a 1,000-word personal essay describing your reason for pursuing a Bryan MBA.

8:00 AM, barely awake, a strong cup of Turkish coffee in one hand and two phones in the other, I sat down awaiting the call. It came. The First transaction of the day, money exchange between Bank Hapoalim in Jerusalem, and Cairo Amman Bank; I am to authorize this deal between the two banks from the living room of my house! Everything else is closed down. There is an official curfew enforced by the incursion of more than 160 military tanks into my town, Ramallah. The early morning hours came accompanied by the ringing sounds of phones, and blasting sounds of missiles striking various places in the city. My fear was not in being harmed by the attacks, but that the nearby Markava 3 tank would not knock down the phone posts in the area. I had work to finish, and for several weeks to come! The year of 2002 was full of political unrest in my country, and due to the many days of closure, Cairo Amman Bank, the bank I worked for then, decided to entrust me with the operations of its treasury department. Practically I had to run the operations from home for the duration of the incursions, which lasted several weeks, over the phone, with no bank notes or computers, just my word for all the operations. This particular experience gave me a great deal of confidence.

Growing up in a country like Palestine meant that life was full of surprises and roadblocks. Sometimes it is peace and other times it is war and frustration. Some days we were able to go to schools and others we had to go to underground gatherings to get some education. At times it seemed that our lives did not have hope, and dreaming of a bright future was just out of the question. Yet in some ways this uncertainty and frustration propelled me to strive for a better life, while still living in Palestine.

When I graduated from high school, peace was underway, at least for a short while, and things started to look hopeful for my generation. In addition to a major in accounting, I was active in the student body. Several times I participated in student congress, which challenged and boosted my self-confidence, and taught me many important lessons in life, especially commitment and loyalty. Later, this experience enhanced my position at Cairo Amman Bank, where I got my first job after graduating from university.

Though life in Palestine is at the least challenging, I learned that nothing in life comes easy, and that one has to work hard for accomplish dreams. I appreciate my life background especially that it did not stop me from continuing to aspire for a better future for myself and those around me. I believe that in order for a nation to flourish, its members have to take up the challenge of the present to create a different future for themselves and the generations to come. This is what I intend to do with my life. Thus, my decision to return to university, to pursue an MBA program at The University of North Carolina at Greensboro after several years of work in the professional world, will broaden my knowledge. The practical work experience gained from 3.5 years of work at the bank, coupled with an advanced degree in business will no doubt better equip me to refine my business skills, and prepare me to excel in the business world.

OLAMIDE ABIBAT AJAO

Because of her lively and very welcoming personality, Olamide was invited to be the hostess of firm's quarterly community events. She took up a leadership role in contributing to the success of other events in the office, particularly the periodic 'Thank God It's Friday' (TGIF) get together, earning the appellation 'Events Planner' in the process.

In spite of her busy schedule, Olamide loves to volunteer and as part of the National Youth Corps program she taught Physics and Mathematics in a girls' only high school located in the less educationally-developed part of Northern Nigeria for a year. She has also being a staunch supporter of Junior Achievement (JA), a body committed to using hands-on business experience to help young people prepare for leadership roles after college.

Olamide graduated with honors from the University of Ibadan, Nigeria with a degree in Physics. While at Ibadan, she was Editor-in Chief of the Physics Press and also the President of her high school Alumni Association with over 90 members on campus. Her independent undergraduate work titled Natural activities of 40K, 238U and 232Th in elephant grass (Pennisetum purpureum) in Ibadan metropolis, Nigeria was highly acclaimed and consequently published by the Journal of Environmental Radioactivity, United Kingdom. More recently, she passed the Level 1 of the Association of Chartered Certified Accountants (ACCA). In addition, Olamide loves to dance and play volley ball.

Stats
GMAT score(s): 620
Undergraduate GPA: 3.2
College attended: University of Ibadan, Nigeria
Year of college graduation: 2002
Hometown: Ibadan
Gender: Female
Race: African

Admissions Information

Business school attended: Goizueta Business School,
Emory University
Accepted: Goizueta Business School, Emory University,
and Hult International Business School, Boston
Denied: N/A
Waitlisted: N/A

Essay Prompt:

What do you expect to accomplish in the Goizueta Business School MBA program? How will your participation in the MBA program fit in with your experiences and responsibilities as well as your short and long-term career goals?

I have always believed that pursuing an MBA at this time in my career life will help enhance my inherent business skills and tendencies which I have observed over the years. Obtaining an MBA from a top US school has been at the forefront of my goals and dreams because I know it will aid in turning my ideas in to action. An MBA will prepare me for the unique and ever increasing challenges of business leadership especially in the global business landscape. The School's approach (Leadership in Action) of building functional expertise with an enterprise perspective fits perfectly into my plan of executing theories and ideas in the real business world. I will be privileged to learn as well as participate in its field studies in real business environments. I also believe Goizueta Business School will expose me to innovative research, opportunities to network, interact and gain from some of the most successful business leaders in the world.

Studying at Goizueta Business School will be a dream come true because of its commitment to the core values namely courage, integrity, accountability, rigor, diversity, team and community. As an individual, I can relate with these values and thrive in an environment that encourages such. As a future leader, I share a similar commitment to these core values. Beyond this, the accelerated nature of the MBA at Goizueta is ideal for me. I want to obtain a world class MBA from a top-notch school in record time, and also learn the tools needed to fast track my career.

Another reason why I think Goizueta Business School will help me achieve my goals is because of its distinct blend and size of students. Its composition of both local and international students will give me an insight into global business factors and prepare me for challenges. I am a very sociable person by nature – I like to make new friends and learn new things. The diverse and multicultural environment at Goizueta Business School will further expose me to people from different cultures and background creating useful business networks in the business world. The role of team work cannot be overemphasized. During my undergraduate days, I had to work in teams during and after classes, which is the same situation at Accenture where different people work together in teams.

My professional experience till date is relevant towards the realization of my goals. I currently work as a senior business analyst with Accenture, a global management and IT consulting firm. I have worked with several major clients in the financial services industry to develop corporate strategies, restructure their organizational workforces, redesign business processes and implement appropriate technology for increased efficiency and higher returns on investments. I am also responsible for gathering, analyzing and presenting information that will help us deliver value to our clients. Specifically, I have worked on two mergers and acquisition (M & A) of banks in the Nigerian banking industry within the last year. Together with other team members, we helped the clients form new entities, develop the entities' corporate strategies, integrate their operations, migrate data from the various existing software to the new software, amongst other value adding roles. Prior to joining Accenture, I worked with Guaranty Trust Bank, a top 5 Nigerian bank as a Customer Service Representative, with specialty in the MICR operations of the bank. At the time, the unit was a central one that served its 52 branches nationwide. I supervised nine staff who were responsible for the requisition, production and distribution of bank instruments to all our branches and to selected customers. The combination of these two roles has helped me in getting closer to achieving my set goals. Working with Accenture has given me both international exposure and diverse roles within the industry. I have had to critically understand my clients' businesses and the attendant dynamics. I know what drives these businesses, how they create value and their success stories. At GT Bank, I learnt the essentials of excellent customer service delivery, importance of perception and professionalism. With the experiences gained, I think I am well positioned to make my dreams come true.

My short term professional goal is to acquire adequate requisite knowledge and practical experience in international businesses. To accomplish this, I have worked with a global firm that has given me the required international exposure and allowed me garner as much experience as needed to further position me to achieve my long term goal of setting up a first class international hospitality business that will provide excellent services and redefine the industry. I have always looked forward to becoming an exceptional business leader in the hospitality business areas and as such, I have planned my short and long term goals to perfectly fit into each other. I hope to aid in promoting business and entrepreneurial development in the Nigerian economy by becoming a major player in international business using the wealth of knowledge to be gained from my professional working experience and MBA to assist start-up ventures and existing businesses in the long run.

To achieve my goals, I will need a repertoire of relevant skills. Most importantly, I need to possess good knowledge of the industry and have a sound understanding of the financial and commercial aspects. I must be both creative and innovative. I need to improve on my management style by effectively managing time, people, projects and relationships with customers and colleagues. Equally necessary are self-motivation, leadership and team playing skills. In other words, I need a distinguished MBA from a world class school – Goizueta Business School.

In summary, I strongly believe Goizueta Business School has an excellent and distinctly conducive and favorable environment that fits with my personality which will enable me maximize my potential and further improve on my abilities while empowering me with necessary skills and knowledge that will contribute towards the success of my entrepreneurial pursuit. The MBA experience will be a very invaluable and absolutely important ingredient in achieving my goals.

TREVOR WINN

I find the business school application process similar in many respects to the job application process and this is intentional. B-schools are judged by their ability to place students in high profile careers and the more apt your are at selling yourself as an applicant, the easier you will be for the career center to find a job. Keep an eye on the big three: GMAT, GPA, and work experience. If they are in the meaty range of accepted applicants from prior years, it makes the admissions officer's job much easier. In addition, visiting the campus to get a feel for the school community (professors, students, and administration) and an understanding of what makes the school worthwhile to you. For me it was easy, I fell in love with Darden during one of many business school visits.

The crucial factors for my application were completing and excelling in business coursework (to compensate for my undergrad GPA) and weaving together a compelling story as to why an MBA would be a fit for me in the context of my past and future goals. Minor points include that I was applying to a Southern school as a history major from California with non-traditional work experience (for business school that translate into not banking or consulting). These factors allowed me to fill diversity needs for geography, experience, and undergraduate majors that admissions offices hope to fill in every accepted class. Good luck!

Stats
GMAT Score: 670
Undergraduate GPA: 3.10
College attended: University of California—Riverside
Year of college graduation: 2001
Graduate school attended: N/A
Hometown: Redlands, CA
Gender: Male
Race: Caucasian

Admissions Information
Business school attended: University of Virginia Darden School of Business
Accepted: University of Virginia Darden School of Business
Denied: University of California—Berkeley Haas School of Business
Wait-listed: N/A

Essay Prompt:

Describe your most rewarding leadership experience and what it means to your development as a potential leader.

Growing up in the home of a single mother in a blue-collar area was challenging. In spite of this adversity, I was the first person in my family to have attended college after completing high school. During college, I landed a teaching position with the Princeton Review that eventually led to full-time work. Most Princeton Review instructors were teaching affluent upper class students how to improve their test scores for college admission. During my full-time tenure at The Princeton Review, I was able to pursue a population of students that no one had served before and address two false notions. The first was that these students were disengaged regarding their college futures and the second was that we would damage our brand by helping the disadvantaged kids. We were able to offer students from the poorest schools in Southern California SAT preparation. It was commonly believed that these students were not interested in being helped. These two issues had prevented Princeton Review from pursuing an aggressive marketing strategy in this market space and I was amongst the few who challenged this notion. I helped to design a program that helped over six thousand students over three years throughout Riverside and San Bernardino Counties significantly improve their SAT scores. Our after-school program had a 95% completion rate that was the highest in history of almost every school we worked with. Two years after the inception of this program, the average number of college-going students from these high schools had risen by twenty percent. I had a tangible impact on the community I grew up in.

In order to accomplish this, I have become a business generalist, forced to master both the intricacies and the holistic nature of my business. I sell the product myself, I train others to deliver the product, I visit the customers, I order the materials, I write the brochures, and I am required to manage the finances of my division. Working with each functional area has taught me that personal commitment and the articulation of a vision do affect great change.

Working with disadvantaged students and underserved schools has been uplifting and, at the same time, a living parable for me. A business that does right will anchor itself within the community. Harvesting the wealth of your surroundings without an appropriate outlet to show your concern for the greater good can create a tenuous relationship with your marketplace. By aligning a business's goals with the improvement of its surroundings, a business intertwines its own fate with that of the community. I learned the relevance and understand the value of making my marketplace better because of my presence.

TROY JOHNSON FOSTER

In college, I spent my senior year at the helm of the university's daily student newspaper. As editor in chief, The Daily Barometer won the state's top award for student journalism excellence for the first time in a decade. The paper later went on to receive the Society of Professional Journalist's top award as the Best All-Around Daily Student Newspaper in the nation in 2001. After college, I worked in media professionally for five years. I began my career at a small newspaper in Madras, Oregon, where I worked as a reporter, photographer, and editor. In 2003, I moved up to a larger paper in Twin Falls, Idaho, where I oversaw a team of reporters and later a team of copyeditors.

Stats
GMAT score(s): 490
Undergraduate GPA: 2.99
College attended: Oregon State University
Year of college graduation: 2001
Hometown: Portland, OR
Gender: Male
Race: Caucasian
Admissions Information
Business school attended: University of Montana
Accepted: University of Montana
Denied: N/A
Waitlisted: N/A

Essay Prompt:

A Letter of Intent (Statement of Goals) explaining why you want an MBA from The University of Montana.

I'm a news junky. Whether it's on nationally, in my local community or on the other side of my neighbor's fence, I like to know what's going on. I read newspapers online, I'm in touch with the bloggosphere, and I watch those all-news channels. All the time.

I'm this way because I'm a journalist. I make it my business to be in the know.

For the past 10 years, as both a student and professional, I've tried my hand in most areas of what we used to call "print" journalism. I've worked as an editor, reporter and photographer. I've been a teacher, a mentor and somebody's boss. I've written stories, cropped photos and penned headlines. I've published Web sites, written manuals and corrected grammar.

When you spend nearly a decade in the news profession, you develop a few quirks. One thing people often tell me is that I ask a lot of questions -- sometimes too many. I can't help it. I've become a curious person.

As a reporter, I never felt comfortable tackling a story I couldn't wrap my mind around. So when I'd go into an interview, it wasn't unusual for me to startle my interviewee with the detailed nature of my questions. But for me to write about something, I have to understand it. If I can't figure something out, I can't stand myself.

So what does all this have to do with an MBA, and my desire to get one from your university?

You see, I was watching one of those all-news channel one day, staring at those guys on the floor of the New York Stock Exchange. As they were shouting, waving their hands wildly, I realized I had no idea what they were doing. Or who they were yelling at. Or what purpose it served. And I *wanted* to know.

So three years ago I enrolled in some economic courses for personal enrichment. I wanted to know why Alan Greenspan was an important man. I wanted to know why the value of the dollar goes up and down. I wanted to know more about interest rates. And I wanted to know why everyone gets so excited about this concept called "free trade."

And with those first two econ classes, my thirst for knowledge increased. I wanted to know more about accounting so I could understand why there was an Enron and WorldCom. I wanted to take finance classes so I could be more prudent in the management of my own checking account. I wanted to watch "Mad Money with Jim Cramer" and know what the hell he's talking about.

Aside from personal enrichment, there is the more traditional reason why I'm seeking an MBA. Two paths lie ahead of me after grad school. One is to join my brother as a business partner in the development of low-income housing; the other more likely option is to go back into journalism. Regardless of which path I choose, I feel I need to take it with an MBA under my belt.

About a year ago my brother asked me whether I'd be interested in leaving newspapers to join him in his fledgling business. My brother is seven years older than me and possesses a law degree. The two of us have sketched out a tentative division of labor that would have me managing the finances of our small corporation. An MBA would be an invaluable asset. It would also put me on comparable ground with my sibling in terms of education.

But if I go back to my first love -- journalism -- I must go back with more tools at my disposal. First of all, a better understanding of the business and economic world would make me a better journalist. Secondly, if journalists in the "print" medium are going to survive, they're going to need new ways of thinking. I spent most of my journalism career as a workhorse in the newsroom, but I always kept my eye on the publisher's office. It was a "one day, maybe" sort of thing. So if I intend to keep that idea in the back of my mind, I'll need to know how to run a business, not just a newsroom. And with today's decline of the traditional newspaper, that's more important than ever.

To understand just how quickly newspapers are fading, you need look no further than my news consumption habits. I spent almost 10 years of my life working for newspapers. They were my lifeblood; my cause. But a few months ago, I canceled my subscription to the newspaper in my own town -- the one I used to work for! -- because I felt the copy landing on my front door was no longer relevant. I take it all online now. And if people like me are canceling their subscriptions, well ... then ... you get the idea.

Assuming everything goes according to plan, I'll have the equivalent of an associate's degree in business by fall and have met all necessary prerequisites for admission into the MBA program. I'm currently enrolled in three classes at the College of Southern Idaho, and I intend to take four courses in Missoula this summer (assuming, again, that everything goes according to plan).

I'm thrilled with the idea of moving to Missoula and attending the University of Montana. The past year has been full of excitement already. I took a break from my career to get some things out of my system: I visited Europe, worked as a bartender and traveled all over the United States, too. I currently work at a ski area -- another one of those things I'd always wanted to try.

Now I'm ready to get back to business. Business school, that is. And I'd be honored to do it at the University of Montana.

VALERIE DE CHARETTE

I probably had more random experience than most of the other applicants. I wrote and edited three Let's Go *travel guides in college, and all my work experience was in retail (three and a half years turning a start-up urban e-tailer into a successful store and one and a half at Macy's Merchandising Group in the young men's market).*

Stats
GMAT score: 740 **Undergraduate GPA:** 3.7 **College attended:** Harvard College **Year of college graduation:** 2002 **Graduate school attended:** N/A **Hometown:** New York City, New York **Gender:** Female **Race:** French/Korean, Caucasian/Asian
Admissions Information
Business school attended: University of Chicago Graduate **Accepted:** GSB **Denied:** Stanford **Waitlisted:** Columbia **Other (explain):** third-round for all apps

Essay Prompt:

Explain the path that has led you to pursue an MBA as the next stop in your professional and personal development. Describe your short and long term post-MBA career goals. What or who influenced your choice of schools, and how specifically will Chicago GSB help you succeed?

Growing up, I never thought of going to business school. As early as elementary school I decided I was going to be a journalist – first as an anchorwoman, then as an investigative reporter for *The New York Times*, then as a touring reviewer and photographer for *Rolling Stone*, and finally as the editor-in-chief of *Vogue*. I settled on fashion magazines because, through my many childhood mutations, fashion was the one subject that always held my interest.

With this goal in mind I became editor-in-chief of my high school newspaper, wrote and edited three Let's Go travel guides during college, and after graduation sent out eager letters to all my favorite fashion editors – without receiving a single response. Instead I ended up with an interview at DrJays.com, a two-year-old e-tailer of urban clothing. I accepted their offer, expecting to continue looking for an editorial position as I worked.

Three years later DrJays.com was a thriving retailer: Amazon.com had chosen the site as their youth anchor when launching apparel, brands that hadn't answered my calls the first year were hounding me, and sales had doubled each year. By then I had also realized that I loved my job. I loved the risk, the negotiations, the buy planning, the merchandising strategies and the marketing. I enjoyed the business as much as I had enjoyed writing and editing – my temporary job had replaced my childhood dream! I decided that if I was going to commit to the business side of fashion I needed broader exposure. Although DrJays.com was an amazing company and had been an incredible opportunity, I resolved to make the move to Macy's Merchandising Group to gain more traditional training.

Working for MMG, an ancient, hulking ship compared to the jet ski that was DrJays.com, introduced me to business at a higher level of detail. I discovered how important the close analysis of numbers and an educated approach to strategy are to the success of a mature company. Although I believe business acumen is gained mostly through experience, working among the highly trained merchants at MMG made me realize that a wider-encompassing education in business would catapult me to a superior level of operation.

I do not know what will happen in the future since I have changed so much in the past, but with my experience up to this point I know I want to stay in the fashion industry, and Chicago is currently an exciting place for fashion. Mayor Daley, towards his goal of establishing Chicago as a prominent US cultural center, has most recently focused on apparel, appointing a city Fashion Advisory Council and instituting an annual Fashion Week. My years at DrJays.com were so inspiring because it was such a young company, and as such offered more opportunity and flexibility than a longer-established corporation could have afforded. The prospect of joining Chicago's fashion industry at a similarly early point in its development is exciting. At this moment Chicago is a good place for someone like me to meet mentors in the business, obtain stimulating internships, and maybe find the right position after school.

In terms of academics, GSB can supply me with the superior quantitative education that I need. Numbers are the weakest link in my chain of skills – I was, after all, going to be a famous journalist, not a businesswoman – and I want a school that will challenge me to improve those skills. I have always been decisive and quick to make educated decisions but in order to maintain this ability as I progress, I need to maximize my quantitative and analytical competence.

Business is more than just number-crunching, though, and no matter what company I end up working for, I envision myself creating and implementing top-line strategies. I have had experience with both the quotidian grind and the holistic steering of a company, and I know that I am better used as a generator of and springboard for ideas. The grind is absolutely necessary to understand and experience because it provides one with the information necessary to initiate feasible strategies, but I aim to effect broader change and improvement. I cannot operate at that high a level with only good intuition and creative thinking, which brought me to where I am now; I also need a solid background in strategic management. GSB's focus on management, leadership, and entrepreneurship is perfectly in line with my goals. The wide gamut of management courses GSB offers, as well as unique programs like LEAD, will arm me with the skills necessary to attain more influential levels within the fashion industry.

Beyond improving my business skills, I also want to use business school as an opportunity to explore related fields like language, history, and law. Variety is important to me because it keeps me inspired. Whenever I start to feel like I am getting wedged in routine at work I know it is time to go competitive shopping, focus on something different for a day, or just read something new to gain fresh perspective. My preference for variety is what attracts me to working for multi-brand/multi-tier retailers (such as Federated) and conglomerates (LVMH, for example). GSB fits my need for range academically because it gives more importance to electives (inside and outside the business school) than other top schools. I can supplement my statistics and economics courses with courses as closely related as the history of commercial culture or mergers and acquisitions law, or as distantly relevant as elementary Korean.

Languages are particularly important to me because intrinsic to fashion is global finance and culture, and the fashion industry is fiercely international. As the child of two immigrants from two different countries, I am personally as well as professionally invested in maintaining a global perspective. GSB, through its International Business Exchange Program can acclimatize me to conducting business with and within other cultures and economies.

There are many schools that can teach me the quantitative skills I need, that offer electives, and that have international programs, but the University of Chicago is the only school to have all these qualities to the degree that I consider sufficient and to be so conveniently located in a city that is actively growing its fashion presence. In addition, the University of Chicago as a whole is known for having rigorous academic standards and correspondingly intellectually-minded students, and this is the foremost reason I want to attend GSB. When I wanted to be a journalist I thought experience was everything and school was unnecessary (oh, the certitude of eighteen-year-olds!), so I went to Harvard simply because I needed a degree. I knew better by senior year, but I wish that I had been more focused from the start. I still may not know exactly what I want down the line, but I understand why further education is necessary for me and I know I want to pursue business school. The scholarliness of the University of Chicago is the perfect complement to what were somewhat random years of undergraduate work and the right place for me to build on my post-college experience.

Essay Prompt:

What is the one thing that most people do not know about you?

Few people know that I was a classical pianist. I used to practice up to four hours a day, I performed across the United States and in France and Japan, I competed in national and international competitions, and I taught piano and theory to the younger students at my music school. Although I no longer play regularly, music will always be an integral part of my life: I still attend concerts often, I surprise friends by identifying classical loops in pop songs, and when I absently drum my fingers on my desk my boss asks if there is construction on our floor.

Essay Prompt:

What book, play, or movie would you recommend to the admissions committee? Why?

I recommend *Defying Hitler* by Sebastian Haffner, a German writer who grew up between the two World Wars. As Haffner's memoir unfolds, the reader observes how interest in his personal affairs blinded Haffner to events in the public sphere.

Suddenly, the Nazis are so powerful he cannot resist without risking death. This book demonstrates that citizens and corporations must constantly mind how their vested interests affect their rights and their environment. The admissions committee is likely familiar with business publications, but schools also need to instill an understanding of consequence and social responsibility in their students and alumni.

Essay Prompt:

It is your first day of business school and people are selecting study groups. How would you describe the value you will bring to a study group?

It is cliché, but I will bring enthusiasm. When I went to college it was out of obligation; I thought I knew everything a school could teach and I was loathe to wait four years to start gaining professional experience. After having my career plans turned on their head, I understand that there is always something to learn and to this end I am anxious to maximize graduate school. In addition, my business experience thus far has been extremely positive and this only piques my interest more and leaves me itching to expand my knowledge.

Essay Prompt:

2. Choose one of the following questions. (500 word maximum) B. You have been asked to write an editorial about the most pressing issue facing humanity. Please identify the issue and justify why you have selected it.

The most pressing issue facing humanity is people's indifference to global problems. Immeasurable effort is needed just to broach wide-reaching issues like establishing world peace, so most individuals disregard larger concerns because they assume their efforts will be negligible. I am a firm believer in the idea that every bit counts, though, and this is how I view my role in combating the indifference around me.

I believe the most important issues facing the world currently are conserving the environment and educating children. Without a healthy environment we may no longer have a habitat, and without education subsequent generations may not be able to thrive together within this habitat. I do my part, however small, to reverse these problems and set an example of participation.

Growing up in Manhattan, I was a true city girl until, during college, my parents bought a house in a sparsely-settled area of upstate New York. There I started riding horses with a neighboring farmer, through untouched forests and across untamed meadows. Around the same time a friend of mine moved to an organic farm. I spent many weeks visiting her, doing things I had never done: weeding fields, building a winter greenhouse, eating vegan, and living without electricity.

Appreciating the beauty of nature made me want to preserve it and living so minimally made me realize how I wasteful I was of precious resources. I started turning off the unnecessary lights and air conditioners in my apartment, I stopped running the water while brushing my teeth, and I arranged a compost system for the country house. At Macy's I initiated a discussion of organic manufacturing practices with our core vendors and upper management, establishing a dialogue that will hopefully result in safer processes within a segment of our business.

A healthy environment is necessary, but combating inequality and prejudice so people can co-exist is just as important, and I believe education is the key to global cooperation. Many years ago my uncle started a foundation to support an elementary school in Nepal. I visited Nepal last April and it was sobering to see 10-year-olds embroidering the cheap blouses sold in stores like Macy's. Upon returning to the United States, I began fundraising for the school and making strides locally by volunteering as an SAT prep teacher at a school in Brooklyn. Last year I also arranged a fashion internship for a promising student from this school.

Although it is not much, I am doing my part to help further the causes that I consider crucial. My small contribution is a mere drop in the ocean of what needs to be done, but, as I become more influential, I will hopefully be able to effect larger change. More importantly, if my actions inspire someone else to make an effort, small or large, then I will have done my part towards decreasing society's indifference.

ABOUT THE AUTHOR

Nedda Gilbert is a graduate of the University of Pennsylvania and holds a master's degree from Columbia University. She has worked for The Princeton Review since 1985. In 1987, she created The Princeton Review corporate test preparation service, which provides Wall Street firms and premier companies tailored educational programs for their employees. She currently resides in New Jersey.

Share your *Princeton Review*® success story with us!

Email **PrincetonReviewGuides@randomhouse.com** with your name, story, and the title of the guidebook that helped you crack a test or pick the perfect school.

By submitting your story, you agree to grant to Princeton Review a perpetual, non-exclusive, royalty-free, worldwide license to use your name and story, in whole or in part, in all media whether now known or hereinafter devised, on and in connetion with Princeton Review's publications and in the advertising and promotion thereof.

More expert advice from
The Princeton Review

Increase your chances of getting into the business school of your choice with **The Prince** **Review**. We can help you get higher test scores, make the most informed choices, and m the most of your experience once you get there. We can also help you make the career m that will let you use your skills and education to their best advantage.

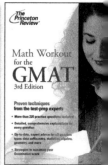

Cracking the GMAT, 2011
978-0-375-42975-0
$22.99/C$26.99

1,012 GMAT Practice Questions
978-0-375-42927-9
$19.99/C$24.99

Verbal Workout for the GMAT, 2nd Edition
978-0-375-76462-2
$19.00/C$27.00

Math Workout for t. GMAT, 3rd Edition
978-0-375-42985-9
$19.99/C$23.99

Cracking the GMAT with DVD, 2011
978-0-375-42976-7
$37.99/C$44.99

The Best 300 Business Schools, 2011
978-0-375-42790-9
$22.99/C$25.99

Word Smart for Business
978-0-679-78391-6
$12.95/C$19.95

The Anxious Test-Taker's Guide to Cracking Any Test
978-0-375-42935-4
$14.99/C$18.99

Available everywhere books are sold and at **PrincetonReviewBooks.com**